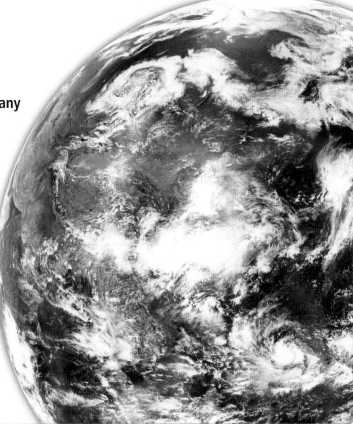

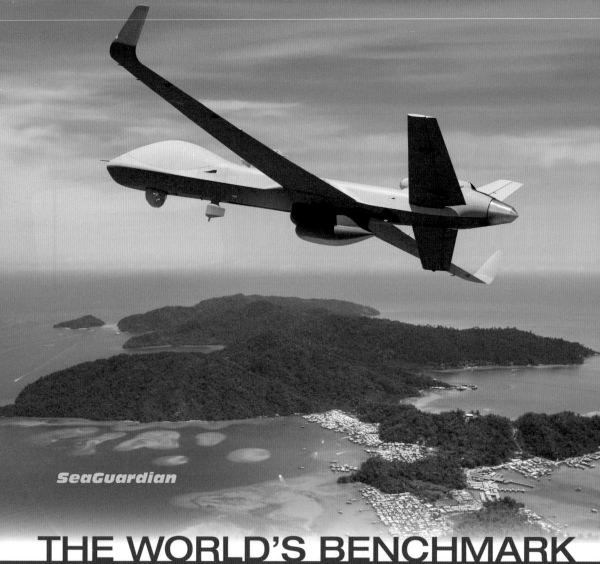

Powering
mission capability

Rolls-Royce pioneers cutting-edge technologies for many of the world's major defence programmes. Delivering next generation power systems and intelligent service solutions, Rolls-Royce is a powerful ally for 160 armed forces and over 70 naval customers world-wide.

Advantage
where it counts

Survival
GLOBAL POLITICS AND STRATEGY
Volume 61 Number 3 | June–July 2019

'Possibly the most important lesson from the history of arms control is that it is very difficult to build disarmament agreements, but quite easy to destroy them. Doing the latter has never enhanced national or international security.'

Alexey Arbatov, Mad Momentum Redux? The Rise and Fall of Nuclear Arms Control, p. 32.

'In the end, an infatuation with a distorted past deluded millions of British citizens, as well as hundreds of pro-Brexit politicians, about the future of their country outside Europe. [The] UK … entered Brexit negotiations convinced that it enjoyed global status and prestige that had actually vanished decades earlier.'

Edoardo Campanella and Marta Dassù, Brexit and Nostalgia, p. 109.

'Moscow and Beijing believe that the West wants to change their political systems. They have decided to mount a proactive defence, by blocking the US and other states from promoting liberal democracy or individual human rights in states where the sitting government is opposed to such developments.'

Nicholas Redman, Moscow Rules, p. 252.

Survival

GLOBAL POLITICS AND STRATEGY

Volume 61 Number 3 | June–July 2019

Contents

Cover: TASS via Getty Images

On the cover
A *Bulava* missile is launched by the *Yuri Dolgoruky*, a Russian *Borei*-class submarine, during a drill in the White Sea in May 2018.

On the web
Visit www.iiss.org/publications/survival for brief notices on new books on Europe, Africa and Latin America.

***Survival* editors' blog**
For ideas and commentary from *Survival* editors and contributors, visit www.iiss.org/blogs/survival-blog.

Survival
GLOBAL POLITICS AND STRATEGY

The International Institute for Strategic Studies

2121 K Street, NW | Suite 801 | Washington DC 20037 | USA
Tel +1 202 659 1490   Fax +1 202 659 1499   E-mail survival@iiss.org   Web www.iiss.org

Arundel House | 6 Temple Place | London | WC2R 2PG | UK
Tel +44 (0)20 7379 7676   Fax +44 (0)20 7836 3108   E-mail iiss@iiss.org

14th Floor, GBCorp Tower | Bahrain Financial Harbour | Manama | Kingdom of Bahrain
Tel +973 1718 1155   Fax +973 1710 0155   E-mail iiss-middleeast@iiss.org

9 Raffles Place | #51-01 Republic Plaza | Singapore 048619
Tel +65 6499 0055   Fax +65 6499 0059   E-mail iiss-asia@iiss.org

Survival Online www.tandfonline.com/survival and www.iiss.org/publications/survival

Aims and Scope *Survival* is one of the world's leading forums for analysis and debate of international and strategic affairs. Shaped by its editors to be both timely and forward thinking, the journal encourages writers to challenge conventional wisdom and bring fresh, often controversial, perspectives to bear on the strategic issues of the moment. With a diverse range of authors, *Survival* aims to be scholarly in depth while vivid, well written and policy-relevant in approach. Through commentary, analytical articles, case studies, forums, review essays, reviews and letters to the editor, the journal promotes lively, critical debate on issues of international politics and strategy.

Editor **Dana Allin**
Managing Editor **Jonathan Stevenson**
Associate Editor **Carolyn West**
Assistant Editor **Jessica Watson**
Production and Cartography **John Buck, Kelly Verity**

Contributing Editors

Ian Bremmer	Bill Emmott	Jeffrey Lewis	Teresita C. Schaffer	Ruth Wedgwood
Rosa Brooks	Mark Fitzpatrick	Hanns W. Maull	Steven Simon	Lanxin Xiang
David P. Calleo	John A. Gans, Jr	Jeffrey Mazo	Angela Stent	
Russell Crandall	John L. Harper	'Funmi Olonisakin	Ray Takeyh	
Toby Dodge	Erik Jones	Thomas Rid	David C. Unger	

Published for the IISS by
Routledge Journals, an imprint of Taylor & Francis, an Informa business.

SUBMISSIONS

To submit an article, authors are advised to follow these guidelines:

- *Survival* articles are around 4,000–10,000 words long including endnotes. A word count should be included with a draft.
- All text, including endnotes, should be double-spaced with wide margins.
- Any tables or artwork should be supplied in separate files, ideally not embedded in the document or linked to text around it.
- All *Survival* articles are expected to include endnote references. These should be complete and include first and last names of authors, titles of articles (even from newspapers), place of publication, publisher, exact publication dates, volume and issue number (if from a journal) and page numbers. Web sources should include complete URLs and DOIs if available.
- A summary of up to 150 words should be included with the article. The summary should state the main argument clearly and concisely, not simply say what the article is about.

- A short author's biography of one or two lines should also be included. This information will appear at the foot of the first page of the article.

Please note that *Survival* has a strict policy of listing multiple authors in alphabetical order.

Submissions should be made by email, in Microsoft Word format, to survival@iiss.org. Alternatively, hard copies may be sent to *Survival*, IISS–US, 2121 K Street NW, Suite 801, Washington, DC 20037, USA.

The editorial review process can take up to three months. *Survival*'s acceptance rate for unsolicited manuscripts is less than 20%. *Survival* does not normally provide referees' comments in the event of rejection. Authors are permitted to submit simultaneously elsewhere so long as this is consistent with the policy of the other publication and the Editors of *Survival* are informed of the dual submission.

Readers are encouraged to comment on articles from the previous issue. Letters should be concise, no longer than 750 words and relate directly to the argument or points made in the original article.

ADVERTISING AND PERMISSIONS

For advertising rates and schedules

USA/Canada: The Advertising Manager, Taylor & Francis Inc., 530 Walnut Street, Suite 850, Philadelphia, PA 19106, USA Tel +1 (800) 354 1420 Fax +1 (215) 207 0050.

UK/Europe/Rest of World: The Advertising Manager, Routledge Journals, Taylor & Francis, 4 Park Square, Milton Park, Abingdon, Oxfordshire OX14 4RN, UK Tel +44 (0) 207 017 6000 Fax +44 (0) 207 017 6336.

SUBSCRIPTIONS

Survival is published bi-monthly in February, April, June, August, October and December by Routledge Journals, an imprint of Taylor & Francis, an Informa Business.

Annual Subscription 2018

Institution	£607	$1,062	€890
Individual	£153	$258	€208
Online only	£524	$917	€769

Taylor & Francis has a flexible approach to subscriptions, enabling us to match individual libraries' requirements. This journal is available via a traditional institutional subscription (either print with online access, or online only at a discount) or as part of our libraries, subject collections or archives. For more information on our sales packages please visit http://www.tandfonline.com/page/librarians.

All current institutional subscriptions include online access for any number of concurrent users across a local area network to the currently available backfile and articles posted online ahead of publication.

Subscriptions purchased at the personal rate are strictly for personal, non-commercial use only. The reselling of personal subscriptions is prohibited. Personal subscriptions must be purchased with a personal cheque or credit card. Proof of personal status may be requested.

Dollar rates apply to all subscribers outside Europe. Euro rates apply to all subscribers in Europe, except the UK and the Republic of Ireland where the pound sterling rate applies. If you are unsure which rate applies to you please contact Customer Services in the UK. All subscriptions are payable in advance and all rates include postage. Journals are sent by air to the USA, Canada, Mexico, India, Japan and Australasia. Subscriptions are entered on an annual basis, i.e. January to December. Payment may be made by sterling cheque, dollar cheque, euro cheque, international money order, National Giro or credit cards (Amex, Visa and Mastercard).

Survival (USPS 013095) is published bimonthly (in Feb, Apr, Jun, Aug, Oct and Dec) by Routledge Journals, Taylor & Francis, 4 Park Square, Milton Park, Abingdon, OX14 4RN, United Kingdom.

The US annual subscription price is $842. Airfreight and mailing in the USA by agent named WN Shipping USA, 156-15, 146th Avenue, 2nd Floor, Jamaica, NY 11434, USA. Periodicals postage paid at Jamaica NY 11431.

US Postmaster: Send address changes to Survival, C/O Air Business Ltd / 156-15 146th Avenue, Jamaica, New York, NY11434.

Subscription records are maintained at Taylor & Francis Group, 4 Park Square, Milton Park, Abingdon, OX14 4RN, United Kingdom.

ORDERING INFORMATION

Please contact your local Customer Service Department to take out a subscription to the Journal: **USA, Canada:** Taylor & Francis, Inc., 530 Walnut Street, Suite 850, Philadelphia, PA 19106, USA. Tel: +1 800 354 1420; Fax: +1 215 207 0050. **UK/ Europe/Rest of World:** T&F Customer Services, Informa UK Ltd, Sheepen Place, Colchester, Essex, CO3 3LP, United Kingdom. Tel: +44 (0) 20 7017 5544; Fax: +44 (0) 20 7017 5198; Email: subscriptions@tandf.co.uk.

Back issues: Taylor & Francis retains a two-year back issue stock of journals. Older volumes are held by our official stockists: Periodicals Service Company, 351 Fairview Ave., Suite 300, Hudson, New York 12534, USA to whom all orders and enquiries should be addressed. *Tel* +1 518 537 4700 *Fax* +1 518 537 5899 *e-mail* psc@periodicals.com *web* http://www.periodicals.com/tandf.html.

The International Institute for Strategic Studies (IISS) and our publisher Taylor & Francis make every effort to ensure the accuracy of all the information (the "Content") contained in our publications. However, the IISS and our publisher Taylor & Francis, our agents, and our licensors make no representations or warranties whatsoever as to the accuracy, completeness, or suitability for any purpose of the Content. Any opinions and views expressed in this publication are the opinions and views of the authors, and are not the views of or endorsed by the IISS and our publisher Taylor & Francis. The accuracy of the Content should not be relied upon and should be independently verified with primary sources of information. The IISS and our publisher Taylor & Francis shall not be liable for any losses, actions, claims, proceedings, demands, costs, expenses, damages, and other liabilities whatsoever or howsoever caused arising directly or indirectly in connection with, in relation to or arising out of the use of the Content. Terms & Conditions of access and use can be found at http://www.tandfonline.com/page/terms-and-conditions.

The issue date is June–July 2019.

The print edition of this journal is printed on ANSI-conforming acid-free paper.

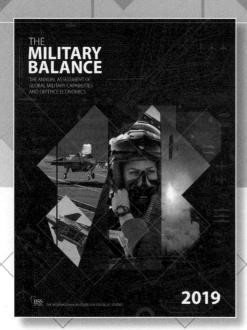

THE MILITARY BALANCE

The annual assessment of global military capabilities and defence economics

2019

The Military Balance is the annual IISS assessment of the military capabilities and defence economics of 171 countries. Now in its 60th year, it is an indispensable handbook for anyone conducting serious analysis of security policy and military affairs.

NEW FEATURES

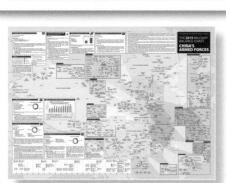

- Complementing its regional analysis, the book carries detailed assessments of defence developments in China, Russia and the United States. There are also features on Belarus, Chile, Iraq, Sweden, South Africa and Thailand, among others.

- New thematic texts analysing challenges in nuclear-arms control: past and present; quantum computing and defence; and defence analysis over the 60 years of *The Military Balance*.

- New global domain-trends section, covering economics, land, maritime, aerospace and cyber.

- New regional opening pages, highlighting major trends and detailing key data points, such as top-ten active military personnel and tactical combat-aircraft fleets.

- New regional arms orders and deliveries sections, outlining significant defence-procurement events in 2018.

- Updated comparative defence-statistics section, with graphics showing key data relating to defence economics and major land, sea and air capabilities, including brigade structures in China, Russia and the US and anti-air-warfare surface combatants and operators.

- Updated summaries of national military capability, at the start of each country entry.

- A new wall chart, focused on China's armed forces and military modernisation.

LAUNCHED/PUBLISHED

15 February 2019

PURCHASE *THE MILITARY BALANCE 2019* ONLINE:
www.iiss.org/militarybalance OR
https://www.tandfonline.com/tmib

IISS THE INTERNATIONAL INSTITUTE FOR STRATEGIC STUDIES

ROUTLEDGE
Routledge
Taylor & Francis Group

Mad Momentum Redux? The Rise and Fall of Nuclear Arms Control

Alexey Arbatov

In a September 1967 speech in San Francisco that attracted little notice at the time, Robert McNamara – then the US secretary of defense and one of the Cold War's most formidable strategic thinkers – took note of the primacy of technological progress in determining the state's policymaking: 'There is a kind of mad momentum intrinsic to the development of all new nuclear weaponry. If a weapon system works and works well, there is strong pressure from many directions to procure and deploy the weapon out of all proportion to the prudent level required.'[1] The enormous destructive power and technical complexity of nuclear arms had made critical political decisions hostage to the weapons' technical characteristics.

With regard to nuclear war, Carl von Clausewitz's classical postulate – that war is the continuation of politics by other means – might have been recast to say that war is the continuation of the technical characteristics of weapon systems that determine doctrines, operational plans and the contingencies of their employment. In the same speech, McNamara pointed out that 'actions – or even realistically potential actions – on each side … trigger reactions on the other side. It is precisely this action–reaction phenomenon that fuels the arms race.'[2] He also recognised something that seldom, if ever, had been acknowledged: 'If we had more accurate information about

Alexey Arbatov is Director of the Center for International Security at the Institute of World Economy and International Relations, and is a full member of the Russian Academy of Sciences. He participated in the START I negotiations in 1990, served as deputy chair of the Defense Committee of the State Duma from 1994–2003, and headed the Non-Proliferation Program at the Carnegie Moscow Center from 2004–17.

Survival | vol. 61 no. 3 | June–July 2019 | pp. 7–38   DOI 10.1080/00396338.2019.1614785

planned Soviet strategic forces, we simply would not have needed to build as large a nuclear force as we have today.'[3]

Coming from a top American official, these insights signified a revolution in the strategic mentality of the time. A half-century later, they remain relevant. Firstly, McNamara proposed a conceptual breakthrough out of the 'mad momentum' of the arms race: 'We do not want a nuclear arms race with the Soviet Union, primarily because the action–reaction phenomenon makes it foolish and futile … Both of our nations would benefit from a properly safeguarded agreement first to limit and later to reduce both our offensive and defensive strategic nuclear forces.'[4] This prompted the start of negotiations on strategic arms between the two nuclear superpowers two years later, which would usher in 40 years of diplomatic interaction between the United States and the Soviet Union (later Russia) that produced nine major treaties and agreements on nuclear forces. The quantities and aggregate destructive power of nuclear weapons were steeply reduced, the probability of nuclear war was drastically lowered, and the unprecedented transparency and predictability of nuclear forces that McNamara desired was ensured.

Secondly, McNamara's ideas have contemporary relevance because legacy Cold War-era arms control is collapsing and an uncontrolled nuclear arms race is threatening to return.

Thirdly, the principal nuclear powers' current generation of leaders, political elites and military officials has an inadequate understanding of the history of the nuclear arms race and nuclear arms control, and therefore an insufficient appreciation of the dangers of the vicious circle of the arms race and the international crises it provoked. Russian President Vladimir Putin recently expressed the hope that 'no new crises of the Cuban type happen in the world', adding that 'if anybody over there want it, they are welcome'.[5]

The world's ability to muddle through the next phase of international tensions without a major crisis, and to prevent such a crisis from escalating to nuclear Armageddon, is in doubt.

Falling dominoes

The evidence of arms-control disintegration is obvious and nowadays broadly discussed among states, within the world's professional community and mass media. Still, the array of emerging systemic crises is worth examining.

The United States' and Russia's withdrawal from the 1987 Intermediate-Range Nuclear Forces (INF) Treaty appears virtually inevitable. Given the US renunciation of the 1972 Anti-Ballistic Missile (ABM) Treaty in 2002, this would remove the remaining cornerstone of the nuclear-arms-reduction regime launched by the 1991 Strategic Arms Reduction Treaty (START I). Eight years have passed since Russia and the United States have discussed any option for the START follow-on agreement – the longest pause in strategic-arms talks for 50 years. Although both parties fulfilled their reduction obligations under the current New START by the February 2018 deadline (albeit with a number of reservations from Russia), the treaty will expire in 2021. The chances for successful negotiations on a new agreement after the abrogation of the INF Treaty, and given deep disagreements between the two parties on ballistic-missile defence (BMD) and other important issues, are bleak indeed. Meanwhile, Washington has been reluctant to extend New START to 2026 under the terms of the treaty, though Russia nowadays tepidly favours such an extension.

Against this background of the apparent abandonment of bilateral nuclear arms control, the United States and Russia are entering a new cycle of the arms race. Unprecedentedly, it will include competition not only in offensive nuclear weaponry but also in offensive and defensive non-nuclear strategic and medium-range weapons, as well as in the development of space weapons and cyber warfare.

Russia has been modernising its strategic triad for more than a decade, deploying and developing two new intercontinental-ballistic-missile (ICBM) systems (the SS-27 Mod 2/3 *Yars* and SS-29 *Sarmat*), one submarine-launched ballistic-missile (SLBM) system (the SS-N-32 *Bulava-30*), two heavy-bomber systems (the Tu-160M *Blackjack* and PAK DA), and long-range nuclear and dual-purpose air-, ground- and sea-launched cruise missiles (the Kh 102/101 (AS-23A/B), 9M2729 (SSC-8) and 3M14 (SS-N-30), respectively). Russia is also developing and deploying a new generation of nuclear and dual-purpose weapon systems unveiled in Putin's 1 March 2018 address: the *Avangard* strategic nuclear boost-glide hypersonic system; *Poseidon* long-range, high-speed, nuclear-propelled and nuclear-armed heavy torpe-does; *Burevestnik* nuclear-powered intercontinental nuclear cruise missiles; *Kinzhal* air-launched hypersonic middle-range missiles; and a number of other sub-strategic nuclear and dual-purpose systems.[6] Given the probable demise of the INF Treaty, intermediate-range land-based *Kalibr*-type cruise missiles and hypersonic missiles may be deployed. (Indeed, the US gov-ernment has alleged that Russia has already deployed a ground-launched cruise missile similar to the *Kalibr* 3M14.)

The United States, for its part, is developing strategic systems for limited nuclear strikes. These include *Trident*-2 SLBMs with low-yield W-76-2 warheads, B-61-12 variable-yield gravity bombs for heavy bombers and tactical-strike aircraft, long-range stand-off air-launched nuclear cruise mis-siles, and nuclear sea-based cruise missiles. The pending US withdrawal from the INF Treaty has lent further momentum to the development of land-based medium-range cruise, ballistic and hypersonic systems. In the longer term, beginning in the mid-2020s, the United States plans to modern-ise its whole strategic triad, replacing heavy bombers, ICBMs and nuclear submarines with SLBMs.[7]

Unlike the Cold War version, the new nuclear arms race will be multilat-eral, involving states such as China, India, Pakistan, Israel and North Korea as well as the United States and Russia. The intensification of the arms race would undoubtedly undermine the nuclear non-proliferation regime. The review conference of the Non-Proliferation Treaty (NPT) in 2015 ended in failure, and the next conference in 2020 is likely to fail as well. The nuclear-weapons states have reneged on their obligation under the NPT's Article VI to 'undertake to pursue negotiations in good faith on effective measures relating to cessation of the nuclear arms race at an early date and to nuclear disarmament'. Further aggravations include the US withdrawal from the 2015 multilateral nuclear deal on the Iranian atomic programme, the dead-lock over the concept of a zone free of weapons of mass destruction in the Middle East, and the deep split between nuclear and non-nuclear NPT states over the Treaty on the Prohibition of Nuclear Weapons approved by the UN General Assembly on 6 July 2017.[8] The probable degradation of NPT norms will prevent the treaty from effectively addressing the challenges of the significant future growth of the world's atomic energy and trade in nuclear materials and technologies. As a consequence, the line between peaceful and military use of nuclear energy through the nuclear fuel cycle will become even blurrier.

The new cycle of the arms race among nuclear-weapons states will probably encourage a new round of nuclear proliferation: Iran and Saudi Arabia could well join the nuclear club, as could Brazil, Egypt, Japan, Nigeria, South Korea, Taiwan and Turkey, among others. This would eventually seal the fate of the Comprehensive Nuclear Test-Ban Treaty (CTBT), which for 23 years has not entered into legal force because of the refusal of the United States and several other nations to ratify it. Under the thunder of nuclear explosions, the Fissile Material Cut-Off Treaty, on which negotiations have been stalled for more than a quarter-century, will die a quiet death. Increased production of weapons-grade uranium and plutonium, and nuclear-arms proliferation in the unstable regions of the world, will sooner or later afford international terrorists access to nuclear explosives. This could end current civilisation, if a war between nuclear states does not do so earlier.

McNamara must have been pleasantly surprised at the 50 years of successful nuclear arms control and non-proliferation that followed his 1967 speech. But the impending implosion of his hopes and ideas would have deeply depressed him.

The political roots of the crisis

The present confrontations between Russia and the West and the US and China are exacerbating the crises of arms control and whipping up the arms race, but the roots of the crisis run deeper. Traditional nuclear arms control emerged on the basis of a predominantly bipolar world order, a more or less symmetrical balance of power between the US and the Soviet Union, and a relatively simple delineation between nuclear and conventional weapon systems. Strategic circumstances have profoundly changed during the last 50 years, and arms control has largely failed to adapt to the changes.

The collapse of the Soviet Union accelerated the emergence of a multipolar world order. Other power centres – China and the EU globally, and India, Iran, Japan, Pakistan, Turkey and others regionally – started playing increasingly important international roles. With few exceptions, nuclear arms control did not figure prominently in their external interests and security concepts. In addition, the transition from confrontation to cooperation among the great powers during the 1990s brought the probability of war between them close to zero. This development redirected the international security agenda to ethnic and religious conflicts, international terrorism, nuclear proliferation, and illegal arms and drugs trafficking. For a time, the unprecedented improvement in relations between Russia and the West actually encouraged monumental breakthroughs in nuclear arms control: huge Cold War-era stockpiles were reduced by roughly an order of magnitude in weapons numbers and, to an even greater extent, in aggregate destructive power.[9] This was accomplished by unilateral reductions on the part of France, Russia, the United Kingdom and the US, and even more through the INF Treaty, START I (1991), START II (1993), the START III Framework Agreement (1997), the Strategic Offensive Reductions Treaty (SORT) in 2002 and finally New START (2010). The deeper trend over the course of these agreements was worrying, however, as the substantial achievements of 1987–97 gave way to complacency.

Despite Moscow's regular appeals to turn the bilateral arms-reduction process into a multilateral one, occasionally joined by Washington, the other seven nuclear states declined. They have routinely asserted that Russia and the US still possessed 90% of the global nuclear arsenal and called for more substantial reductions as a precondition for their participation in multilateral disarmament efforts. Some multilateral agreements were achieved: indefinite extension of the NPT (1995), the signing of the CTBT (1996) and the adoption of the Additional Protocol to the NPT, which expanded International Atomic Energy Agency (IAEA) safeguards (1997). Nevertheless, the two leading powers failed to elaborate consistent and equitable principles of multilateral nuclear-arms limitations (parity, strategic stability, national or aggregate quotas for the third nuclear-weapons states), to propose a sensible sequence by which third states could join the process, or to put forward a practical substantive agenda for negotiations on classes and types of weapon systems and realistic verification methods.

In the context of ongoing proliferation of medium- and long-range bal-listic and cruise missiles, the two leading powers proved unable to adapt existing arms-control treaties (in particular, this relates to the ABM and INF treaties, and the New START follow-on) to the new military environment. Instead, the probable emergence of a multilateral nuclear and missile world became a convenient argument for the abrogation of such agreements. Another mistake was the common assumption that improved political and economic relations between states made arms control irrelevant. In reality, there was a large gap between merely ceasing to be enemies and becom-ing allies, and arms control remained useful, if not crucial, for narrowing that gap. The nuclear arms race between Russia and the United States actu-ally stopped during the 1990s and 2000s.[10] But other types of technological developments tangibly affected military capabilities of states and non-state entities. As a result, traditional demarcation lines between nuclear and con-ventional arms, offensive and defensive weapons, and global and regional systems were eroded.

When START I was about to expire in 2009, it fell to the Barack Obama and Dmitry Medvedev administrations to hastily work out New START (the Prague Treaty), which effectively legalised the strategic nuclear force levels set by SORT seven years earlier. Having been a useful stopgap measure, the treaty now failed to address new weapons developments and was quite relaxed in its traditional limits, including the counting rules and verification regime.[11] There has been no material progress since. The effective hiatus of aggressive arms control after 1997, and still more after 2010, has led to the wholesale disintegration of the arms-control system and the beginning of a new cycle of the arms race.

Technological drivers of disintegration

Trends in military technology have been blurring the fundamental arms-control delineation between nuclear and conventional offensive systems. The development of high-precision, long-range non-nuclear air- and sea-launched cruise missiles relying on advanced electronics and command-control and information systems, increasingly based in space, have been especially consequential. Such weapons were effectively demonstrated in the wars in

Iraq (1990, 2003), Kosovo (1999), Libya (2011) and Syria (2014–18).[12] New long-range, precision-guided offensive arms are degrading the nuclear threshold in several ways. Firstly, most of them are using dual-purpose delivery systems such that the other side would not know whether it was under conventional or nuclear attack before actual explosive impact.[13] Secondly, many of the weapons are able to hit the nuclear forces and command-and-control information systems of the opponent, potentially prompting nuclear retaliation or pre-emption. The threats posed by US long-range cruise missiles to Russian strategic missiles may be exaggerated, as Russia's silo launchers and underground command centres are super-hardened.[14] The fact remains that the American weapons can hit early-warning radars, light shelters for mobile ICBMs, missile submarines at bases and heavy bombers at airfields, as well as command-and-control and communications sites that are not hardened.

Russia is vaguer on limited nuclear warfare

A much larger potential threat to strategic targets may come from prospective boost-glide weapons. The United States has been developing and testing several systems of this type.[15] Recently, Russia overtook the US with its analogue, called the *Avangard*, and in 2019 will start deploying it on modified SS-19-X-Mod4 ICBMs and later possibly on new heavy SS-29 ICBMs (*Sarmat*), which are to replace SS-18 (*Satan*) missiles.[16] The US and Russia are not the only countries to develop high-precision long-range conventional (including boost-glide hypersonic) weapons. China is working on its project at an accelerated pace; India is developing these weapons as well, and other countries are likely to follow.

The concepts and systems for limited nuclear strikes ('tailored options') are also obscuring the nuclear–conventional threshold. The United States is apparently associating such options with strategic/tactical gravity bombs (B-12-61), W-76-2 low-yield warheads for a portion of its *Trident*-2 SLBMs, the nuclear long-range air-launched cruise-missile system, and new medium-range sea-based (nuclear) cruise-missile systems.[17] Russia is vaguer on the notion of limited nuclear warfare, but some unofficial sources relate it to tactical nuclear platforms, such as the boost-glide *Avangard* and various sub-strategic systems.[18]

Another avenue of technical development is dissolving the border separating defence and offence. In 2007, the United States initiated deployment of a global missile-defence system with regional segments in the Euro-Atlantic and the Pacific. Over Russia's objections, the US refused to develop a joint system, or to accept binding obligations not to calibrate its missile-defence system to intercept Russian missiles. Starting in 2011, Russia started an air–space defence programme that includes missile defence.[19] Some senior Russian military and military-industrial authorities have indicated that the US system's defensive capability against Russian strategic forces is negligible because the Russian ICBMs and SLBMs are sufficiently numerous, survivable and equipped with effective BMD penetration aids.[20] Many Russian and American defence and security experts share this view.[21] Nevertheless, Russia's political leadership has continued to insist that US BMD is undercutting Russian nuclear deterrence and bilateral strategic stability. While such claims are to a significant degree politically motivated, the open-ended nature of the US BMD programme and an American rejection of any technical or strategic limitations or predictability regime for that programme could raise legitimate strategic concerns.

The upshot is that new US defensive programmes are conceptually erasing the strategic demarcation that McNamara established between 'offensive' BMD (intended to negate an opponent's second-strike capability) and 'defensive' BMD (intended to protect strategic retaliatory forces against a disarming strike, or defend against a third nuclear state's attack).[22] This line is also being diluted at the operational level. For Russia, the US *Aegis* and *Aegis Ashore* BMD Standard-3 (SM-3) interceptor launchers on ships, and at land bases in Romania and Poland, are indistinguishable from the universal Mk-41 launchers for ship-based *Tomahawk* cruise missiles. Hence, Russia is able to claim that the US is in violation of the INF Treaty, which prohibited deployment of land-based, long-range cruise missiles and their launchers.

The development of BMD systems with anti-satellite capabilities is also destabilising. In the US, the most advanced system of this class is a modified version of the *Aegis* Mk7 naval anti-missile/anti-satellite system equipped with SM-3 missiles and a self-guided kinetic warhead, tested against a satellite in 2008.[23] Russia envisions anti-satellite capability for the S-500 surface-to-air missile complexes, as well as for the long-range kinetic-kill *Nudol* missile interceptor (an analogue of the US ground-based interceptor system in Alaska and California) for the new A-235 Moscow BMD system.[24] China has also joined the anti-satellite arms race, having tested its system in 2008, and India conducted its first test in 2019. Talks between Moscow and Washington on space weapons were conducted in the late 1970s and 1980s and in a multilateral format in the 2000s, but failed. Substantial dialogue on cyber-warfare capabilities, which will have an undoubted but as yet unclear effect on strategic stability, has not developed further than preliminary consultations.

Yet another victim of technological developments is the delineation between global and regional offensive and defensive weapons. This has never been ironclad – recall the Cold War debates about Soviet missiles in Cuba, and American forward-based missiles and strike aircraft – but now is creating growing strategic problems. US regional BMD in Europe and in Asia, aimed at Iranian and North Korean missiles, is perceived in Russia and China as intended to intercept their strategic ICBMs and SLBMs at boost phase, thus degrading their respective deterrents. Accordingly, the two powers are developing a range of missile systems to penetrate these defences. The United States is planning to counter these programmes with new nuclear arms of its own, as proclaimed in the US Department of Defense's Nuclear Posture Review of 2018.

Russia and China perceive the United States' employment of long-range, precision-guided conventional systems (subsonic and, in the future, hypersonic) against hostile regional states and terrorists as implicitly threatening non-nuclear counterforce strikes. Russia is countering with its air–space defence and long-range dual-purpose offence programmes, China with analogous conventional offensive systems. The US Nuclear Posture Review interpreted these measures as new threats, to be deterred by, among other means, threatened nuclear retaliation.[25]

Russia's concern about third states' medium-range missiles in Asia within reach of its territory has prompted its criticism of the 1987 INF Treaty at a high official level, since it bans only Russian and American weapons of that variety.[26] In 2018, Washington echoed this argument, claiming the right to deploy medium-range missiles to counter comparable Chinese weapons. Against that political background, mutual accusations of treaty violations gained momentum and contributed to its collapse.

In light of the growing impact of such systems on strategic stability, leaving them out of arms-control agreements would diminish the effects of nuclear disarmament. Including such weapons in agreements would create tough problems in terms of definitions, counting rules and verification, all the more so given that conventional systems have been and most probably will be extensively used by the US, Russia and other powers in local military operations.

A sharp turn in global politics dealt an especially devastating blow to the nuclear arms-control system. After 2012, Moscow embarked on strengthening Russia's control of the post-Soviet space (Georgia, Ukraine) and its projection of force beyond it (Syria, Venezuela), modernising its conventional forces, and energising the implementation of a nuclear modernisation programme that had begun earlier. In response, the United States and its allies imposed economic sanctions and revived the strategy of isolation, containment and arms build-up against Moscow. A fierce propaganda fight broke out, amped up by hacker sabotage operations. Military competition between Russia and the United States intensified in Eastern Europe, the Baltic and Black Sea areas, and the Arctic and Asia-Pacific regions.

Yet the main problem now is not the technical complexity of the strategic relationships, as intricate as they are, nor the degree of turmoil in the world order, as chaotic as it is. It is rather the distinct failure on the part of the new generation of political and military elites on both sides to appreciate the high strategic importance and priority of arms control.

Lessons of the Cold War arms race

The expectation at the top level of the Harry Truman administration was that it would take a generation or more for the Soviet Union to break the US nuclear monopoly established at the end of the Second World War.[27] With some help from espionage, however, it happened only four years later. The US attempt to restore its preponderance with a thermonuclear-weapon test at the Pacific Eniwetok Atoll on 31 October 1952 was thwarted even sooner – by the Soviet hydrogen-bomb test on 12 August 1953. As Daniel Ellsberg, once one of McNamara's 'whiz kids', has noted, during the ensuing decades the crash production of fission and then fusion nuclear weapons went on, apparently without any rational justification. The United States was simply matching growing production rates with an ever-expanding target list, while the Soviet Union was just catching up.[28] This course produced insane levels of destructive overkill on both sides.

The United States' plan for the actual use of nuclear weapons, set out in the Strategic Air Command's first Single Integrated Operational Plan (SIOP-62), called for quickly following any armed conflict with the Soviet Union with massive airstrikes, conducted by 1,850 heavy and medium bombers, that would drop 4,700 atomic and hydrogen bombs on cities and military installations across the Soviet Union, China and their allies.[29] The Pentagon's estimates were that this attack would have resulted in 800 million casualties in the targeted and adjacent neutral countries.[30] That amounted to approximately one-third of the global population at the time.

The US nuclear build-up peaked around 1965 at about 34,600 warheads, and by the end of the 1980s this had declined to 24,700 weapons. The Soviet stockpile was consistently rising and, according to the highest available assessment, reached a plateau of 46,100 warheads by the end of the 1980s. The cumulative destructive power of the US arsenal was at its maximum of 19,000 megatons in 1960, while that of the Soviet Union peaked at 19,700 megatons in 1975. Taken together, the two superpowers accumulated the maximum destruction potential of 26,000 megatons (equivalent to 1.3m Hiroshima bombs) in 1973–74.[31]

William Perry, the US secretary of defense in 1993–96, wrote in 2015:

> When I look back on those years, I see a historically all-too-familiar irrational, impassioned thinking that … drove the frenzied debates on nuclear strategy, drove the huge additions in destructiveness we made to our nuclear forces, and brought us to the brink of blundering into a nuclear war … Even before the nuclear arms buildups of the 1970s and 1980s, our nuclear forces were more than enough to blow up the world

> … Yet we obsessively claimed inadequacies in our nuclear forces. We
> fantasized about a 'window of vulnerability'. Both governments – ours
> and that of the Soviet Union – spread fear among our peoples. We acted as
> if the world had not changed with the emergence of the nuclear age, the
> age in which the world changed as never before.[32]

The rivalry of the two superpowers in new nuclear-delivery vehicles had
four distinct but overlapping rounds. In the late 1940s and 1950s, it involved
bombers and medium-range missiles; in the 1960s and early 1970s strategic
land- and sea-based ballistic missiles; in the 1970s and early 1980s ballistic
missiles with multiple individually targeted re-entry vehicles (MIRVs); and
in the 1980s medium-range cruise missiles and strategic ballistic missiles
with enhanced hard-target kill capability (that is, against hardened ICBM
silo launchers and command centres). Until the end of the 1980s, arms-race
cycles went through intensive build-ups of new generations of delivery
systems that fully or partially replaced the preceding ones.

Various weapon systems affected the probability of nuclear war in different
ways. Some, such as sea-based long-range ballistic missiles and ICBMs in
hardened silos and on ground-mobile launchers, lowered that probability
insofar as they provided for survivable retaliatory capability. Others, such
as ICBMs and SLBMs with enhanced counterforce (that is, disarming-strike)
capability, increased the threat of first strike or pre-emption. McNamara in
San Francisco nonetheless recognised the crowning irony of nuclear weapons:

> While thermonuclear power is almost inconceivably awesome and
> represents virtually unlimited potential destructiveness, it has proven
> to be a limited diplomatic instrument … There is a strong psychological
> tendency to regard superior nuclear forces as a simple and unfailing
> solution to security … What must be understood is that our nuclear
> strategic forces play a vital and absolutely necessary role in our security
> and that of our allies, but it is an intrinsically limited role.[33]

McNamara's paradox is the fundamental lesson of the 70-year nuclear
arms race. Just two or three decades ago, in the late 1980s and 1990s, the

notion was commonly accepted in the Euro-Atlantic and post-Soviet political and strategic communities, but now is increasingly questioned. Although today the number and megatonnage of the weapons in the US and Russian arsenals are many times lower than they were in McNamara's time, the current nuclear balance still reflects massive overkill: about 1,600 megatons, or some 80,000 Hiroshimas.[34] Furthermore, modern nations have far lower tolerances for war casualties and face considerably greater economic and social fragility than they did during the Cold War. Even though societies are weaker and more risk-averse, the US and Russia consider their existing destructive potentials insufficient for effective deterrence. Thus, policymakers do not appear to have learned McNamara's lesson. They seem more focused on technological breakthroughs for the sake of gaining a decisive theoretical military advantage than on actual improvements in national and international security by enhancing arms-control systems and regimes.

The history of the nuclear arms race is full of examples of initial strategic breakthroughs that have led to serious damage to national security. Having been the first to create nuclear weapons, the US assumed it would enjoy long-term world dominance. At the time, this implied using the nuclear threat to contain Joseph Stalin's communist expansion and, if necessary, dropping atomic bombs on major Soviet cities. As John Newhouse has recounted, after warily considering the so-called 'Baruch Plan' – which called for the transfer of atomic weapons and technology to the IAEA, a UN body – in 1946, the Truman administration adopted an 'anti-Soviet line … combined with a conviction that Soviet science would always lag well behind America's, whose security … must lie in doing whatever it took to preserve a long lead in advanced weapons over the enemy'.[35]

Only three years later, of course, the US lost its nuclear monopoly and in another ten years – after Soviet development of long-range bombers and ICBMs – the United States was once and forever deprived of its traditional invulnerability to conflicts and wars sourced beyond the two oceans that surrounded its territory. Thirty years after Hiroshima, the People's Republic of China could target the US with nuclear missiles, and in another 50 years North Korea could do so. The creation of the atomic bomb may have been inevitable. But clearly Truman and other American officials of his time did not foresee the long-term outcome of the nuclear arms race and proliferation, and had they done so would have been horrified.

A less dramatic but still instructive example is the US initiative in the deployment of MIRVed sea- and land-based strategic missiles. The US began to develop them in the mid-1960s to trump any robust ABM defence that the Soviets might deploy in the future. In 1969, however, the US–Soviet Strategic Arms Limitation Talks (SALT) generated the prospect of stringent mutual limits on ABM systems, which materialised with the ABM Treaty in 1972. Once that treaty came into view, there was no longer any urgent need to deploy MIRVed missiles. But McNamara's successors proceeded with the deployment of MIRVed *Minuteman*-3 ICBMs in 1970 and *Poseidon* SLBMs in 1971 in order to gain superiority over the Soviet Union in nuclear warheads after missile launchers had been limited by the SALT I agreement. This move was seen as enabling the expansion of the United States' target

The other side caught up swiftly

list in the Soviet Union and returning to a counterforce strategy (that is, attacking the strategic military forces of the opponent), which was officially declared in 1974 with the 'retargeting doctrine' of secretary of defense James Schlesinger.[36] Once again, Washington was establishing a lead in advanced military technology. And once again, the other side caught up swiftly, deploying one new MIRVed SLBM and three MIRVed ICBM systems. In the late 1970s, this provoked a panic in the United States with respect to the 'window of vulnerability' of its land-based missile force that cast fatal doubt on the SALT II Treaty and lasted throughout the 1980s.

A more recent and revealingly analogous case involves conventional high-precision, long-range systems. Initially, the technology was incorporated into dual-purpose air-launched cruise missiles (ALCMs) and sea-launched *Tomahawk* cruise missiles (SLCMs), developed and deployed by the US starting in the mid-1970s. The Soviet Union followed suit in the early 1980s, but, due to inadequate guidance systems, only with missiles carrying nuclear warheads. American conventional SLCMs were mass-produced and extensively used in local conflicts, but eventually were integrated into the US strategic doctrine and began to affect the nuclear balance as an instrument of 'conventional deterrence' against nuclear opponents – namely, Russia and China.[37] In this area, American superiority continued for much longer – about 30 years – but eventually Russia caught up and by 2010 started mass production of conventional precision-guided SLCMs (the *Kalibr* 3M14 (SS-N-30A)) and ALCMs (Kh-555 (AS-22) and Kh-101 (AS-23A)). Their number by 2018 increased 30-fold, and they were effectively demonstrated in Syria after 2015.[38] Current Russian military doctrine postulates: 'In the context of implementing the missions of strategic deterrence by use of force the Russian Federation envisions employment of high precision weapons.'[39]

In the meantime, since old cruise missiles are subsonic, with long flight times and limited range, the United States initiated a programme dubbed 'prompt conventional global strike' to develop boost-glide weapons capable of hitting any target in the world with precision-guided conventional warheads within 60 minutes after launch.[40] Supposedly, such arms were intended to counter terrorists and rogue states, but Moscow, keeping in mind the US concept of strategic 'conventional deterrence', suspected that this qualitatively new American capability would also be a strategic threat to Russia. Speaking at the Valdai Discussion Club in 2015, Putin said: 'A strategy already exists for a so-called first disarming strike, including with the use of long-range, high-precision non-nuclear weapons, the effect of which may be compared to that of nuclear arms.'[41]

In tests of boost-glide systems in 2010–11, the United States seemed to take the lead over Russia. By 2018, however, Russia conducted a series of successful tests of the boost-glide *Avangard* system and commenced deployment of two missile regiments in 2019. Obviously impressed by Russian advances in cruise missiles and hypersonic systems, the Pentagon, in the 2018 Nuclear Posture Review, for the first time officially expressed concern over this threat: 'Extreme circumstances could include significant non-nuclear attacks. Significant non-nuclear strategic attacks include, but are not limited to, attacks on the US, allied, or partner civilian population or infrastructure, and attacks on US or allied nuclear forces, their command and control, or warning and attack assessment capabilities.'[42] It is uncertain whether *Avangard* gliders carry nuclear or conventional warheads, whether they can be MIRVed, whether their accuracy is sufficient for non-nuclear strikes, and whether Russia will keep its advantage in boost-glide hypersonic systems for a sustained period. But an emerging US vulnerability to conventional missile attacks would represent a major strategic shift.

The Soviet Union also experienced comparable 'boomerang effects' of the arms race. Its launch of the first artificial satellite *Sputnik* in 1957 demonstrated its primacy in space and intercontinental-missile technology. Prompted by Soviet leader Nikita Khrushchev's bravado ('we are forging missiles like sausages' and 'we will bury you'), John F. Kennedy campaigned in part on the existence of a 'missile gap' favouring the Soviet Union (it turned out to be illusory), and was obliged to initiate a crash missile build-up.[43] From 1961 to 1967, the United States' strategic-missile force increased 40 times over and achieved a 4:1 superiority over the Soviet Union's force.[44] Khrushchev's desperate attempt in 1962 to curtail the United States' growing superiority by deploying medium-range missiles to Cuba provoked a crisis in which only sheer luck and some timely political acumen saved the world from catastrophe. The crisis ended with Moscow's withdrawal of the missiles and, while American officials had confidentially indicated to their Soviet counterparts that the US would remove medium-range nuclear missiles from Turkey at a later date, Moscow's international humiliation. Khrushchev's successors invested immense resources to close a missile gap they now perceived to favour the US and thus achieve strategic parity in the 1970s.

Kennedy initiated a crash missile build-up

Another example was the development of BMD systems. The Soviet Union made an early start in 1953 and initially got ahead of the US, achieving the first successful intercept of a medium-range missile in 1961.[45] Once again, Khrushchev could not refrain from reckless boasting: 'We can without missing hit a fly in the outer space.'[46] But the American BMD programme, started in 1958, had outpaced the Soviet one by 1963. Since the late 1960s, American BMD programmes – the *Safeguard* system from 1969–72, Reagan's Strategic Defense Initiative (SDI, or 'Star Wars') after 1983 and European BMD since 2007 – have plagued Moscow. As noted, the Soviet BMD programme in the mid-1960s incentivised the development of the American MIRVed systems, leading to two massive and costly arms-race cycles in the 1970s and 1980s involving fivefold increases in strategic-warhead numbers and the destabilisation of the nuclear balance.

Perhaps the most striking example was the deployment of the Soviet RSD-10 *Pioneer* (SS-20) land-based, intermediate-range ballistic missiles (IRBMs), which started in 1976. Allegedly, it was designed to replace obsolete SS-4 and SS-5 missiles and maintain regional balance vis-à-vis US forward-based nuclear-attack aircraft and French and British nuclear forces. In reality, this Soviet deployment was hugely excessive, reflecting the absence of any rational civilian control over the military–industrial complex. The total number of SS-4 and SS-5 missiles was about 700, but the new ground-mobile SS-20 IRBMs were MIRVed, and constituted a radical qualitative improvement and manifold build-up of nuclear forces in terms of aggregate warheads.[47] As revealed later, the planned total deployment of missiles of this type was 650, of which two-thirds were to be located in Europe and one-third in Asia. Of those, 405 (carrying 1,215 warheads in total) were already deployed by 1987.

Responding in 1979, the United States and NATO decided to bring 108 *Pershing*-2 IRBMs and 464 BGM-109G US ground-launched cruise missiles to Europe. According to Oleg Grinevsky, a patriarch of Soviet diplomacy, the Soviet Foreign Ministry (in particular, the deputy minister Georgy Kornienko) timidly proposed stopping or limiting the SS-20 build-up so as to preclude the US deployment. But Marshal Dmitry Ustinov, the defence minister, and Marshal Nikolay Ogarkov, head of the General Staff, consolidating the hardline position of the Communist Party Politburo under Yuri Andropov, flatly refused.[48] The US deployment started in 1983, and led to a second dangerous crisis in superpower relations and a breakdown of arms-control negotiations in Geneva. But Moscow's view of the situation soon changed dramatically: while Soviet missiles could not reach American territory, those of the United States could easily cover all of the Soviet Union's European territory. Worse still, as seen from the Kremlin, *Pershing*-2 missiles were capable of striking targets with high-precision, ground-penetrating warheads and, in an ominously short (seven-minute) flight time, destroying hardened underground national command centres. Furthermore, ground-launched cruise missiles, with their low trajectory, could not be tracked by radars and therefore afforded almost zero warning time – and, according to Soviet military estimates, might destroy up to 65% of other military and civilian targets across the European part of the Soviet Union.[49]

The upshot was that Moscow's attempt to redress the theatre nuclear balance with NATO turned into a major blunder that deeply undercut its security. As a matter of damage control, Mikhail Gorbachev, the new Soviet leader, in 1987 was compelled to agree to the INF Treaty, based on the principle of 'double global zero'. It effectively required the elimination of 1,846 Soviet medium- and shorter-range deployed and reserve missiles – 1,000 missiles more than corresponding US missile cuts and covering three times as many nuclear warheads. The medium-range-missile saga of the 1980s is of particular relevance to the present prospect of the collapse of the INF Treaty.

Ignoring the lessons

Vasily Klyuchevsky, a Russian historian who lived in the nineteenth century, is supposed to have observed: 'History does not teach anybody anything – it just punishes for not learning its lessons.' It looks as though the nuclear powers are on the verge of once again living up to this grim insight.

The main novelty of the current US nuclear strategy and weapons programmes is the concept of a limited or selective nuclear war, which originated in the 1960s with massive deployments of tactical nuclear arms in Europe and Asia. From the early 1970s, the United States promoted various options for selective and limited strategic strikes against Soviet military targets.[50] In the 2018 Nuclear Posture Review, this concept once again took on a central role and was addressed to Russia:

> Recent Russian statements on this evolving nuclear weapons doctrine appear to lower the threshold for Moscow's first-use of nuclear weapons. Russia demonstrates its perception of the advantage these systems provide through numerous exercises and statements. Correcting this mistaken Russian perception is a strategic imperative … To address these

types of challenges and preserve deterrence stability, the United States
will enhance the flexibility and range of its tailored deterrence options.[51]

As noted, this concept would rely on the full range of sea- and air-launched
nuclear and dual-purpose systems, and possibly medium-range land-based
ones, though the US has not as yet indicated that it will deploy INF-covered
land-based systems in Europe.[52]

As for Russia, it played with this idea in 2003, when an official Ministry
of Defence document announced plans for the 'de-escalation of aggression
… [by] the threat to deliver or by the actual delivery of strikes of various
intensity using conventional and (or) nuclear weapons'. Thus, the document assumed the possibility of 'dosed combat employment of selected
components of the Strategic Deterrence Force'.[53] Current Russian military
doctrine and other official documents make no mention of such concepts,
but they have been frequently discussed in professional military circles,
including those associated with governmental institutions, which stressed
'the limited nature of a first nuclear strike, which is designed not to harden,
but rather to sober up an aggressor, to force it to halt its attack and move
to negotiations'.[54]

In an address to the Russian Federal Assembly on 1 March 2018, Putin
said: 'Any use of nuclear weapons against Russia or its allies, weapons of
small, medium or any yield at all, will be considered as a nuclear attack on
this country. Retaliation will be immediate, with all the attendant consequences.'[55] This statement does not appear to countenance the concept of
limited nuclear response, though it also does not negate it. Russian military doctrine postulates: 'The Russian Federation shall reserve the right to
use nuclear weapons in response to the use of nuclear and other types of
weapons of mass destruction against it and/or its allies, as well as in the
event of aggression against the Russian Federation with the use of conventional weapons when the very existence of the state is in jeopardy.' The
purpose of a nuclear strike is defined as 'the infliction of the assigned level
of damage on an aggressor in any conditions'.[56] These formulations too do
not embrace the notion of limited nuclear war, but do not exclude them
either. It is not clear when and how exactly the 'existence of the state' can be

considered in jeopardy, and what 'level of damage' to the enemy might be interpreted as sufficient.

Moscow has often followed the US example by adapting its strategy and doctrine to fit its technology. No matter how much the deterrence doctrine is used to justify supposedly limited nuclear capabilities, they actually lower the nuclear threshold and increase the likelihood of any armed clash between the superpowers escalating into a nuclear conflict with a subsequent exchange of mass nuclear strikes. Having retained more sub-strategic nuclear arms than the rest of the world combined, Russia could be shifting its emphasis to conventional or dual-purpose systems.[57] Nevertheless, if the US is really concerned about neutralising Moscow's suspected concept of limited nuclear use, the best way to do so would be to flatly deny such a possibility instead of responding in kind. Still better would be a joint US–Russia declaration excluding any nuclear first strike or first use, as voiced in the 1970s and 1980s with respect to 'winning and fighting nuclear war', especially if it were substantiated by a follow-on to START and a radical reduction in sub-strategic nuclear forces.

Putin compared the test with the Sputnik launch

The same boomerang dialectics may arise with advanced hypersonic weapon systems. Russia's programme has been justified by the need to penetrate the American BMD system on the US continent, in Europe, in Asia and on surface ships. Putin declared the last successful test of the boost-glide *Avangard* in December 2018 as 'a New Year's present to the country' and even compared it with the *Sputnik* launch of 1957.[58] Describing its unique qualities, he said: 'It flies to its target like a meteorite, as a burning ball, fireball ... As you understand nobody in the world has anything comparable ... Sometime probably there will be, but in the meantime our guys will invent something else.'[59] On cue, the United States has accelerated its hypersonic-development programme.[60] The future strategic importance of the new weapon systems remains uncertain. It will be defined by their cost and scale of deployment, accuracy and class of warhead (nuclear or conventional), resistance of command-and-control and navigation assets to countermeasures, and the availability of opposing tracking and intercept systems.

From a strategic perspective, such a system might be needed if the United States could create a BMD system capable of defending against 1,500 Russian ballistic missiles' nuclear warheads, or at least a few hundred of those surviving a counterforce strike. But this is impossible in the foreseeable future, and the expansion of US BMD, envisioned by the ballistic-missile-defence review of 2019, does not imply anything like SDI's notional capabilities.[61] (In fact, the Soviet Union initiated development of a nuclear boost-glide system called *Albatross* in the mid-1980s as a countermeasure to SDI.) Hence, *Avangard*, like a number of other advanced arms programmes that Putin announced in 2018, may look exciting to Russia as a technological achievement, but is obviously excessive as a response to the United States' BMD systems. If deployed at limited scale, hypersonic arms will not tangibly affect the strategic balance. But if both sides were to deploy them in large numbers, with nuclear or highly accurate conventional warheads, they could disrupt Moscow's nuclear deterrence strategy and Russia's national security.

At the Valdai Discussion Club in Sochi in October 2018, Putin formulated the main concept of the Russian nuclear doctrine:

> Our concept is based on a launch-on-warning strike … This means that we are prepared and will use nuclear weapons only when we know for certain that some potential aggressor is attacking Russia, our territory … A missile attack early warning system … monitors the globe, warning about the launch of any strategic missile … and identifying the area from which it was launched. Second, the system tracks the trajectory of a missile flight. Third, it locates a nuclear warhead impact zone. Only when we know for certain – and this takes a few seconds to understand – that Russia is being attacked we will deliver a retaliatory strike.[62]

This launch-on-warning concept is extremely controversial, leaving supreme national command authority only a few minutes for a decision, which may be triggered by a technical mishap, strategic miscalculation or psychological stress. Some 50 years ago, Herbert York warned about 'a state of affairs in which the determination of whether or not doomsday has arrived will be made either by an automatic device … or by a pre-programmed President who, whether he knows it or not, will be carrying out orders written years before by some operations analyst'.[63]

Hypersonic systems are prone to making the situation still more dangerous. Launched to fly at an altitude of 50–60 kilometres, their trajectory goes largely under the BMD radars' beams with broadly changing azimuths, which makes their flight path unpredictable and precludes interception at a pre-programmed rendezvous point. Moscow emphasises this very characteristic in its BMD penetration strategy. At the same time, however, the characteristic precludes confirmation of a missile attack by tracking radars after the launch of hypersonic boosters is detected by early-warning satellites (at least as long as there are no space-based infrared systems for tracking hypersonic gliders). After satellites detect a missile launch 60 to 90 seconds later, the next time they will see a hypersonic glider will be three to four minutes before impact, which does not leave time for authorisation of a launch-on-warning strike.[64] While the air-defence challenges presented by hypersonic systems may be addressable through the deployment of different sensors and other technical innovations, this remedy would take time to develop and its feasibility remains uncertain.

If the US and Russia broadly introduce hypersonic arms, both nations will face this problem. But, according to Putin, launch on swarning amounts to Russia's main deterrence concept. About half of its strategic warheads are deployed on silo-based ICBMs (including the forthcoming *Sarmat* heavy missiles and *Avangard* boosters). They are the primary weapon systems for launch on warning due to both their vulnerability to counterforce strike and their high ('hair-trigger') launch readiness. For the US, the concept is secondary since only a quarter of its force (by actual loading) is deployed on silo-based ICBMs. Thus, Moscow, having initiated the hypersonic arms race, may in the future face the threat of a disarming strategic strike and would have to consider several fraught options. One would be to sustain 'the infliction of the assigned level of damage on an aggressor in any conditions', envisioned by the current military doctrine, without launch on warning.[65] This would imply mammoth costs in relocating the strategic force in sufficient numbers to highly survivable ground-mobile, sea- and air-basing modes, along with their command-and-control complexes.

Another option might be to retain the launch-on-warning concept, under which retaliation should be authorised upon receiving information from early-warning satellites. This would mean neglecting the history of satellites' false alarms over the course of their decades of service. In addition, the reliability of space systems could become compromised by growing anti-satellite capability or cyber warfare.

The third option would be to reduce 'the assigned level of damage on an aggressor' and rely primarily on ground-mobile and sea-based systems, while gradually phasing out silo-based ICBMs. This move would save a lot of money and might be facilitated by lowering the overall force numbers under the follow-on START. This would be in line with the rational strategic programme elaborated in 1998 by a Russian version of a 'blue ribbon' military–civilian panel commissioned by then-minister of defence Marshal Igor Sergeyev and headed by Nikolay Laverov, vice-president of the Russian Academy of Sciences.[66] Rational considerations would seem to dictate this option, but times have dramatically changed since 1998.

Given the parlous state of US–Russia relations, the arms-control crisis, and the nature and ideology of Moscow's decision-making system, the first or second alternative, or some combination of the two, seems more likely in the foreseeable future if hypersonic systems become a key element of the arms race.

Reflections on disarmament

One lesson from the last half-century of arms control is that shifts in the military balance make the sides periodically alternate their stances on the limitation or prohibition of certain weapon systems. Arms-control negotiators have frequently joked that Moscow and Washington have the same positions on all arms-control issues, just at different times. An important moment in strategic arms control occurred at a June 1967 meeting in Glassboro, New Jersey, between American president Lyndon Johnson and Soviet prime minister Alexei Kosygin. McNamara urged Kosygin to appreciate the destabilising effect of ABM systems. Kosygin categorically rejected this viewpoint, indignantly asserting: 'Defense is moral, offense is immoral.'[67] By that time, the Soviet Union had decided to deploy the Moscow area A-35

Galosh missile-defence system, while McNamara was dragging his feet on the proposed US *Nike*-X BMD. In just two years, Moscow would embrace McNamara's philosophy, regarding BMD as destabilising and sticking to this position for the ensuing half-century, while Washington would adopt Kosygin's position, during the 1980s and thereafter.

The reason for the flip is obvious: each party is trying to limit arms in which the opponent is superior and maximise its own military advantages. But in the course of the arms race the sides regularly match or overtake each other and correspondingly change arms-control priorities. For example, Russia has for many years emphasised the threat of US precision-guided, long-range conventional systems, portrayed by Putin as weapons of 'the first global disarming strike'.[68] After Russia recently built up its conventional cruise-missile capability and achieved a breakthrough in hypersonic systems, this threat all but disappeared from the Russian list of strategic concerns. Likewise, Russian deployment of the new-generation ground-mobile conventional A-235 *Nudol* and S-500 BMD systems may change its attitude towards missile defence. One conclusion is that it is not worthwhile to ideologically demonise the other side's advantages in arms programmes or differences in negotiating positions. These asymmetries regularly alternate and require clear-headed professional assessments rather than shrilly politicised pronouncements on various 'gaps'.

Another important lesson is that arms-control treaties, even if concluded in a tense international environment, have usually enhanced mutual security and facilitated detente. The ABM Treaty and SALT I agreement of 1972 were concluded despite the opposition of Soviet hardliners in the Politburo soon after the escalation of US bombing of Vietnam and its mining of Haiphong Harbor, which damaged Soviet ships. These agreements stimulated broader progress in nuclear-arms limitation, reduction and elimination, enhancing international security, improving US–Soviet relations and helping to end the Vietnam War.

Conversely, the breakdown of arms-control negotiations or refusal to ratify agreements has always damaged security and never helped resolve other international problems. Washington's rejection of SALT II ratification due to the Soviet invasion of Afghanistan in 1979 hindered strategic arms control, and in no way facilitated peace in Afghanistan or great-power cooperation on international security. Likewise, the Russian political elite's indignation over NATO expansion and the use of force in Yugoslavia prevented timely ratification of START II and the conclusion of the treaty on the basis of the START III Framework Agreement of 1997. This was counterproductive for arms control and did not alleviate mutual grievances and mistrust in NATO–Russia relations. Finally, Moscow's refusal to start negotiations on the START follow-on after 2012 contributed to the ensuing crisis of arms control and to new strategic tensions between Russia and the West.

Possibly the most important lesson from the history of arms control is that it is very difficult to build disarmament agreements, but quite easy to destroy them. Doing the latter has never enhanced national or international security, and has invariably compromised them. For instance, the United States denounced the ABM Treaty in 2002, citing the missile threat of rogue states. Eighteen years later, the US has 44 strategic ground-based, mid-course defence-system interceptors in Alaska and California, increasing to 64 by 2023.[69] Yet, under the 1974 protocol to the ABM Treaty of 1972, each side was permitted 100 interceptor missiles, which the US could base in North Dakota. The treaty did not envision any restrictions on technical characteristics of interceptors (that is, as to range, guidance system or warhead type), while the location, if necessary, could be easily renegotiated as an amendment to the treaty. The US Standard-3 *Aegis*-type interceptors in Europe and Asia or on surface ships, for use against medium-range ballistic missiles, could come under the documents included in the 1997 agreement on the delineation of strategic and theatre missile-defence systems.[70] So the ABM Treaty could easily have been preserved with light amendments that would have permitted the United States to do everything it has done since 2002, or is planning to do in the foreseeable future.

In the event, US withdrawal from the ABM Treaty did not alleviate overall strategic tensions, and in fact made them worse. Missiles and missile technologies have proliferated. North Korea withdrew from the NPT in 2003, started nuclear tests in 2006 and had been testing missiles of ever-growing range up to 2018. Iran agreed to curtail its nuclear programme in 2015 not because of US BMD development but for unrelated reasons, and continues to develop and test missiles. After New START in 2010, US–Russia strategic negotiations stopped, the main objection on Moscow's side being the absence of the ABM Treaty and cooperative development of defence systems by the two nations. In 2018, Russia unveiled a package of new offensive programmes to counter the US BMD, which is seen in Moscow as an open-ended programme. China is emulating Russia on this score.

Another example is Russia's 'suspension' of its participation in the Treaty on Conventional Armed Forces in Europe (CFE) in 2007 and 'final suspension' in 2015. Initially, Moscow justified these steps as a means of applying pressure on NATO to ratify the 1999 CFE Adaptation Agreement. But in 2011, NATO states responded by also ceasing their adherence to the terms of the treaty. Presently, there is no functioning conventional-forces-limitation regime in Europe. Russia has been building up its forces in its Western and Southern military districts, as in Crimea, South Ossetia and Abkhazia. On the other side of their borders, NATO has undertaken defensive deployments in the Baltic states, Poland and Romania, and US military units and heavy arms and equipment are returning to the continent. Substantial NATO superiority over Russia in all military and economic dimensions, alongside American logistics and power-projection capabilities, make the prospects for Russian security along its western borders quite precarious. Moscow would probably have felt more comfortable if NATO forces in Eastern Europe had been tangibly limited by CFE national and territorial quotas, and open to confidence-building and transparency regimes.

Still greater near-term threats may emerge after the expected collapse of the INF Treaty and expiration of START without extension of a follow-up. The loss of their stabilising effects cannot be offset by any medium-range or strategic-weapons programme on either side. Possible deployment of new US medium-range missiles in Europe and Asia occasioned by the end of the INF Treaty would, due to their short flight time and low trajectory, render a Russian deterrent based on launch on warning unconvincing, as there would be no time for its implementation. According to a statement by one respected Russian military commander, this might force Russia to move to the highly risky concept of a pre-emptive nuclear strike.[71] If the United States were to follow suit by adopting a similar concept, crisis stability would be practically impossible to maintain.

        *   *   *

There has been a proliferation of well-intended studies on various substitutes for formal arms control in the absence of the INF Treaty or START.[72] All of the options are considerably less effective than existing arms-control treaties with respect to preserving strategic stability and predictability, and managing the arms race. Furthermore, if the present political elites of leading nations lack the will or knowledge to sustain formal arms control, they are unlikely to acquire the disposition to replace it with dubious surrogates, never mind to resurrect it. While thinking about a bleak future for arms control and entertaining other purportedly tolerable arrangements may be professionally supportable for strategic analysts, that vocation could turn counterproductive. Politically, it would service the illusion that living without formal arms control might not be so bad and that the damage from its disintegration could be limited. Instead, they should be providing politicians with a realistic picture of the myriad future dangers of a world without arms control.

Saving the INF Treaty and START while there is still time would be much easier and more productive than searching for palliatives after their demise. The problems of INF Treaty compliance could be quickly fixed by agreeing on additional short-notice, on-site inspections at Russian *Iskander/ Novator* missile bases and US *Aegis Ashore* bases in Romania and Poland in order to remove mutual suspicions. Extending START for another five years would be even easier. Negotiating a START follow-on would be more challenging, but still possible before 2021 if there were firm political directives from the Kremlin and the White House. After all, New START was negotiated in just one year.

McNamara finished his luminous San Francisco speech with these words: 'In the end, the root of man's security does not lie in his weaponry, it lies in his mind. What the world requires in its third decade of the Atomic Age is not a new race towards armament, but a new race towards reasonableness. We had all better run that race.'[73] Those words have never been as relevant as they are now – in the eighth decade of the Atomic Age.

Notes

1   Quoted in Robert S. McNamara, *The Essence of Security: Reflections in Office* (New York: Harper & Row, 1968), p. 166.

2   *Ibid.*, pp. 58–9.

3   *Ibid.*, p. 58.

4   *Ibid.*, p. 62.

5   'Putin predostereg SSHA protiv novogo Karibskogo Krizisa' [Putin Warned the United States Against a New Cuban Crisis], RIA Novosti, 20 February 2019, https://ria.ru/20190220/1551153828.html.

6   'Poslanie Prezidenta Federal'nomu Sobraniyu. 1 marta 2018 g.' [Statement of the President of Russia to the Federal Assembly], Kremlin, 1 March 2018, http://www.kremlin.ru/events/president/ news/5695.

7   Office of the Secretary of Defense, 'Nuclear Posture Review', February 2018, p. 23, https://media.defense.gov/2018/Feb/02/2001872886/-1/-1/1/2018-NUCLEAR-POSTURE-REVIEW-FINAL.

8   Treaty on the Prohibition of Nuclear Weapons, adopted 7 July 2017, United Nations, http://undocs.org/en/A/CONF.229/2017/8.

9   Calculations are based on *SIPRI Yearbook 2017: Armaments, Disarmament and International Security* (Oxford: Oxford University Press, 2017), pp. 648–717; and *SIPRI Yearbook 1990: World Armaments and Disarmament* (Oxford: Oxford University Press, 1991), pp. 3–51.

10 Examples of small-scale and slow remaining modernisation programmes of the time are the US refitting its missile submarines with *Trident*-2 instead of *Trident*-1 missiles, and Russian deployment of the SS-25 *Topol* ground-mobile ICBM as a replacement for older ICBMs, SLBMs, strategic submarines and bombers.

11 SORT in 2002 fixed ceilings of 1,700–2,200 warheads per party, while New START reduced them to 1,550 warheads in 2010. However, its new counting rules provided substantial 'discounts'. For example, strategic bombers counted as one delivery vehicle and one warhead, while each could carry 12–20 nuclear cruise missiles and gravity bombs. Submarines in overhaul and other de-alerted weapons were not counted under the main ceilings. Hence, the actual force loading by the START I counting rules is closer to 2,000 warheads per party.

12 This applies to US systems such as the *Tomahawk* sea-launched cruise missile (BGM-109) and air-launched cruise missiles (AGM-84, AGM-158B, JASSM-ER). Russian non-nuclear cruise missiles are the *Kalibr* 3M-54 and 3M-14 sea-launched cruise missiles, and the Kh-55SM, Kh-555 and Kh-101-type air-launched cruise missiles.

13 These are heavy and medium bombers, tactical-strike aircraft, ships, and attack submarines with missiles capable of carrying both nuclear and conventional warheads: the *Kalibr* and *Tomahawk* sea-based cruise missiles (some of which will again be armed with nuclear warheads), air-launched cruise missiles of the Kh101/102 type or the AGM-158, and *Iskander*-type ground-launched tactical ballistic and cruise missiles.

14 See Alexey Arbatov and Vladimir

Dvorkin (eds), *Nuclear Proliferation: New Technologies, Weapons, Treaties* (Moscow: Carnegie Moscow Center, 2009), pp. 85–103; and Alexey Arbatov, Vladimir Dvorkin and Natalia Bubnova (eds), *Missile Defense: Confrontation and Cooperation* (Moscow: Carnegie Moscow Center, 2013), pp. 183–225.

15 James M. Acton, *Silver Bullet? Asking the Right Questions About Conventional Prompt Global Strike* (Washington DC: Carnegie Endowment for International Peace, 2013), pp. 33–63, http://carnegieendowment. org/2013/09/03/ silver-bullet-asking-right-questions-about-conventional-prompt-global-strike-pub-52778.

16 'Statement of the President of Russia to the Federal Assembly'.

17 'Nuclear Posture Review', p. xii.

18 See N. Boitzov, 'Terminologiia v Voennoi Doktrine' [Terminology in the Military Doctrine], *Nezavisimoe voennoe obozrenie*, no. 40, 3 October 2014; and D. Akhmerov and M. Valeev, 'Aerostat – Drug "Sarmata"' [Balloon – A Friend of 'Sarmat'], *Voenno–Promyshlennyi Kur'er*, no. 39, 12–18 October 2016, p. 6, available at http://www.vpk news.ru.

19 'Expanded Meeting of the Defence Ministry Board', Kremlin, 19 December 2014, http://eng.kremlin.ru/transcripts/23410.

20 *Ibid*.

21 Vladimir Dvorkin and Vladimir Pyriev, 'The US/NATO Program and Strategic Stability', in Arbatov, Dvorkin and Bubnova (eds), *Missile Defense*, pp. 183–203.

22 McNamara, *The Essence of Security*, pp. 63–6.

23 Vladimir Dvorkin, 'Space Weapons Programs', in Alexey Arbatov and Vladimir Dvorkin (eds), *Outer Space: Weapons, Diplomacy, and Security* (Washington DC: Carnegie Endowment for International Peace, 2010), pp. 30–45.

24 A. Mardasov, '"Nudol": Ubiitza Amerikanskich MBR i Sputnikov' ['Nudol': A Killer of the US ICBMs and Satellites], *Free Press*, http://svpressa.ru/war21/article/174898/.

25 'Nuclear Posture Review', p. 21.

26 See 'Meeting of the Valdai International Discussion Club', Kremlin, http://news.kremlin.ru/news/19243; and 'INF Treaty Can't Last Endlessly, Ivanov Said', RIA Novosti, http://ria.ru/defense_safety/20130621/945019919.html.

27 Daniel Ellsberg, *The Doomsday Machine: Confessions of a Nuclear War Planner* (New York: Bloomsbury, 2017), pp. 266–8.

28 *Ibid.*, p. 270.

29 Fred Kaplan, *The Wizards of Armageddon* (New York: Simon & Schuster, 1983), p. 269.

30 Ellsberg, *The Doomsday Machine*, pp. 100–4.

31 Thomas B. Cochran, William M. Arkin and Milton M. Hoeing, *Nuclear Weapons Databook: Vol. IV – Soviet Nuclear Weapons* (New York: Harper & Row, 1989), pp. 22–7, 42–3.

32 William Perry, *My Journey at the Nuclear Brink* (Palo Alto, CA: Stanford University Press, 2015), p. 55.

33 McNamara, *The Essence of Security*, pp. 59–60.

34 K. Sivkov, 'Razoruzhen i ochen' opasen' [Disarmed and Very Dangerous], *Voenno–Promyshlennyi Kur'er*, no.

11, 22–28 March 2017, pp. 1–4.

35 John Newhouse, *War and Peace in the Nuclear Age* (New York: Alfred A. Knopf, 1989), p. 69.

36 See Ronald L. Tammen, *MIRV and the Arms Race* (New York: Praeger, 1973), p. 114; and 'Third Annual Report to the Congress on United States Foreign Policy', 9 February 1972, in *Public Papers of the Presidents of the United States, Richard M. Nixon, 1972* (Washington DC: US Government Printing Office, 1974), p. 307.

37 Robert Einhorn and Steven Pifer, *Meeting U.S. Deterrence Requirements: Toward a Sustainable National Consensus* (Washington DC: Brookings Institution, 2017), https://www.brookings.edu/wp-content/uploads/2017/09/fp_20170920_deterrence_report.pdf.

38 'Statement of the President of Russia to the Federal Assembly'.

39 Kremlin, 'The Military Doctrine of the Russian Federation', http://news.kremlin.ru/media/events/files/41d527556bec8deb3530.pdf.

40 See Acton, *Silver Bullet?*.

41 'Meeting of the Valdai International Discussion Club', President of Russia, 22 October 2015, http://en.kremlin.ru/events/president/news/50548.

42 'Nuclear Posture Review', p. 21.

43 L. Glazkova, *Mozhet li povtorit'sya Karibskii krizis?* [Can the Cuban Crisis Be Repeated?], https://www.pnp.ru/politics/mozhet-li-povtoritsya-novyy-karibskiy-krizis.html.

44 McNamara, *The Essence of Security*, p. 57.

45 Pavel Podvig, 'The Development of Soviet and Russian Ballistic Missile Defense in the 20th Century', in Arbatov, Dvorkin and Bubnova (eds),

Missile Defense, pp. 33–51.

46 Cited by A. Kislyakov, *PRO 'Verbu', Mukhu, 'Kaktus' i 'Krota'* [ABM, 'Verba', Mukha, 'Kaktus', and 'Krota'], RIA Novosti, https://ria.ru/20071217/92808803.html.

47 O. Grinevskiy, *Perelom. Ot Brezhneva k Gorbachevu* [The Break. From Brezhnev to Gorbachev] (Moscow: Olimpia, 2004), p. 13.

48 *Ibid.*, pp. 18–23.

49 *Ibid.*, p. 23.

50 Secretary of Defense James R. Schlesinger, *Annual Defense Department Report, FY 1975* (Washington DC: US Government Printing Office, 4 March 1974), http://history.defense.gov/Portals/70/Documents/annual_reports/1975_DoD_AR.pdf?ver=2014-06-24-150705-323.

51 'Nuclear Posture Review', p. 21.

52 *Ibid.*

53 'Current Goals in the Development of the Armed Forces of the Russian Federation', *Red Star*, 11 October 2003, http://old.redstar.ru/2003/10/11_10/3_01.html.

54 Yevgeny Akhmerov, Marat Valeev and Dmitry Akhmerov, 'The Balloon Is a Friend of "Sarmat"', *Military–Industrial Courier*, 12 October 2016, https://vpk.name/news/165525_aerostat__drug_sarmata.html.

55 'Statement of the President of Russia to the Federal Assembly'.

56 'The Military Doctrine of the Russian Federation'.

57 According to independent estimates, Russia has about 1,850 units of such nuclear weapons. *Ezhegodnik SIPRI 2017. Vooruzheniya, razoruzhenie i mezhdu-narodnaya bezopasnost* [SIPRI Yearbook 2017: Armaments, Disarmament and

International Security] (Moscow: Nauka, 2018), p. 338.

58 'Putin Warned the United States Against a New Cuban Crisis'.

59 'Statement of the President of Russia to the Federal Assembly'.

60 Patrick Tucker, 'The US Is Accelerating Development of Its Own "Invincible" Hypersonic Weapons', Defense One, 2 March 2018, https://www. defenseone.com/technology/2018/03/ united-states-accelerating- development-its-own-invincible- hypersonic-weapons/146355/.

61 Office of the Secretary of Defense, 'Missile Defense Review', January 2019, https://media.defense.gov/2019/ Jan/17/2002080666/-1/-1/1/2019- MISSILE-DEFENSE-REVIEW.PDF.

62 Transcript of meeting of the Valdai Discussion Club, 18 October 2018, http://en.kremlin.ru/events/president/ news/58848.

63 Herbert York, *Race to Oblivion* (New York: Simon & Schuster, 1970), p. 232.

64 Acton, *Silver Bullet?*, p. 70.

65 'The Military Doctrine of the Russian Federation'.

66 See Alexey Arbatov, 'Understanding the US–Russia Nuclear Schism', *Survival*, vol. 59, no. 2, April–May 2017, pp. 33–66.

67 Newhouse, *War and Peace in the Nuclear Age*, p. 205.

68 Transcript of meeting of the Valdai Discussion Club, Sochi, 24 October 2014, http://news.kremlin.ru/ transcripts/46860.

69 'Missile Defense Review'.

70 This agreement permitted tests of BMD interceptors against missile targets with a speed of no more than 5 km per second and range of 3,500 km. For the future, it was permitted to develop land- and air-based interceptors with a speed of up to 5.5 km/sec, and sea- based interceptors of up to 4.5 km/sec. Such BMD subsystems were exempted from the limitations of the ABM Treaty.

71 In an interview, Colonel General Viktor Esin, former chief of staff of the Russian Federation Strategic Missile Forces, said: 'If the Americans begin to deploy their missiles in Europe, we will have no choice but to abandon the doctrine of launch-on-warning and move to a doctrine of preemptive strike.' See 'Interview with Colonel General Viktor Esin', *Zvezda Weekly*, 8 November 2018, https://zvezdaweekly. ru/news/t/2018117102-0iaAI.html.

72 See Sergey Karaganov, 'On the New Nuclear World: How to Strengthen Deterrence and Maintain Peace', *Russia in Global Politics*, vol. 15, no. 2, March–April 2017; Andrey Kortunov, 'The End of the Bilateral Era: How the US Withdrawal from the INF Treaty Changes the World Order', Carnegie Moscow Center, 23 October 2018, https://carnegie.ru/commentary/77551; and Vincent Manzo, 'Nuclear Arms Control Without a Treaty? Risks and Options After the New START: CNA's Strategy, Policy, Plans, and Programs Division (SP3)', Deterrence and Arms Control Paper no. 1, April 2019.

73 McNamara, *The Essence of Security*, p. 67.

Debating Nuclear No-first-use, Again

Brad Roberts

The debate about US nuclear declaratory policy is as old as US nuclear weapons themselves. Presidential promises about when nuclear weapons would be used (positive security assurances) and when they would not (negative security assurances) are widely seen as a critical factor in shaping the political and military environments, as they can directly affect perceptions of deterrence, assurance and strategic stability by both friends and adversaries. Over the years, many have advocated that the United States adopt a policy of no-first-use (NFU) of nuclear weapons. But no US president has so far heeded this advice. The NFU debate has resurfaced in the new 116th Congress. House Armed Services Committee Chairman Adam Smith joined with Senator Elizabeth Warren to offer NFU legislation, with the statement that 'our current nuclear strategy is not just outdated – it is dangerous'. They went on to argue that NFU would 'help us maintain our moral and diplomatic leadership in the world'.[1]

With the political debate about US nuclear policy again heating up, it is a good time to recall prior debates. Understanding how they took shape and why they concluded the way they did can help inform current policy development. With this policy baseline in mind, it is easier to assess whether and how changed circumstances might dictate changed policies.

Brad Roberts is Director of the Center for Global Security Research at Lawrence Livermore National Laboratory. He served as US Deputy Assistant Secretary of Defense for Nuclear and Missile Defense Policy from 2009 to 2013. The views reflected here are the author's personal views and should not be attributed to any institution with which he is or has been affiliated.

Survival | vol. 61 no. 3 | June–July 2019 | pp. 39–56   DOI 10.1080/00396338.2019.1614788

The 2009 Strategic Posture Commission and NFU

The last significant congressional discussion of US nuclear declaratory policy occurred late in the George W. Bush administration. It arose in the context of a highly charged debate over nuclear policy driven by an unpopular administration seeking new nuclear warheads. Stoking the controversy was the call to substantially revise deterrence practices made by former secretaries of state Henry Kissinger and George Shultz, former secretary of defense William Perry, and former senator Sam Nunn in their now famous series of *Wall Street Journal* op-eds.[2]

Faced with division and confusion on nuclear policy generally, congressional leaders established a bipartisan Strategic Posture Commission. Its 2009 report, in turn, underscored the necessity of a bipartisan nuclear strategy given the enduring nature of the nuclear problem. The crux of the matter was that the lifespan of nuclear-modernisation programmes and of arms control (from negotiation through ratification to full implementation) is measured in decades – far longer than a two-year Congress. As the congressional balance of power can be expected to shift periodically, continuity of policy purpose requires some basic bipartisan agreement about the means and ends of policy, and some restraint on the exercise of bold departures that are unlikely to enjoy broad support. Toward this end, the commission recommended a nuclear strategy combining political means to reduce and eliminate nuclear weapons with military means of maintaining deterrence so long as they remain deployed. Despite its bipartisan cast, the commission was unequivocal and unanimous in rejecting NFU. It did so with the argument that NFU would be harmful to extended deterrence: 'potential aggressors should have to worry about the possibility that the United States might respond by overwhelming means at a time and in a manner of its choosing'.[3]

This unanimous position materialised despite the presence on the commission of long-time NFU advocate Morton Halperin. Having joined the consensus in 2009, Halperin subsequently set out his own personal views on the subject, arguing that NFU was 'a good idea whose time has not come' and 'can and should be put off for another day'.[4] In making this case, he noted that a declaratory policy of NFU would generate political discord that would impede efforts to accomplish other steps that would go further in reducing nuclear dangers.

The 2010 Nuclear Posture Review and NFU

The Barack Obama administration ended up taking the commission's advice on both bipartisanship and declaratory policy, but not without significant deliberation. Advocates within and outside the administration made the case for adopting NFU. The insiders saw NFU as beneficial for signalling a move away from Cold War thinking, which the president had promised in his April 2009 speech in Prague. Those outside government generally reinforced this view, while also deriving new arguments from a changing security environment. Scott Sagan, for example, argued that the threat of nuclear first use was no longer necessary to deter non-nuclear attack by other weapons of mass destruction (WMD) or by large-scale conventional military forces, and that the benefits of adopting NFU for US non-proliferation objectives had been seriously underestimated.[5]

While considering its options but before deciding what formulation of declaratory policy to adopt, the Obama administration sought out the views of the broader community of interest. It encountered many different opinions about the wisdom of NFU from a wide range of stakeholders. Among non-governmental organisations (NGOs), it found both supporters and opponents. Among allies, there were also varied attitudes, sometimes even within the same government. Some allies felt more secure than ever before in 2009 and thus were inclined to support a US NFU policy; others were under new pressure from hostile neighbouring powers, small and large, and felt rising anxiety about both nuclear and non-nuclear threats to their integrity and sovereignty. They also conveyed rising anxiety about the credibility of US security guarantees in light of new nuclear threats to the US homeland from 'rogue states' and given new questions about the end of unipolarity and possible US retreat.

Although attracted to bold policy initiatives, the Obama administration was also focused on practical steps toward the long-term disarmament goal. The White House characterised these as steps that would increase the safety and security of the United States and its allies, and also of other nuclear-armed states, thereby presumably increasing their willingness to take additional steps to reduce the numbers and roles of nuclear weapons. While the president wanted to take significant steps toward the long-term disarmament goal, he did not want to undermine strategic stability, weaken extended deterrence and assurance of allies, or erode the non-proliferation regime. Quite a few bold ideas that were judged to fall short of these criteria were left on the cutting-room floor. NFU ended up there for several reasons.[6]

Firstly, the administration rejected the claim that there are no plausible circumstances in which the US might be the first to employ nuclear weapons. It saw such circumstances as extremely remote but did not regard them as completely implausible. It conceived a narrow range of contingencies, much narrower than in the Cold War, in which the vital interests of the United States or its allies might be put at risk by non-nuclear WMD or overwhelming conventional forces.

Calculated ambiguity served deterrence well

Secondly, the administration did not share the confidence of many NFU advocates that US conventional forces, though pre-eminent, would be sufficient to deter such threats to the vital interests of US allies. Considerable damage could be done to allies in the time it would take the US to project conventional forces in sufficient scale to prevent a catastrophe for those allies.

Thirdly, the administration concluded that the United States and its allies could reduce their reliance on nuclear weapons but not eliminate their role entirely. While building up missile defences and non-nuclear counter-force capabilities would facilitate a reduced role, these measures could not obviate the need for nuclear weapons. This was because the supplemental, non-nuclear tools of deterrence were unlikely to have the same influence as US nuclear threats on the calculus of cost and risk that would crucially inform an enemy's decision to go to war against a US ally.

Fourthly, administration leaders assessed that the tradition of calculated ambiguity had served deterrence well and should not be set aside at a time of continued concern about the effectiveness of deterrence for new challenges. Fraught experience with US red lines in Libya, Syria and Ukraine did nothing to increase their willingness to experiment with red lines in the nuclear realm.

Fifthly, some in the administration judged that the views of worried allies needed to be prioritised over those of more secure allies. This was a moral choice. But it also reflected a desire to ensure that decisions about NATO's nuclear policy and posture be made by the allies collectively rather than individually and separately. Had such unilateral decisions become the norm, it is likely that NATO's collective nuclear deterrent would have collapsed, stranding those more worried allies without a nuclear umbrella and generating among them resentment about the disengagement of NATO's long-standing members from their defence.

Sixthly, there was a desire to align US nuclear declaratory policy with the policies of its two nuclear allies, the United Kingdom and France, which were not prepared to adopt or support NFU.

Finally, the administration was broadly inclined to take the advice of the Strategic Posture Commission on tailoring nuclear strategy to promote bipartisanship. This approach was considered valuable in gaining congressional support for its nuclear-policy agenda, covering both arms control and force modernisation.[7]

After considerable deliberation, and after hearing the views of many experts inside and outside government, Obama rejected NFU. The administration's 2010 Nuclear Posture Review report thus stated that the employment of US nuclear weapons would be considered only in extreme circumstances, when the vital interests of the United States or an ally were at risk. But the Obama administration did significantly restrict the place of first use in US nuclear strategy by amending the negative security assurance. Under the so-called 'clean NSA', the US limited the threat of first use to only nuclear-armed states and other states not in compliance with their nuclear non-proliferation obligations.

In rejecting NFU, the Obama administration was not instead embracing first use as its preferred strategy. This is a continuing point of confusion and concern about the implications of rejecting NFU. In US strategy, the fundamental role of nuclear weapons has always been to deter nuclear attack by threatening nuclear retaliation. The fundamental role is not for pre-emptive or preventive nuclear war. Reserving the right to 'go first' in a certain narrow range of circumstances does not alter that fact.

The president also rejected the 'sole purpose' formulation. That is, having agreed that the fundamental purpose of US nuclear weapons is to deter and retaliate against nuclear attack, he was not willing to state that this was their sole purpose. This stance followed from the assessment that there remains a narrow range of contingencies in which an enemy's use of chemical, biological or conventional capabilities could jeopardise the vital interests of the United States or its allies and thus create the extreme circumstances in which the US might employ nuclear weapons. At the same time, however, the 2010 Nuclear Posture Review expressed a commitment to work to create the conditions that might make it possible to safely adopt such a formulation in the future.

Subsequent Obama reviews

With these decisions, the administration's policy review concluded. But its internal debate did not end. The Obama team reviewed, re-assessed and re-deliberated its nuclear policy throughout its eight-year term. It periodically asked itself what more should and could be done to fulfil the Prague vision. The White House first revisited these questions in 2011 and 2012, in its preparation of new presidential guidance on planning for the employment of nuclear weapons. Toward that end, it undertook a comprehensive review of nuclear deterrence strategy. The review was strategy-driven in that it began with first-order policy objectives and determined how they should be reflected in operational plans and capabilities. Those objectives were drawn directly from the 2010 Nuclear Posture Review, but explicitly included the requirement of achieving presidential objectives in case deterrence were to fail, and revalidated the administration's positive and negative security assurances.

In its final year, the administration undertook another sweeping review of nuclear policy, which again resurrected the NFU issue. Outside advocates again made the case for NFU, this time with the implied message of 'better late than never'. Bruce Blair, for example, called for NFU adoption as part of 'a bold move to fix an outdated strategy' that would, in his view, make the world dramatically safer by reducing the concerns of US adversaries that the United States might use nuclear weapons first.[8] And Sagan's 2009 arguments were revisited – especially the contention that the non-proliferation benefits of NFU had been undervalued.

This so-called 'internal review', however, came to the same conclusion on NFU as all of its predecessors. Administration leaders were not persuaded that a change in policy had been undervalued. Instead, there was a rising frustration with the constant demands of NGOs on the United States and the disappointing impact of prior decisions and actions in generating support for more robust non-proliferation actions. Nor was the administration persuaded that US adoption of NFU would significantly reduce the likelihood of nuclear threats or attack by Russia or China, whose declaratory policies and nuclear doctrines seemed to have little to do with US declaratory policy.

A coda to this review arose during the administration's last few days. In a review of the administration's legacy in implementing the agenda set out in Prague eight years earlier, then-vice president Joseph Biden asserted that both he and the president wanted to endorse the 'sole purpose' formulation because of the administration's progress in reducing nuclear dangers.[9] Oddly, he did not go on to explain why the president had chosen not to change declaratory policy. Nor did he make any case that the 'narrow range of contingencies' that drove the policy in the first place had been meaningfully narrowed.

In fact, this would have been, and would still be, a difficult case to make. The non-nuclear threats to the sovereignty and integrity of US allies cannot be said to have eased during that period. Significant chemical, biological and conventional threats remain in all three regions where the United States extends security guarantees.[10] And the crisis of confidence in the multilateral disarmament regime has only intensified.

Subsequent commentary on the results of the 2016 internal review raised an additional issue of continuing importance: the proper impact of allies on US declaratory policy. In the internal review as in the Nuclear Posture Review, stakeholders were consulted. Given that US allies had almost unanimously welcomed the findings of the 2010 Nuclear Posture Review, it is hardly surprising that they again opposed NFU. The executive departments again found their thinking about the requirements of extended deterrence compelling, and the secretaries of defense, state and energy (Ash Carter, John Kerry and Ernest Moniz) again lined up against NFU.[11]

NFU advocates criticised both the grumbling of US allies and the Obama administration's deference to their complaints.[12] Such critics were far off the president's policy course. Obama had arrived in office in 2009 committed to renewing US alliances and more effectively engaging US allies in meeting contemporary international challenges of many kinds. His dedication to assuring them deepened as his personal relationships with allied leaders developed. In close parallel, his commitment to extended deterrence intensified, as allied leaders communicated their concerns about emerging threats, and about the ability and will of the United States to deter those threats. Thus, Obama was particularly unprepared to reject their counsel on the requirements of their assurance. The advice of NFU advocates to override allied concerns might have been better received by the administrations that preceded and succeeded Obama.

The 2018 Nuclear Posture Review and NFU

The Trump administration also took up declaratory policy as part of its own Nuclear Posture Review. Its internal deliberations are not yet a matter of public record, but the result on NFU is clear enough. Although motivated by some very different principles and foreign- and defence-policy objectives, the administration settled for direct repetition of the nuclear declaratory policy of the Obama administration. NFU was rejected again, as was 'sole purpose'. The review concluded that 'significant non-nuclear strategic attacks' could create the 'extreme circumstances' in which the US president might employ nuclear weapons. The Trump administration also maintained the 'clean NSA', word for word.[13]

Debate renewed

Now, in 2019, the advocates of 'bold action' via NFU are back. As of spring 2019, it remained unclear whether Representative Smith and Senator Warren actually expected to succeed in imposing a new declaratory policy on the executive branch. Their effort may instead reflect their intent to line up Democrats so that NFU is a pre-agreed input and not merely an option for the next Democratic administration's Nuclear Posture Review.

In any case, the renewal of congressional debate has brought with it a resurgence of NGO advocacy and familiar arguments. The Arms Control Association's Daryl Kimball has staked out a leading role in this new debate with a forceful case for NFU that reflects current concerns and factors.[14] He has reformulated one of the key arguments of NFU advocates, while adding a timely new argument. The point of departure for Kimball's analysis is the observation that nuclear risks are increasing. This assessment is incontestable, and all partisans in the debate about NFU should find it easy to concur in it. The renewal of major-power rivalry, North Korea's steady progress toward a viable nuclear force, the decay of the non-proliferation regime, the crisis of multilateral disarmament diplomacy, and rising doubts about the intention and ability of the United States to safeguard the global and regional order are all driving new sources of nuclear risk, danger and instability. Following three decades of concerted bipartisan US effort to mitigate these factors, this is a lamentable result.

Kimball goes on to reformulate the argument that existing policy is both outdated and dangerous. In Kimball's view, 'retaining the option to use nuclear weapons first is fraught with unnecessary peril'. He characterises contemporary US nuclear strategy as 'largely the same' as Cold War strategy, with what he believes to be a focus on large-scale nuclear attacks, dangerously high alert levels for such a contingency and a reliance on the threat of first use as a way to use US nuclear capabilities before losing them. In this framework, he judges that enemies have a high incentive to strike first against the United States with nuclear weapons in a time of crisis. To stabilise this tenuous situation, he concludes, NFU would make a dramatic difference by eliminating the use-or-lose incentive. In making this argument, he is echoing the arguments of Michael Gerson from nearly a decade earlier.[15]

The problem with this analysis is that its assumptions about current US nuclear policy are wrong. US nuclear strategy is not 'largely the same' as in the Cold War. The focus on large-scale nuclear attack disappeared along with the Single Integrated Operational Plan nearly two decades ago.[16] The Obama administration's Deterrence Requirements Review further shifted the focus onto what it called twenty-first-century contingencies, which it later defined as regional conflicts in which aggressors attempt to escalate their way out of failed aggression against a US ally.[17] The alert practices of US nuclear forces were significantly altered by the presidential nuclear initiatives of the 1990s; only a portion of those forces remain capable of prompt action. The Obama administration also further downgraded planning for the Cold War-vintage, bolt-from-the-blue, all-out attack by a peer enemy and took steps to increase presidential decision time during a crisis. It did, however, opt to retain the technical capability for launch under attack. A key factor in its decision to do so was the desire to ensure that no enemy ever thinks that a disarming first nuclear strike on the United States can be attempted with acceptable risk. But so long as the US maintains nuclear forces capable of surviving a surprise pre-emptive attack, there seems no significant prospect of ever needing to employ forces in this manner.

Kimball's analysis focuses on the risks of all-out strategic warfare when the major risks today are at the regional level. Russia has established an approach to regional war that integrates a broad and diverse set of weapons (nuclear and non-nuclear, kinetic and non-kinetic) to conduct strategic operations aimed at destroying critically important targets. The potential value to Russia of escalatory action is not to use or lose its strategic arsenal. Rather, it is to sober the US and its allies by awakening them to the underlying reality that Russia has a higher stake and greater interest in prevailing in the conflict, and thus bring NATO to a Clausewitzean 'culminating point' at which it chooses not to bear the costs and risks of further war.[18]

The option for first use was retained to address this new problem. The scenarios that most concern deterrence planners today are those involving adversary nuclear blackmail and brinkmanship in regional contingencies and, potentially, limited nuclear attacks by challengers aimed at breaking the will of US allies, and perhaps separately the United States, to stay in the fight. The instabilities in such contingencies flow from the calculus that adversaries – principally Russia – may be able to escape significant escalatory risks by using conventional forces backed by nuclear threats to put in jeopardy allied and US interests.

The United States and its NATO allies have focused on this problem as a result of Russia's military annexation of Crimea and revelations about the advanced state of Russian preparations for a war in Europe. Against this backdrop, NFU would be a step in the wrong direction. It would not decrease the risk of Russian nuclear use in a regional war in Europe. On the contrary, it would increase that risk by nourishing Russia's expectations that its actions putting the vital interests of NATO members at risk would not be met with a military reply that would be too costly for Russia to bear. The United States' adoption of NFU would also put the US at odds with its two nuclear-armed allies – the UK and France – and with the NATO tradition of calculated ambiguity. This would reinforce Russia's expectation of Western disagreement and disarray in a time of burgeoning crisis, which could encourage risk-taking by Russian leaders.

The timely new argument advanced by Kimball concerns the proper role of Congress in authorising nuclear employment – a question brought to the fore by President Donald Trump's 'cavalier and reckless statements' (Kimball's words) about nuclear weapons. Kimball argues that 'continuing to vest such destructive power in the hands of one person is undemocratic, irresponsible, unnecessary, and increasingly untenable'. Thus, he concludes, a congressionally imposed NFU policy could help reduce a significant new peril.[19]

The president's talk of nuclear war has been alarming

Indeed, the president's talk of nuclear war and the nuclear arms race has at times been alarming. Naturally and appropriately this has produced consideration of how to limit his authority to initiate nuclear war. Whether Congress has the authority to legislate constraints on the power of the commander-in-chief in a major international crisis is uncertain. Whether a president would in fact feel constrained by such a legislative requirement in time of war is also an open question. Moreover, a legal limitation on the president's authority to employ nuclear weapons could be seen by potential adversaries as further increasing the likelihood that the US would be fearful, divided and paralysed in a strategic crisis (as autocrats generally want to believe democracies to be). This consideration could embolden them to attempt to impose a military fait accompli. Thus, even successful legislation might simply trade one set of risks for another.

NFU: a 2019 net assessment

The arguments for NFU have not proven persuasive for policymakers for decades. Are they now, given the lessons of recent experience and the heightened dangers of the new period? An answer to this question requires subsidiary assessments of what impacts NFU adoption by the United States would have on deterrence, on assurance of allies, on non-proliferation and disarmament, and on the broader future of US nuclear policy.

Regarding the impact of the United States' NFU adoption on deterrence, the positive case is built on two main arguments. One, already discussed, is that it would actually strengthen deterrence by decreasing the adversary's incentive to strike first in a crisis. The second is that NFU would not harm deterrence because US conventional forces are credible deterrents for all non-nuclear contingencies, given the United States' presumed overwhelming conventional military edge. In fact, the ability of the US to fight and win 'major theater wars' slipped away while Washington was harvesting the peace dividend, fighting the 'war on terrorism' and engaging in prolonged counter-insurgency campaigns in Iraq and Afghanistan. Moreover, when the United States awakened to the problem of major-power rivalry in 2014–16, it discovered how much progress Russia and China had made in adapting their military strategies and capabilities to achieving a conventional fait accompli in a regional war and to protecting that gain with escalatory threats and actions in the all-domain context.

The situation has grown genuinely perilous. Reporting in late 2018, the bipartisan National Defense Strategy Commission offered this stark assessment:

> Previous congressionally mandated reports … warned that this crisis was coming. The crisis has now arrived … a crisis of American power. Should war occur, America will face harder fights and greater losses than at any time in decades … Put bluntly, the US military could lose the next state-vs.-state war it fights … Russia and China are leveraging existing and emerging technologies to present US forces with new military problems … Detailed, rigorous operational concepts for solving these problems and defending US interests are badly needed, but do not appear to exist.[20]

This implies that the presumptively 'narrow' range of contingencies facing the US military has not in fact narrowed. The circumstances in which the United States can now credibly threaten decisive non-nuclear military action against an aggressor have diminished relative to a decade ago, and significantly so. Amplifying the problem is the continued non-compliance of numerous states with their chemical and biological arms-control obligations. The upshot is that NFU adoption would not have a positive or benign impact on deterrence. Rather, it would generate new dangers and new risks.

On the impact of NFU adoption on the assurance of allies, the positive case is that NFU assures allies that the United States remains committed to reducing nuclear dangers and to restraining its own nuclear policies and posture. But for many allies, this argument misses the point. Yes, they seek assurance that a cavalier and sometimes reckless president will not generate new nuclear dangers for them. But for a significant number of allies, the deeper assurance they seek is that the United States will be prepared to use all means available when their vital interests are at risk. They want to be convinced that a neighbour who might contemplate putting those interests at risk understands that there would be a terrible price to be paid. They also want to rest easy that the United States understands this requirement and is proceeding, in partnership with them, to strengthen the means of their common defence.[21]

For these anxious allies, NFU is troublesome in every way. It signals clearly that the US will not be prepared to use all means available to it when their vital interests are at risk, declining to do so unless the enemy is foolish enough to cross the nuclear red line. NFU thus sends a message of restraint to dangerous neighbours, encouraging conventional provocations and risk-taking. It signals that the United States doesn't understand the unique value for their defence of the US threat of the first use of its nuclear weapons. The preference of some Americans to deter by non-nuclear means reinforces their anxiety that they will be left to die in large numbers while the US masses, dispatches and assembles its conventional forces rather than issuing threats of nuclear first use. For some allied experts, the US flirtation with NFU is one more sign that the United States no longer has the will to do what is necessary for their security, which could portend significant shifts in the political allegiance of US allies.

The impact of NFU on the assurance of allies ought to be especially salient for the 116th Congress. That session began with abundant indications of bipartisan efforts to reassure allies at a time of unhelpful presidential statements about the value to the United States of its alliances. Perhaps the best example was the 'reassurance tour' to the February 2019 Munich Security Conference by a bipartisan congressional delegation. In the words of one of its members, 'We can go a long way to satisfying our allies that support for the relationship is not only strong but it is bipartisan, even if it is not always reflected in the Oval Office.'[22] Adoption of NFU would thwart this effort by signalling that Congress puts a unilateral assessment of the requirements of stability and reactions to presidential unpredictability above the near-term requirements of those whom the United States has pledged to defend. Congress cannot have it both ways.

The positive case for NFU adoption with respect to non-proliferation and disarmament is widely asserted by NFU advocates. Smith and Warren, for example, argue that NFU adoption would 'help us maintain our moral and diplomatic leadership'.[23] But precisely how this would be so, and how such leadership would result in improved non-proliferation and disarmament performance by the international community, is far from clear.

My own experience points me to the following conclusion: while NFU would be welcomed by the many advocates of more action on disarmament by the nuclear-armed states, its actual impact on non-proliferation and disarmament would be at best modest and short-lived. This assessment follows the experience of the Obama administration, which took numerous steps to reduce the number and role of US nuclear weapons, many of which had been recommended to it by NGO advocates. These helped to contribute to a successful Non-Proliferation Treaty (NPT) review conference in 2010 (assuming the measure of success is the agreement of a final statement). But the actual practical result in the disarmament community was the negotiation of a workaround to the NPT – namely, the Treaty on the Prohibition of Nuclear Weapons – and the creation of the International Campaign to Abolish Nuclear Weapons, which aims to pressure and shame the democracies in reaction to their supposed bad faith in negotiating the elimination of nuclear weapons.

In my view, leadership of the global nuclear order cannot be achieved with palliatives like NFU. Leadership requires a proper blend of idealism and pragmatism. There is too much of the former and too little of the latter in the claim that NFU adoption by the United States would make a positive impact on non-proliferation and disarmament.

Finally, regarding the impact NFU adoption would have on the broader future of US nuclear policy, we should be wary. We have already seen an erosion of the bipartisanship on nuclear policy in the US Congress that was one of the legacies of the Obama administration. NFU adoption would accelerate that erosion. Other special nuclear projects would likely come to the political fore from other parts of the political spectrum (there are plenty waiting on the sidelines). The drift of events is back toward a time that few in the current Congress would remember – the deep division and paralysis of 2009 and 2007. This brings us to a simple question: is the advice of the bipartisan Strategic Posture Commission from a decade ago still relevant and useful?

As noted above, the Strategic Posture Commission concluded that US nuclear policy must have a long lifespan and thus must enjoy a measure of bipartisan support sufficient to ensure continuity as the congressional majority shifts back and forth. Toward that end, they recommended adoption of a balanced approach to strategy encompassing political measures to reduce nuclear threats and military measures to deter nuclear attack so long as nuclear weapons remain. They advised policymakers to eschew bold policy debates and instead seek compromise sufficient to ensure policy continuity.

Today, congressional leaders should again shore up this consensus. To help do so, they should refrain from bold actions that are deeply opposed by one side or the other.

*   *   *

Halperin argued in 2010 that NFU is 'a good idea whose time has not come'.[24] It still hasn't come. NFU adoption at this time would undermine deterrence in significant ways at a time when deterrence is already weakening for other reasons. It would contribute to a further erosion of the assurance of allies and at a time when such assurance is already being tested for other reasons. It would add no meaningful leadership to non-proliferation and disarmament efforts. And it would have a corrosive impact on the residual elements of bipartisanship on nuclear policy in the Congress. At a time of rising nuclear dangers, such results would only magnify those dangers. No-first-use is a step in the wrong direction.

Notes

1   See Joe Gould, 'Warren, Smith Introduce Bill to Bar US from Using Nuclear Weapons First', *Defense News*, 30 January 2019, https://www.defense-news.com/congress/2019/01/30/warren-smith-introduce-bill-to-bar-us-from-using-nuclear-weapons-first/.

2   For the full set of op-eds, see 'Vision and Steps for a World Free of Nuclear Weapons', Nuclear Threat Initiative, 1 November 2013, https://www.nti.org/analysis/articles/vision-and-steps-world-free-nuclear-weapons/.

3   United States Institute of Peace, 'America's Strategic Posture: The Final Report of the Congressional Commission on the US Strategic Posture', May 2009, https://www.usip.org/sites/default/files/America's_Strategic_Posture_Auth_Ed.pdf.

4   Morton Halperin, 'Forum: The Case for No First Use – An Exchange', *Survival*, vol. 51, no. 5, October–November 2009, p. 22.

5   Scott D. Sagan, 'The Case for No First Use', *Survival*, vol. 51, no. 3, June–July 2009, pp. 163–82.

6   See US Department of Defense, 'Nuclear Posture Review Report', April 2010, pp. viii, 15–17, https://dod.defense.gov/Portals/1/features/defenseReviews/NPR/2010_Nuclear_Posture_Review_Report.pdf.

7   James R. Schlesinger and William J. Perry, 'Nuclear Review Shows Bipartisanship', Politico, 14 April 2010, https://www.politico.com/story/2010/04/nuclear-review-shows-bipartisanship-035747.

8   Bruce Blair, 'How Obama Could Revolutionize Nuclear Weapons Strategy Before He Goes', Politico, 22 June 2016, https://www.politico.com/magazine/story/2016/06/barack-obama-nuclear-weapons-213981.

9   'Remarks by the Vice President on Nuclear Security', 11 January 2017, https://obamawhitehouse.archives.gov/the-press-office/2017/01/12/remarks-vice-president-nuclear-security.

10   See US Department of State, Bureau of Arms Control, Verification and Compliance, Reports on Adherence to and Compliance with Arms Control, Nonproliferation, and Disarmament Agreements and Commitments, available at https://www.state.gov/t/avc/rls/rpt/.

11   Paul Sonne, Gordon Lubold and Carol E. Lee, '"No First Use" Nuclear Policy Assailed by US Cabinet

Officials, Allies', *Wall Street Journal*, 12 August 2016, https://www.wsj.com/articles/NFU-nuclear-policyproposal-assailed-by-u-s-cabinet-officials-allies-1471042014.

12 Nina Tannenwald, 'The Vanishing Nuclear Taboo? How Disarmament Fell Apart', *Foreign Affairs*, vol. 97, no. 6, November/December 2018, p. 21.

13 US Department of Defense, 'Nuclear Posture Review, 2018', pp. 21–2, https://dod.defense.gov/News/Special Reports/2018NuclearPostureReview.aspx.

14 Daryl G. Kimball, 'The Case for a US No-First-Use Policy', *Arms Control Today*, October 2018, https://www.armscontrol.org/act/2018-10/focus/case-us-first-use-policy.

15 See Michael S. Gerson, 'No First Use: The Next Step for U.S. Policy', *International Security*, vol. 35, no. 2, Fall 2010, pp. 7–47.

16 Paul Bernstein, 'Post-Cold War Nuclear Strategy', in Jeffrey A. Larsen and Kerry M. Kartchner (eds), *On Limited Nuclear War in the 21st Century* (Palo Alto, CA: Stanford University Press, 2014), p. 89.

17 US Department of Defense, 'Quadrennial Defense Review, 2014', p. 14, http://archive.defense.gov/pubs/2014_quadrennial_defense_review.pdf.

18 Dave Johnson, 'Russia's Conventional Precision Strike Capabilities, Regional Crises, and Nuclear Thresholds', Livermore Papers on Global Security No. 3, 2018, https://cgsr.llnl.gov/content/assets/docs/Precision-Strike-Capabilities-report-v3-7.pdf.

19 Kimball, 'The Case for a US No-First-Use Policy'.

20 United States Institute of Peace, 'Providing for the Common Defense: The Assessment and Recommendations of the National Defense Strategy Commission', November 2018, https://www.usip.org/sites/default/files/2018-11/providing-for-the-common-defense.pdf.

21 See, for example, Yukio Satoh, 'U.S. Extended Deterrence and Japan's Security', Livermore Papers on Global Security No. 4, 2017, pp. 58–9.

22 Paul Kane, 'Democrats on "Reassurance Tour" for European Allies Worried about Trump', *Washington Post*, 16 February 2019, https://www.washingtonpost.com/powerpost/democrats-on-reassurance-tour-for-european-allies-worried-about-trump/2019/02/16/061e6e18-3157-11e9-8ad3-9a5b113ecd3c_story.html?utm_term=.62c5fcef33d1.

23 Quoted in, for example, Paul Sonne, 'Top Democrats Introduce Bill to Prevent U.S. from Striking First with Nuclear Weapons', *Washington Post*, 30 January 2019, https://www.washingtonpost.com/world/national-security/top-democrats-introduce-bill-to-prevent-us-from-striking-first-with-nuclear-weapons/2019/01/30/a5959ee6-24bc-11e9-ba08-caf4ff5a3433_story.html?utm_term=.bd22a317dc15.

24 Halperin, 'Forum', p. 22.

Arms, Influence and the Treaty on the Prohibition of Nuclear Weapons

Kjølv Egeland

The 2017 Treaty on the Prohibition of Nuclear Weapons (TPNW) has correctly been described as a 'challenge to nuclear deterrence'.[1] But what, precisely, is the nature of the challenge? Prohibiting the development, hosting and use of nuclear weapons, as well as any assistance, encouragement or inducement of prohibited acts, the TPNW was negotiated with a view to amplifying anti-nuclear norms and galvanising nuclear-disarmament processes. Delegitimising nuclear weapons, supporters believe, will help create the conditions for the abolition of nuclear weapons and enhance international security in the long term.[2] For its most strident opponents, however, the TPNW constitutes little more than moralistic posturing or, worse, an enabler for clandestine nuclear-weapons programmes or withdrawals from the Non-Proliferation Treaty (NPT).[3] Others have praised the intentions of those seeking to abolish nuclear weapons, but hypothesised that the TPNW could produce dangerous unintended effects, such as unbalanced stockpile reductions or the destabilisation of deterrence relations and US alliances in Europe and East Asia.[4] Still others have expressed concern about the apparent polarisation of the nuclear-security debate, urging more intellectual engagement across the divide between 'righteous abolitionists' and 'dismissive realists'.[5]

Kjølv Egeland is a Fellow of the Norwegian Academy of International Law (NAIL) and a Lecturer in International Security at Sciences Po in Paris, France.

Survival | vol. 61 no. 3 | June–July 2019 | pp. 57–80   DOI 10.1080/00396338.2019.1614786

This article constitutes an attempt to bridge this gulf. Its purpose is not to pass judgement on the morality of nuclear-deterrence practices or to debate whether the aspiration of nuclear abolition is desirable. Instead, it aims to unpack the concept of deterrence and investigate the ways in which adherence to the TPNW could affect nuclear-deterrence relationships. A number of observers have contended that the TPNW 'bans' nuclear deterrence. Against these commentators, I maintain that the treaty prohibits overt nuclear-deterrence practices and, if fully implemented, could greatly reduce the risk of nuclear confrontation, but will not in and of itself eliminate the conditions for nuclear deterrence. Nuclear rearmament would remain a threat – and hence a potential source of deterrence – even in a world without nuclear weapons. Moreover, pending the advent of such a world, non-nuclear-weapons states allied to nuclear-armed states, also known as nuclear 'umbrella states', could continue to benefit from extended nuclear deterrence even as parties to the TPNW. All else being equal, adherence to the TPNW by a nuclear-umbrella state would produce only an incremental reduction of the salience of nuclear weapons in its security doctrine. Attaining and maintaining a world without nuclear weapons will most likely require a range of supporting politico-legal instruments and actions.

Deterrence in theory and practice

The English term 'deterrence' comes from the Latin word *deterre*, which means 'to frighten from or away'.[6] In the words of the British theorist and civil servant Michael Quinlan, the practice of deterrence provides a means of 'helping to influence others against taking action that would be unwelcome to us, by putting clearly before them the prospect that the action will prompt a response that will leave them worse off than if they had not taken it'.[7] In international relations, the concept of deterrence is most often used to describe the act of convincing, or seeking to convince, an adversary not to attack militarily. To 'convince', in this context, means, in the words of Patrick Morgan, 'to penetrate and manipulate the thought processes of the opposing leaders so that they draw the "proper" conclusion about the utility of attacking'.[8] In practice, it is difficult to isolate the independent deterrent effect of a country's nuclear assets from its other military capabilities: conventional weapons, cultural factors and natural obstacles such as mountains or oceans may also function as deterrents. Conceptually, however, nuclear deterrence occurs when an actor is discouraged from taking a course of action that would be unwelcome to another through fear of *nuclear* reprisals by the aggrieved party. Extended nuclear deterrence occurs when an actor is discouraged from taking a course of action that would be unwelcome to another through fear of nuclear reprisals by a third party. For the renowned deterrence theorist Thomas Schelling, the difference between deterring aggression against the national homeland and deterring aggression against 'everything "abroad" is the difference between threats that are inherently credible, even if unspoken, and the threats that have to be made credible'.[9] Nevertheless, the underlying logic of deterrence – refraining from undertaking an action out of fear of adverse consequences – remains the same irrespective of whether the adverse consequences are to be administered by a direct opponent or by a third party. Strategists commonly also differentiate between deterrence and compellence. While compellence involves the act of convincing an adversary to do something, deterrence involves the act of convincing an adversary *not* to do something.[10]

Four points about deterrence are worth stressing here. Firstly, the practice of deterrence must be carefully distinguished from the psychological phenomenon of deterrence. This distinction is often lost in the policy literature on nuclear deterrence and disarmament, including that on the TPNW. Secondly, successful deterrence does not necessarily require the deterrent threat to be wholly or even moderately credible. The potential impact of a nuclear strike is of such a magnitude that even a sliver of credibility could be enough to convince an opponent that the possibility of nuclear retaliation outweighed any potential benefit of aggression. Equally, even credible threats sometimes fail to deter. Thirdly, contrary to conventional wisdom, nuclear deterrence based on 'mutually assured destruction' is not obviously based on 'rational' premises in the social-scientific sense of the term. Lastly, the concept of deterrence is not a neutral analytical category, but interdependent with the social world its users seek to explain. There is constant slippage between the scholarly discussion of deterrence and the practice of deterrence by political actors.

Deterrence as practice and phenomenon

Deterrence is often associated with nuclear strategy, but is in fact pervasive throughout the animal kingdom, including human societies. As Lawrence Freedman points out, manipulating the behaviour of others through threats is a natural phenomenon: 'The fittest often survive through persuading potential predators that they are too fast to be caught, that they will fight back if they are, and that even if they can be overwhelmed, they are inedible.'[11] For the purposes of this article, however, it is crucial to differentiate between the *practice* of deterrence on the one hand, and the *phenomenon* of deterrence on the other. While the former refers, as Schelling puts it, to the art and science of 'influencing the choices that another party will make, and doing it by influencing his expectations of how we will behave',[12] the latter refers to the fact, says Quinlan, that 'people customarily seek, whether consciously or not, to take into account the probable consequences of what they do. They refrain from actions whose bad consequences for them seem likely to outweigh the good ones.'[13]

Drawing on social theory, the practice of nuclear deterrence may be conceived as an 'open-ended, spatially-temporally dispersed nexus of doings and sayings' related to the art and science of nuclear deterrence.[14] This nexus of doings and sayings – development and deployment of nuclear forces, talk of 'fire and fury' and so on – is independent from the actual, psychological phenomenon of nuclear deterrence. As Richard Ned Lebow argues, threat-based strategies 'can provoke the very kind of behaviour they are implemented to prevent if they are perceived as offensive in intent':

> Khrushchev made grossly exaggerated claims about Soviet strategic capability in the aftermath of the launching of Sputnik in 1957, and exploded gigantic nuclear devices in the early 1960s, to intimidate and restrain the US. The Eisenhower and Kennedy administrations played the same game; in 1961, Kennedy advertised publicly and privately the superiority of American strategic forces and his willingness to conduct a first strike under certain circumstances, left largely undefined. He hoped to deter Khrushchev from making another move against Berlin. Evidence from Soviet sources indicates that Kennedy's threats were a principal incentive for Khrushchev to send missiles to Cuba.[15]

The practice of deterrence, Lebow points out, can sometimes produce the opposite of its intended effect. Adversaries may be impervious to risk or simply fail to comprehend the message. But not only do practices of deterrence sometimes not translate into the psychological phenomenon of deterrence on the receiving end, the phenomenon of deterrence can occur without any one actor having deliberately engaged in the practice of deterrence. For example, criminal punishment motivated only by a desire for revenge could in many cases deter future crime. Equally, brutal sentencing practices aimed at deterrence could foment civil unrest and revolution. The occurrence of the phenomenon of deterrence, in other words, is not up to the one issuing the deterrent threat, but to those on the receiving end.

The credibility of deterrent threats

Actors seeking to deter others from taking a particular course of action typically endeavour to make their implicit or explicit deterrent threat as *credible* as possible. Deterrence theorists such as Schelling and Bernard Brodie devoted much of their intellectual capacity to the study of credibility. After all, if actor A does not believe that actor B will ever carry out its deterrent threat, A is unlikely to be deterred. It is important to note, however, that successful deterrence does not require convincing the opponent that punishment is *inevitable* (although threats of inevitable punishment could certainly strengthen the deterrent effect).[16] For example, a state leader may judge the likelihood of being caught meddling in another state's elections to be extremely low, but still be deterred from authorising any meddling based on the calculus that any possibility of punishment outweighed the benefits of disrupting the other state's democratic process. From the perspective of an attacker, aggression constitutes a risk. In this view, an attacker assesses the feasibility of aggression by combining the credibility of punishment with the severity of that punishment.

Nuclear threats typically score low on credibility and extraordinarily high on severity. These dimensions are of course intimately connected; the low credibility of a nuclear threat is in large measure a consequence of its severity. The implication is that nuclear threats lack credibility against anything short of serious violations of vital interests. However, on the higher end of the scale of provocations, nuclear threats may well be just about credible enough to deter. An actor may also be deterred from taking a particular course of action through fear of provoking a spiral of escalation that ultimately could lead to a nuclear confrontation. In his 1989 memoir, the former UK defence minister Denis Healey argued that 'it takes only five percent credibility of American retaliation to deter the Russians [from invading Western Europe] but ninety-five percent credibility to reassure the Europeans'.[17]

The irrationality of nuclear retaliation

The use by influential deterrence theorists of rational-choice theory and formal modelling has contributed to the widespread perception that mutually assured destruction (MAD) rests on rational premises. Scholarship on MAD has often been referred to as 'Rational Deterrence Theory',[18] and one of the standard critiques of nuclear-deterrence strategies is that 'rogue states' and terrorist groups cannot be deterred because they are not rational. But MAD is derived neither from rational premises nor from game theory. In the words of Hedley Bull, 'It is not the case, as is sometimes argued, that these ideas are derivable from formal game theory or that in Schelling's case they have in fact been derived in this way: they represent an imaginative, conceptual exercise.'[19] While Rational Deterrence Theory may be logical and analytically elegant, the basic assumptions on which it rests are not necessarily rational. In fact, several theorists have pointed out that launching a nuclear second strike in response to a large-scale nuclear assault is not, strictly speaking, rational. After all, the infliction of retaliatory nuclear violence would not mitigate the damage caused by the initial strike, but add to the destabilisation it had caused to the earth's climate. As the authors of '"Blunt Not the Heart, Enrage It": The Psychology of Revenge and Deterrence' put it:

> Classic theories of deterrence emerged in the wake of the nuclear revolution and required that for deterrence to be stable, both actors had to commit to an otherwise seemingly irrational course of action: nuclear retaliation in response to a first strike. Such a commitment is awkward

within a rationalist framework because, as many theorists have pointed out, a second-strike attack cannot undo or mitigate the apocalyptic damage delivered in a first strike.[20]

At the same time, however, the irrationality of nuclear retaliation does not imply that threats of nuclear retaliation are never credible: 'In short, despite arguments and assumptions that deterrence rests on assumed calculated rationality, the only truly credible aspect of deterrence lies in the authentic emotional power and psychological persuasion of the human drive for revenge in the face of violation or attack.'[21]

Deterrence and the double hermeneutic

Scientific theories such as the laws of thermodynamics have no direct impact on, or engagement with, the subject matter they explain. Energy does not care or know about the first law. Many social-science theories, by contrast, including deterrence theories, are deeply intertwined in society. Anthony Giddens describes this phenomenon as the 'double hermeneutic'. For Giddens, 'the subjects of study in the social sciences and the humanities are concept-using beings, whose concepts of their actions enter in a constitutive manner into what those actions are'.[22] Social-scientific concepts, then, do not just explain the world, they also shape it. For example, Jean Bodin and Niccolò Machiavelli did not simply describe an independently occurring series of social changes, 'They helped constitute the state forms that emerged from those changes. Modern states could not exist at all were not concepts such as "citizen", "sovereignty", and "government" itself, mastered by the individuals who administer them and those subject to their rule.'[23] Deterrence, in this view, is not a neutral analytical concept detached from the social world. The concept and theories of deterrence have direct impacts on the world through the scholarship of experts and the use and questioning of those theories by the actors whose behaviour the theories are supposed to explain. Benoît Pelopidas put this succinctly when he observed that the concept of deterrence does 'double work'.[24] Deterrence theorists typically seek both to *describe* the world and, at the same time, to *act* on it:

> Saying that deterrence works is intended to make it work or at least to help
> it work better. It is meant to be a self-fulfilling prophecy. As a consequence,
> for these utterances to be able to work better, their authors have to deny
> their intention to produce an effect. They have to appear authoritative as
> descriptions and nothing more in order to have the intended effect.[25]

Nuclear weapons may well have fostered stability and restraint in many instances, but, as noted by the author Martin Amis, 'the trouble with [nuclear] deterrence is that it can't outlast the necessary time-span, which is roughly between now and the death of the sun'.[26] Many long-standing nuclear-arms-control proposals, such as the de-alerting of nuclear forces, aim precisely at hedging against the prospect that an irrational outburst of emotions may be quickly translated into catastrophic nuclear violence. One of the central challenges to the long-term viability of nuclear deterrence is the danger of technological malfunction and inadvertent escalation.[27]

The fact that the effectiveness of nuclear deterrence relies, in part, on the degree to which political leaders accept the basic premises of deterrence theories has led many theorists to view efforts at devaluing and delegitimising nuclear weapons with hostility. Criticising deterrence practices, says Pelopidas, is 'portrayed as both perverse and jeopardizing', as weakening the deterrent effect of such practices and thereby undermining international stability.[28] In the late 1950s, for example, Henry Kissinger argued vigorously against the adoption of a ban on nuclear testing, maintaining that such a step would undercut deterrence and cause a dangerous rift in NATO.[29] Just like many contemporary critics of the TPNW, Kissinger saw the West's alleged insistence on 'moral perfection' as a dangerous weakness.[30] US allies' squeamishness about nuclear war had to be dispelled:

> One of the chief tasks of United States policy in NATO … is to overcome the
> trauma which attaches to the use of nuclear weapons and to decentralize
> the possession of nuclear weapons as rapidly as possible. Nothing would
> so much dispel the mystery of nuclear weapons as their possession by the
> Continental powers. Nothing would do more to help restore a measure of
> consistency to allied military planning.[31]

In hindsight, the 'trauma which attaches to the use of nuclear weapons' appears to have helped curb proliferation and avoid war with nuclear weapons.[32] Taking the opposite view to the one propounded by Kissinger in the 1950s, the 189 parties to the NPT agreed in 2010 on the need 'for further progress in diminishing the role of nuclear weapons in security policies'.[33] The logical end point of this process – the abolition of nuclear weapons – remains a stated goal of virtually all states. Of course, the goal of creating a nuclear-free world has often been criticised. Schelling and others have argued that a nuclear-free world would provide the most dangerous of all possible nuclear balances, incentivising rapid rearmament and pre-emptive nuclear strikes.[34] While a full discussion of this claim falls outside the scope of this article, suffice it to point out that several commentators have disputed Schelling's hypothesis. While it is true that nuclear weapons cannot be disinvented, fissile material can be controlled, warheads can be verifiably eliminated and norms can be cultivated.[35]

The impact of the TPNW on nuclear-deterrence relations

Adopted in July 2017, the TPNW prohibits its parties from possessing, hosting, using or threatening to use nuclear weapons, as well as from assisting, encouraging or inducing prohibited activities.[36] A perfunctory reading of these prohibitions would suggest that the TPNW rules out any reliance on nuclear deterrence. Indeed, both proponents and opponents of the TPNW have contended that the new treaty 'bans deterrence'. Hirofumi Tosaki avers that the TPNW 'legally prohibits reliance on nuclear deterrence'.[37] Paul Meyer and Tom Sauer have likewise argued in this journal that nuclear deterrence will become 'illegal':

> The ban treaty will forbid the development, production, testing, acquisition, stockpiling, transfer, possession and stationing – as well as the use and threat of use – of nuclear weapons. Consequently, the decades-old doctrine of nuclear deterrence will become illegal for the signatory states, and in the eyes of the hundreds of millions of citizens around the world who support the treaty.[38]

Commentators have also maintained that the TPNW prohibits reliance on *extended* nuclear deterrence. For example, Ramesh Thakur suggests that the TPNW 'could be interpreted to read that it prohibits extended nuclear deterrence'.[39] Matthew Harries argues that the treaty 'implicitly prohibits a state party from receiving any kind of nuclear deterrence guarantee'.[40] The authors of a Harvard Law School study assert that the treaty's prohibitions 'make it unlawful for a state party to benefit from the protection of a nuclear umbrella arrangement'.[41] I maintain that these assertions are inaccurate. As long as nuclear rearmament and use remain possible, the conditions for nuclear deterrence will exist. The effect of the TPNW on deterrence relations will in large part depend on how states frame and implement their own, and their allies', obligations under the treaty.

'Threatening to use' nuclear weapons

The practice of nuclear deterrence is often conceptualised as a strategy based on the implicit or explicit 'threat' to use nuclear weapons. During the TPNW negotiations, certain participants argued strongly in favour of including in the treaty an explicit prohibition against threatening to use nuclear arms. The Japanese non-governmental organisation Peace Boat – one of the organisations represented in the Steering Group of the International Campaign to Abolish Nuclear Weapons (ICAN) – submitted a working paper to the negotiating conference asserting that the 'threat of use of nuclear weapons is at the core of nuclear deterrence policy'. The concept of nuclear deterrence 'has provided the basis of justification' for the retention of nuclear weapons, Peace Boat observed, concluding that it was therefore important that the TPNW 'clearly prohibit the threat of use of nuclear weapons so that the policy of nuclear deterrence is provided unlawful'.[42] Accordingly, Article 1 of the TPNW enjoins its parties never, under any circumstances, to 'use or threaten to use' nuclear weapons. But does the prohibition against threatening to use nuclear weapons legally foreclose nuclear deterrence?

The legal literature on the concept of threats and their relationship to nuclear deterrence is inconclusive.[43] There is no consensus among legal scholars on what constitutes a 'threat' in general, the specific conditions under which threatening to use nuclear force is lawful or unlawful, or the legal status of nuclear-deterrence practices such as MAD or the extension of nuclear security guarantees to third parties.[44] It seems highly doubtful, however, that the possession of nuclear weapons could be said *ipso facto* to constitute a threat to use them in the legal sense. In his recently published legal commentary on the TPNW, Stuart Casey-Maslen argues that the prohibition against threatening to use nuclear weapons enshrined by Article 1 of the TPNW does not encompass either the mere possession of nuclear weapons or membership in alliances that include nuclear-armed states.[45] The TPNW's prohibition against threatening to use nuclear weapons, then, does not rule out either the practice of, or the passive reliance on, nuclear deterrence. Israel, for example, has long been seen to practise nuclear deterrence without ever having acknowledged its possession of nuclear arms. It would be difficult to argue that Israel has 'threatened' to use nuclear weapons in accordance with the accepted usage of that term.

'Possessing' and 'using' nuclear weapons

The effectiveness of the TPNW's claimed prohibition on nuclear deterrence does not rest solely on the prohibition against 'threatening to use' nuclear weapons. The TPNW also prohibits the hosting, possession and stockpiling of nuclear arms. However, even the full catalogue of prohibitions contained in the TPNW arguably does not preclude either the practice or the phenomenon of nuclear deterrence. In fact, even in a nuclear-free world, each state would know that other states, in particular those with large civilian nuclear programmes, could manufacture nuclear weapons within a relatively short period of time. Parties to the TPNW with civilian nuclear technology and materials could thus engage in a form of 'weaponless' or 'virtual' nuclear deterrence.[46] Other states could conceivably be deterred from taking particular courses of action through fear of escalation and rearmament. Weaponless nuclear deterrence would operate at 'one remove' from the possession of nuclear weapons,[47] possibly lessening the risk of accidents or inadvertent nuclear escalation, but nuclear deterrence would remain a feature in strategic affairs. That said, the TPNW would deem any acquisition (or reacquisition) and use of nuclear weapons illegal under international law, meaning that any practice of weaponless nuclear deterrence would rest on the possibility of future violations of the prohibitions against development, production, possession and use. Yet, while a legal prohibition and verification arrangements could help stigmatise nuclear weapons and constrain access to nuclear material, the existence of a legal regime would not in and of itself guarantee that nuclear arms could not nevertheless be acquired and used.

The abolition of current nuclear arsenals would not eliminate the risk of future nuclear rearmament and war. In the 1950s, several renowned authors therefore argued that the risk of nuclear war could only be satisfactorily managed through the institution of a world government that would monopolise the use of force, eliminate all nuclear weapons, and control nuclear materials and technology.[48] In such a world, the conditions for nuclear deterrence would be constrained to an absolute minimum, and would for all practical purposes be an insignificant feature of world politics. Yet in theory, nuclear deterrence could still exist. For example, sub-state groupings could position themselves tactically in relation to the means of force or strategic sectors of the economy, deterring others from taking particular courses of action. The TPNW contains no provisions rendering such actions unlawful, and it is difficult to imagine how any legal document could comprehensively prohibit subtle attempts at influencing behaviour through the manipulation of nuclear fear – let alone nuclear fear itself. The conspicuousness of nuclear deterrence in world politics, in this view, is a matter of degree. The security doctrines of each of the world's states could be conceived as falling on a spectrum between aggressive nuclear grandstanding at one end, and a total rejection of any use of nuclear weapons at the other, with the de-alerting of nuclear forces, adoption of no-first-use policies, explicit reliance on extended nuclear deterrence and general alignment with nuclear-armed states constituting intermediary positions. All else being equal, each of these steps away from aggressive nuclear grandstanding would reduce the salience of nuclear weapons and deterrence in world affairs, likely strengthening the stigma associated with nuclear weapons.

Extended nuclear deterrence and 'encouragement' of prohibited activities
A number of observers have maintained that the TPNW renders extended nuclear deterrence unlawful. The textual justification for this claim is the

prohibitions in Article 1(1) against providing or seeking 'assistance', 'encouragement' or 'inducement' to carry out prohibited activities. According to a commentary on the Chemical Weapons Convention, 'encouragement' means contributing to another actor's 'resolve' to commit a prohibited activity.[49] The current practices of many so-called umbrella states would appear to fall foul of this standard. For example, NATO's 2010 Strategic Concept establishes that the allies will 'maintain an appropriate mix of nuclear and conventional forces'.[50] Endorsement of this statement could reasonably be read as a contribution to the 'resolve' of France, the United Kingdom and the United States to retain nuclear weapons. The UK government has consistently justified the construction of a new class of ballistic-missile submarines with reference to NATO documents and the demands for nuclear reassurance by allies,[51] and successive US administrations have framed spending on nuclear-weapon systems as necessary to fulfil 'extended deterrence commitments' enshrined in Alliance documents. Ostensibly, these commitments oblige the United States to 'retain numbers or types of nuclear capabilities that it might not deem necessary if it were concerned only with its own defense'.[52]

Several observers, including the foreign minister of Norway, have maintained that ratification of the TPNW would not be legally incompatible with NATO membership.[53] However, to comply with its international obligations, any party to the treaty would have to distance itself from statements or alliance documents endorsing the potential use of nuclear weapons. In theory, an umbrella state could accomplish this by issuing a declaration disavowing any possession or use of nuclear weapons appended to its instrument of ratification of the treaty. As argued by Casey-Maslen, ratification of the legally binding TPNW would then, as a matter of international law, 'override' previous support for political documents such as NATO's Strategic Concept.[54] That said, the legal compatibility of the treaty with membership in NATO and other alliances does not imply that adherence to the TPNW would be compatible with a signatory's actual good standing in NATO or other alliances. While collective-defence treaties typically do not contain provisions to expel existing parties, individual allies could suspend technical cooperation, withhold data and intelligence, cancel joint exercises or sow doubt about their willingness to come to the TPNW adherent's aid. Such actions on the part of a signatory's allies would arguably have a much more profound effect on deterrence relations than would the act of acceding to the treaty.

Assuming, for the sake of argument, that it would be possible for an umbrella state to join the TPNW without being ostracised from its alliance, such adherence would not *ipso facto* prohibit it from 'benefiting' from extended nuclear deterrence. After all, accession to the TPNW by a nuclear-umbrella state would not preclude that state's nuclear-armed allies from using nuclear armaments against a third party. The same applies to other non-universally banned weapons such as landmines, cluster munitions and chemical weapons. For example, Denmark's adherence to the Convention on Cluster Munitions would not legally prevent the United States from using cluster munitions in a conflict against a common enemy – including if the United States' involvement in the conflict had emanated from a Danish invocation of NATO's collective-defence clause. Denmark would of course be prohibited from requesting or assisting US use of cluster munitions, but could not be held legally responsible for the discretional actions of the US government. Equally, accession to the TPNW by Denmark would prohibit Copenhagen from assisting, encouraging or inducing the United States to use nuclear weapons – for example by hosting US tactical nuclear munitions on Danish territory – but would not prevent the United States from using nuclear weapons against a common enemy. It should also be pointed out that, in the scenario described above, Denmark's status as a de facto nuclear-weapon-free zone under the TPNW would survive only as long as Denmark or the major powers considered it in their interest to respect that status.[55] Denmark's potential adversaries would of course be aware of this fact. As an illustration of this dynamic, Germany's adherence to the NPT has hardly convinced Russia that the US nuclear warheads stationed on German territory could not be (illegally) transferred to and used by German dual-key aircraft in the event of escalation.

A hypothetical Danish ratification of the TPNW, in other words, would not provide Swedish, Chinese or Russian leaders with a guarantee that aggression against Denmark (and thus NATO) could not escalate into a wider confrontation with Copenhagen's nuclear-armed allies. Were the

United States, the United Kingdom or France to find themselves in a state of war with Russia, Denmark's views on the legality of strategic nuclear strikes against Moscow would be beside the point. As a 1995 US strategy document put it, 'nuclear weapons always cast a shadow over any crisis or conflict in which the US is engaged'.[56] This argument holds even for states without a formal security guarantee. As Schelling argued in *Arms and Influence*, the credibility of extended deterrent threats does not rely on formal guarantees. The credibility, such as it was, of the United States' commitment to defend West Germany and Greece during the Cold War relied not primarily on the North Atlantic Treaty, but on the fact that the United States could not 'afford to let the Soviets overrun West Germany or Greece, irrespective of [US] treaty commitments to Germany or to the rest of Western Europe'. Indeed, the US may well have recognised 'an implicit obligation to support Yugoslavia, perhaps Finland, in a military crisis'.[57] The import of Schelling's argument is that the phenomenon of deterrence, nuclear or conventional, does not rely on formal security guarantees or declarations, but on the enemy's belief that aggression could lead to allied involvement and escalation. Accession to the TPNW by an umbrella state would not eliminate this risk.

The TPNW and the credibility of extended nuclear deterrence

Accession to the TPNW by an umbrella state would not provide its adversaries with a guarantee that aggression against that state could not ultimately escalate into a nuclear war. Accordingly, the conditions for the psychological phenomenon of extended nuclear deterrence would remain. Moreover, alignment with a nuclear-armed state could be interpreted as a nuclear-deterrence practice not prohibited by the TPNW. Under the definition provided above, alignment with a nuclear-armed state would constitute a deterrence practice if it was conceived as such by the umbrella state. From the point of view of an adversary, however, this would be a distinction without a difference.

While an umbrella state's accession to the TPNW would not necessarily eliminate the conditions for nuclear deterrence, it could reduce the credibility of nuclear deterrence in at least two ways. Firstly, as suggested above, an umbrella state's adherence to the TPNW could undercut the viability of certain nuclear-response options, such as the deployment of tactical nuclear weapons to the territory of the umbrella state. The overall strategic balance, however, would arguably remain largely unchanged. Admittedly, the incumbent US government has adopted the position that credible deterrence demands that the United States and NATO match Russia's and other potential adversaries' capabilities on every potential step of the escalation ladder, from hybrid actions via conventional operations to 'low-yield' tactical nuclear strikes and ultimately strategic nuclear war. This view has been challenged by a large section of the expert community.[58] For example, it could be argued that having 'high-yield' strategic weapons as one's only response option could deter adversaries from conventional aggression or 'low-yield' tactical nuclear strikes due to the potential of rapid escalation to strategic nuclear war.[59] As alluded to above, such debates are often particularly acrimonious because they operate on the level of the double hermeneutic of nuclear deterrence; Washington's suggestion that it might be self-deterred from responding to a 'low-yield' nuclear strike with a 'high-yield' response could potentially influence the choices of Washington's adversaries.

Secondly and more importantly, an umbrella state's accession to the TPNW could undermine the credibility of nuclear deterrence by adding to the stigma associated with the use of nuclear weapons. Already in the 1950s, policymakers in the United States and the United Kingdom were cognisant that anti-nuclear norms could increase the reputational costs of using nuclear weapons, and thus decrease the credibility of nuclear use.[60] Operating again on the level of the double hermeneutic, the implicit argument is that the deterrent value of nuclear weapons could diminish if the use of such weapons came to be seen as socially unacceptable. For many supporters of the TPNW, however, the fact that the treaty could strengthen anti-nuclear norms and over time undermine the legitimacy and credibility of nuclear deterrence is precisely the point. As they see it, delegitimising and stigmatising nuclear weapons could reduce the risk of nuclear use and remove one of the key obstacles to nuclear disarmament, namely the 'prestige value' of nuclear weapons.

Opponents of the TPNW have argued that any normative impact of the ban is likely to be asymmetric – that the treaty could foster unbalanced disarmament and instability. The NATO official Michael Rühle, for example, maintains that the TPNW 'will only affect Western democracies' because the 'delegitimisation of nuclear weapons can only work in places with a vibrant civil society'.[61] This statement is not obviously correct – authoritarian states and non-Western democracies also appear to have been affected by nuclear norms[62] – but even if we assume that the TPNW will only have an impact on Western democracies, it is not clear that asymmetric pressure will necessarily yield asymmetric outcomes. On the contrary, increased anti-nuclear pressure in and on France, the United Kingdom and the United States could just as likely translate into an increased willingness in those countries to engage the other nuclear-armed states in meaningful negotiations. In the late 1950s and early 1960s, popular mobilisation against atmospheric nuclear testing in the Western and non-aligned worlds led to the negotiation by the Soviet Union, the United Kingdom and the United States of the 1963 Partial Nuclear-Test-Ban Treaty – not to unilateral measures by the Western powers.[63]

Most of the world's states have agreed to nuclear disarmament

Most, if not all, of the world's states have nominally agreed to enact nuclear disarmament. Supporters of the dominant 'step-by-step' approach to disarmament often point to the large stockpile reductions undertaken since the mid-1980s as proof that the world is on course to achieve the elimination of nuclear weapons. Yet the question remains whether such reductions (quantitative alterations of the status quo) can be used as evidence that the international community is truly on a path to abolition (a fundamental, qualitative transformation of the post-war international structure). While the arms-control approach may have made the world safer, it has arguably never challenged the norms and power structures that sustain nuclear-weapons programmes.[64] And while the established major powers have downsized their arsenals, they continue to value their nuclear weapons, retaining stockpiles more than large enough to cause a nuclear winter.[65] The 'doomsday clock' of the Bulletin of the Atomic Scientists has never been closer to midnight. Furthermore, notwithstanding important cases of 'de-proliferation' by Belarus, Kazakhstan, South Africa and Ukraine, the number of nuclear-armed states has grown since the end of the Cold War. It is thus far from clear that the international community is on a path to nuclear abolition. Many observers have maintained that this is likely to remain the case for as long as nuclear weapons are framed as legitimate instruments of security. From this perspective, delegitimising nuclear weapons would appear to constitute a necessary condition for the achievement of long-term solutions to the problem caused by the nuclear revolution.[66]

*   *   *

The TPNW constitutes a serious challenge to the legitimacy of nuclear-deterrence practices, but does not 'ban' nuclear deterrence. The treaty prohibits overt nuclear-deterrence practices such as threatening to use nuclear weapons, hosting nuclear weapons, possessing and deploying nuclear weapons, and encouraging allies to engage in such activities, but it does not comprehensively foreclose either the phenomenon or the practice of nuclear deterrence. For example, the TPNW does not prohibit civilian nuclear programmes and thus allows for the practice of 'virtual' or 'weaponless' nuclear deterrence. The abolition of nuclear weapons would make nuclear deterrence less salient, but would not eliminate it as a factor in strategic affairs. Furthermore, the TPNW does not prohibit its parties from engaging in military alliances with nuclear-armed states so long as they refrain from any assistance, encouragement or inducement of prohibited activities. *Ceteris paribus*, such states could still 'benefit' from extended nuclear deterrence – whether they wished to or not. The fact that the TPNW does not actually outlaw nuclear deterrence is not an outcome of poor drafting on the part of the TPNW negotiators, but a consequence of the elusive nature of nuclear deterrence. A comprehensive prohibition on nuclear deterrence would necessitate a comprehensive prohibition on nuclear fear. This, however, is unlikely to be feasible – or desirable.

The TPNW has often been framed as a competitor to the step-by-step approach to nuclear disarmament favoured by the nuclear-armed states and most of their allies. According to this approach, nuclear disarmament should be accomplished through the completion of a series of mutually reinforcing, incremental steps. On closer inspection, however, adherence to the TPNW by non-nuclear-weapons states and umbrella states would appear to be not only compatible with, but even complementary to, this approach. Framing nuclear weapons as fundamentally unacceptable instruments of warfare, the TPNW could help build a normative environment more conducive to nuclear disarmament. While adherence to the treaty by nuclear-umbrella states would not comprehensively eliminate extended nuclear deterrence, it would constitute a meaningful step on a path to reducing the salience of nuclear weapons in world affairs. Creating a stronger norm against nuclear weapons will not alone be sufficient to create a world without such weapons, but it may well be necessary.

Notes

1   Edward Ifft, 'A Challenge to Nuclear Deterrence', *Arms Control Today*, March 2017, https://www.armscontrol.org/act/2017-03/features/challenge-nuclear-deterrence.

2   See, for example, Beatrice Fihn, 'The Logic of Banning Nuclear Weapons', *Survival*, vol. 59, no. 1, February–March 2017, pp. 43–50; and Nick Ritchie, 'The Real "Problem" with a Ban Treaty? It Challenges the Status Quo', Carnegie Endowment for International Peace, 3 April 2017, http://carnegieendowment.org/2017/04/03/real-problem-with-ban-treaty-it-challenges-status-quo-pub-68510.

3   See, for example, Michael Rühle, 'The Nuclear Weapons Ban Treaty: Reasons for Scepticism', *NATO Review*, 19 May 2017, https://www.nato.int/docu/review/2017/also-in-2017/nuclear-weapons-ban-treaty-scepticism-abolition/en/index.htm; and Heather Williams, 'Does the Fight over Nuclear Weapons Ban Threaten Global Stability?', *Bulletin of the Atomic Scientists*, 9 February 2017, http://thebulletin.org/does-fight-over-nuclear-weapons-ban-threaten-global-stability10500.

4   See, for example, Matthew Harries, 'The Real Problem with a Nuclear Ban Treaty', Carnegie Endowment for International Peace, 15 March 2017, https://carnegieendowment.org/2017/03/15/real-problem-with-nuclear-ban-treaty-pub-68286; and Scott Sagan and Benjamin A. Valentino, 'The Nuclear Weapons Ban Treaty: Opportunities Lost', *Bulletin of the Atomic Scientists*, 16 July 2017, https://thebulletin.org/2017/07/the-nuclear-weapons-ban-treaty-opportunities-lost/.

5   See, for example, Lars-Erik Lundin,

'Inquiry into the Consequences of a Swedish Accession to the Treaty on the Prohibition of Nuclear Weapons', Swedish Ministry of Foreign Affairs, January 2019, p. 175; and Jenny Nielsen, 'A Summer of Discontent: The Consolidation of Nuclear Disarmament and Deterrence Divides', European Leadership Network, 15 August 2016, https://www.europeanleadershipnetwork.org/commentary/a-summer-of-discontent-the-consolidation-of-nuclear-disarmament-and-deterrence-divides/. The (somewhat leading) distinction between 'righteous abolitionists' and 'dismissive realists' originates in Michael Quinlan, 'Abolishing Nuclear Armouries', *Survival*, vol. 49, no. 4, Winter 2007–08, p. 8.

6   Lawrence Freedman, *Nuclear Deterrence* (London: Penguin, 2018), p. 1.

7   Michael Quinlan, *Thinking About Nuclear Weapons: Principles, Problems, Prospects* (Oxford: Oxford University Press, 2009), p. 20.

8   Patrick M. Morgan, 'Saving Face for the Sake of Deterrence', in Robert Jervis et al. (eds), *Psychology and Deterrence* (Baltimore, MD: Johns Hopkins University Press, 1985), p. 125.

9   Thomas C. Schelling, *Arms and Influence* (New Haven, CT: Yale University Press, 1966), p. 36.

10   *Ibid.*, pp. 69–71.

11   Lawrence Freedman, *Deterrence* (Cambridge: Polity, 2004), p. 6.

12   Thomas C. Schelling, *Strategy of Conflict* (Cambridge, MA: Harvard University Press, 1980 [1960]), p. 13.

13   Quinlan, *Thinking About Nuclear Weapons*, p. 20.

14   Theodore R. Schatzki, 'A Primer on Practices', in J. Higgs et al. (eds), *Practice-Based Education* (Rotterdam: Sense Publishers, 2012), p. 14.

15   Richard Ned Lebow, 'Deterrence: Then and Now', *Journal of Strategic Studies*, vol. 28, no. 5, 2005, pp. 766–7.

16   Schelling, *Arms and Influence*, p. 35.

17   Cited in Matthew Fuhrmann, 'On Extended Nuclear Deterrence', *Diplomacy & Statecraft*, vol. 29, no. 1, 2018, p. 65.

18   See, for example, Christopher H. Achen and Duncan Snidal, 'Rational Deterrence Theory and Comparative Case Studies', *World Politics*, vol. 41, no. 2, 1989, pp. 143–69.

19   Hedley Bull, 'The Theory of International Politics 1919–1969', in Brian Porter (ed.), *The Aberystwyth Papers: International Politics, 1919–1969* (Oxford: Oxford University Press, 1972), reproduced in Andrew Linklater (ed.), *Critical Concepts in Political Science* (London: Routledge, 2000), p. 66.

20   Rose McDermott, Anthony C. Lopez and Peter K. Hatemi, '"Blunt Not the Heart, Enrage It": The Psychology of Revenge and Deterrence', *Texas National Security Review*, vol. 1, no. 1, 2017, p. 70.

21   *Ibid.*, p. 73.

22   Anthony Giddens, *Social Theory and Modern Sociology* (Cambridge: Polity Press, 1987), pp. 18–19.

23   *Ibid.*, p. 20.

24   Benoît Pelopidas, 'Nuclear Weapons Scholarship as a Case of Self-Censorship in Security Studies', *Journal of Global Security Studies*, vol. 1, no. 4, 2016, p. 329.

25   Benoît Pelopidas, 'Re-imagining

Global Nuclear Ordering Beyond
Proliferation and Deterrence', paper
prepared for POSSE, 2015, p. 8.

26   Martin Amis, *Einstein's Monsters*
(London: Vintage, 1999), p. 17.

27   See Patricia Lewis et al., 'Too Close
for Comfort: Cases of Near Nuclear
Use and Options for Policy', Chatham
House, 2014, p. 9.

28   Pelopidas, 'Re-imagining Global
Nuclear Ordering Beyond
Proliferation and Deterrence', p. 14.

29   Henry A. Kissinger, 'Nuclear Testing
and the Problem of Peace', *Foreign
Affairs*, vol. 37, no. 1, 1958, pp. 1–18.

30   Henry A. Kissinger, 'Missiles and the
Western Alliance', *Foreign Affairs*, vol.
36, no. 3, 1958, p. 400.

31   Henry A. Kissinger, *Nuclear Weapons
and Foreign Policy* (New York: Harper
& Brothers, 1957), p. 311.

32   See Nina Tannenwald, *The Nuclear
Taboo: The United States and the Non-
Use of Nuclear Weapons Since 1945*
(Cambridge: Cambridge University
Press, 2007).

33   Review Conference of the Parties to
the Treaty on the Non-Proliferation of
Nuclear Weapons, Final Document,
Doc. NPT/CONF.2010/50 (Vol. I), 2010,
p. 13.

34   Thomas C. Schelling, 'The Role of
Deterrence in Total Disarmament',
Foreign Affairs, vol. 40, no. 3, 1962.

35   See Harald Müller, 'Icons off the
Mark: Waltz and Schelling on a
Perpetual Brave Nuclear World',
Nonproliferation Review, vol. 20, no. 3,
2013, pp. 545–65.

36   'Treaty on the Prohibition of Nuclear
Weapons', 7 July 2017, Article 1.

37   Hirofumi Tosaki, 'Japan's Nuclear
Disarmament Diplomacy Following

the Adoption of the Treaty on the
Prohibition of Nuclear Weapons
(TPNW)', AJISS-Commentary, 20
October 2017, http://www2.jiia.or.jp/
en_commentary/201710/20-1.html.

38   Paul Meyer and Tom Sauer, 'The
Nuclear Ban Treaty: A Sign of Global
Impatience', *Survival*, vol. 60, no. 2,
April–May 2018, p. 62.

39   Ramesh Thakur, 'Nuclear Turbulence
in the Age of Trump', *Diplomacy &
Statecraft*, vol. 29, no. 1, 2018, p. 117.

40   Matthew Harries, 'US Extended
Nuclear Deterrence Arrangements',
in Shatabhisha Shetty and Denitsa
Raynova (eds), *Breakthrough or
Breakpoint? Global Perspectives on the
Nuclear Ban Treaty* (London: European
Leadership Network, 2017), p. 51.

41   International Human Rights Clinic,
'Nuclear Umbrella Arrangements
and the Treaty on the Prohibition
of Nuclear Weapons', Harvard Law
School, 2018, p. 5.

42   Peace Boat, 'Developing a Robust
Nuclear Weapons Ban Treaty', United
Nations Conference to Negotiate
a Legally Binding Instrument to
Prohibit Nuclear Weapons, Leading
Towards Their Total Elimination, UN
doc. A/CONF/229/2017/NGO/WP.19,
17 April 2017, p. 3.

43   See, for example, International Court
of Justice, 'Legality of the Threat or
Use of Nuclear Weapons', Advisory
Opinion, 1996; Yoram Dinstein,
'The Threat of Force in International
Law', *American Journal of International
Law*, vol. 102, no. 4, 2008, p. 919; and
Nikolas Stürchler, *The Threat of Force
in International Law* (Cambridge:
Cambridge University Press, 2007).

44   In its advisory opinion on the

'Legality of the Threat or Use of Nuclear Weapons', the International Court of Justice held that it was unlawful to issue threats that would be illegal if carried out in practice, and suggested that the use of nuclear weapons would generally be contrary to international humanitarian law. The court declined to pass judgement on whether the use of nuclear weapons would be unlawful when the 'survival' of the state using nuclear weapons was in jeopardy. This could be interpreted to suggest that the threat or use of nuclear weapons would not be permissible if carried out on behalf of another state, as the survival of the user would presumably not be in jeopardy. See Nobuo Hayashi, 'Legality Under *Jus ad Bellum* of the Threat of Use of Nuclear Weapons', in Gro Nystuen, Stuart Casey-Maslen and Annie G. Bersagel (eds), *Nuclear Weapons Under International Law* (Cambridge: Cambridge University Press, 2014).

45 Stuart Casey-Maslen, *The Treaty on the Prohibition of Nuclear Weapons: A Commentary* (Oxford: Oxford University Press, 2019), para. 1.81.

46 See, for example, Michael J. Mazarr, 'Virtual Nuclear Arsenals', *Survival*, vol. 37, no. 3, Autumn 1995, pp. 7–26.

47 Quinlan, *Thinking About Nuclear Weapons*, p. 161.

48 See Campbell Craig, 'Solving the Nuclear Dilemma: Is a World State Necessary?', *Journal of International Political Theory*, 9 September 2018, https://doi.org/10.1177/1755088218795981.

49 See Walter Krutzsch, 'Article 1: General Obligations', in Walter Krutzsch, Eric Myjer and Ralf Trapp (eds), *A Commentary on the Chemical Weapons Convention* (Oxford: Oxford University Press, 2014), p. 67.

50 NATO, 'Active Engagement, Modern Defence: Strategic Concept for the Defence and Security of the Members of the North Atlantic Treaty Organization', November 2010, para. 19.

51 See Theresa May, 'UK's Nuclear Deterrent', *House of Commons Hansard*, 18 July 2016, http://hansard.parliament.uk/Commons/2016-07-18/debates/7B7A196B-B37C-4787-99DC-098882B3EFA2/UKSNuclearDeterrent; and Tom Batchelor, 'Defence Secretary Says World More "Dangerous & Unpredictable" Now than During the Cold War', *Express*, 22 January 2016, http://www.express.co.uk/news/uk/637003/Trident-weapons-Michael-Fallon-UK-nuclear-submarines-dangerous-world.

52 William Perry et al., *America's Strategic Posture: The Final Report of the Congressional Commission on the Strategic Posture of the United States* (Washington DC: United States Institute for Peace Press, 2009), p. 8.

53 See Ine Eriksen Søreide, remarks in the Norwegian parliament (Stortinget), 14 November 2018, https://www.stortinget.no/no/Saker-og-publikasjoner/Publikasjoner/Referater/Stortinget/2018-2019/refs-201819-11-14?m=1.

54 Casey-Maslen, *The Treaty on the Prohibition of Nuclear Weapons*, paras 1.88–1.118. See also International Human Rights Clinic, 'Nuclear Umbrella Arrangements and the Treaty on the Prohibition of Nuclear Weapons'.

55 This point was raised during the

debate about a potential Nordic nuclear-weapon-free zone in the 1980s. See Johan J. Holst, 'The Pattern of Nordic Security', *Dædalus*, vol. 113, no. 2, 1984, p. 217.

56 US Strategic Command, 'Essentials of Post-Cold War Deterrence', 1995, p. 7, http://www.nukestrat.com/us/stratcom/SAGessentials.PDF.

57 Schelling, *Arms and Influence*, p. 52.

58 See, for example, Michael Krepon, 'The Folly of Tactical Nuclear Weapons', Defense One, 2 October 2017, https://www.defenseone.com/technology/2017/10/folly-tactical-nuclear-weapons/141440/.

59 See Cheryl Rofer, 'On the Lack of Analytical Utility of the Concept of Deterrence', Nuclear Diner, 19 February 2019, https://nucleardiner.wordpress.com/2019/02/19/on-the-lack-of-analytical-utility-of-the-concept-of-deterrence/.

60 See, for example, Simon J. Moody, 'Enhancing Political Cohesion in NATO During the 1950s or: How It Learned to Stop Worrying and Love the (Tactical) Bomb', *Journal of Strategic Studies*, vol. 40, no. 6, 2017, p. 828; and Tannenwald, *The Nuclear Taboo*, pp. 143, 169–70.

61 Rühle, 'The Nuclear Weapons Ban Treaty'.

62 See T.V. Paul, 'Nuclear Taboo and War Initiation in Regional Conflicts', *Journal of Conflict Resolution*, vol. 39, no. 4, 1995, pp. 696–717.

63 See Rebecca Johnson, *Unfinished Business: The Negotiation of the CTBT and the End of Nuclear Testing* (Geneva: UNIDIR, 2009), pp. 11–15.

64 See David Mutimer, 'From Arms Control to Denuclearization', *Contemporary Security Policy*, vol. 32, no. 1, 2011, pp. 57–75; and Keith Krause, 'Leashing the Dogs of War', *Contemporary Security Policy*, vol. 32, no. 1, 2011, pp. 20–39.

65 See, for example, Alan Robock and Owen B. Toon, 'Self-assured Destruction: The Climate Impacts of Nuclear War', *Bulletin of the Atomic Scientists*, vol. 68, no. 5, 2012, pp. 66–74.

66 Craig distinguishes between 'reformist' and 'radical' approaches to nuclear security, placing normative efforts such as the humanitarian initiative and negotiation of the TPNW in the former bracket. It could be argued, however, that delegitimising nuclear weapons would be a necessary condition for the implementation of certain 'radical' proposals, such as the abolition of nuclear weapons by a world government. See Craig, 'Solving the Nuclear Dilemma'.

Artificial Intelligence and Nuclear Command and Control

Mark Fitzpatrick

In early June, a series of alarming reports roiled relations among the major powers, sparking concerns of a nuclear war. A low-level conflict between Russian and US special-operations forces in Syria apparently left three American soldiers dead from nerve gas. YouTube videos of family members of cabinet officials and senators hurriedly fleeing Washington, and social-media accounts of missile silos in the prairie states going on high alert, triggered Moscow's strategic-warning systems to warn the Kremlin leadership that a US missile launch could be imminent. Separately, satellite imagery appeared online of the South China Sea that utilised new, cutting-edge technology rendering the oceans effectively 'transparent' and revealed the location of three Chinese submarines. Assuming a US government connection, Chinese leaders saw it as a sharp escalation in Washington's presumed encirclement strategy. Meanwhile, management software in several Chinese nuclear power plants generated false-positive safety reports that triggered shutdown decisions. Some wondered if this, too, was due to adversarial misfeasance. Luckily, officials in all countries soon came to realise that the culprit in most of these actions was a shadowy non-governmental organisation seeking to spark conflict through falsified information on social media and the exploitation of private-sector technology breakthroughs.

Mark Fitzpatrick is an IISS associate fellow, was executive director of IISS–Americas from 2015 through 2018, and headed the IISS Non-Proliferation and Nuclear Policy Programme for 13 years. He had a 26-year career in the US Department of State, including as deputy assistant secretary of state for non-proliferation.

Survival | vol. 61 no. 3 | June–July 2019 | pp. 81–92   DOI 10.1080/00396338.2019.1614782

The year was 2021. The fictionalised events occurred in an IISS tabletop exercise in London in November 2018, for a project funded by the Carnegie Corporation of New York designed to examine the potential impact of artificial intelligence (AI) on nuclear strategic stability. Experts from China, Russia, the United States, the United Kingdom and the Czech Republic played roles as decision-makers in Beijing, Moscow and Washington as they sought to understand, address and take advantage of the scenarios and variations posed by the IISS control team.

The major powers' nuclear command-and-control systems increasingly rely on AI programmes, or, more precisely, expert systems and machine-learning algorithms, to enhance information flow, situational awareness and cyber security. Such capabilities can provide such systems with a larger window of opportunity in which to respond in the event of a crisis and thereby support de-escalation. Malevolent actors, however, can also use new technologies offensively to deceive, disrupt or impair command-and-control systems and their human controllers. The IISS tabletop exercise sought to explore several of these malfeasance pathways and vulnerabilities in plausible crisis scenarios. It demonstrated how an AI arms race could reduce strategic stability as the nuclear-weapons states become more reliant on AI for strategic warning in relation to nuclear command-and-control functions.[1]

Escalation via 'deep fakes'

A key danger played out in the exercise was the potential for third parties to spoof warning systems and embed disinformation to fool human operators. In the scenario, a hitherto unknown non-state actor, the World Peace Guardians, circulated falsified videos and photographs on social-media platforms to create the impression that three US special-operations-forces soldiers had been killed by nerve gas in clashes with Russian military advisers in Syria. Some US pundits argued the legal case for the use of tactical nuclear weapons in response. Doctored videos then appeared on American and Chinese media platforms that showed the families of several prominent US officials hurriedly departing Washington DC. Further eyewitness accounts on social media claimed that missile silos in the western US had gone to high alert, and that the crews of two had even opened the silo doors. As a result of these and other secondary indicators used by Russian AI-driven situational-awareness algorithms, Moscow's strategic-warning systems began informing the Kremlin leadership that a US missile launch could be imminent. In the first situation report generated by the control team, Chinese President Xi Jinping cautioned the US not to conduct a nuclear strike against any country and warned that if the US did not provide 'credible evidence' that it was not mobilising for war, China would have to take unspecified defensive actions.

Generally speaking, the scenario was a plausible example of escalation by third parties. In this case, a non-state actor made a deep fake sufficiently believable that it generated a crisis between two nuclear states. A workshop background paper explained how offensive AI capabilities could widen the psychological distance between the attacker and its target. The paper fore-warned that a third-party actor might attempt to use AI-driven adversarial inputs, data-poisoning attacks, and audio and video manipulation to create escalatory effects between nations. While other early-warning systems would eventually discredit the spoof, it would still create high levels of uncertainty and tension in a short period of time. Doctored videos would likely force both parties to put their respective militaries on high alert. They would utilise overhead imagery, signals intelligence or human reporting to determine the reality on the ground. Collecting and processing the intelligence would take precious time during an escalatory crisis in which AI algorithms were urging immediate response actions.

In round two of the exercise, set two days later, Russian and US conventional military forces were on alert and beginning to prepare for possible contingencies. Russian Tu-160 Tupolev supersonic, nuclear-capable bombers were airborne and conducting flights over international waters in the Bering Strait and northern Atlantic Ocean, and US satellite imagery identified numerous Russian transport-erector-launcher units moving within Russian territory. Several US B-52H *Stratofortress* nuclear-capable bombers were airborne and US missile silos were on alert. US AI-driven situational-awareness algorithms downplayed the gravity of the situation, however. Another AI system assessed that the viral images of asphyxiated US soldiers were inauthentic, based on their pixilation and online propagation.

Meanwhile, though, many US citizens were spontaneously departing major cities on the eastern seaboard, overwhelming transportation routes.

In the denouement of round three, trilateral information sharing conducted by the respective computer emergency-response teams and law-enforcement agencies of China, Russia and the US concluded that the images, videos and other social-media postings by the World Peace Guardians organisation were falsified. Both Russia and the US publicly acknowledged that no chemical-weapons attack had occurred in Syria. As a result, both countries' militaries returned to standard operating procedures. Public fears of nuclear war and mass evacuations of cities also subsided. Yet relations between Russia and the US, in particular, remained testy at best.

Skewed early-warning assessments

Deep fakes by third parties can be magnified by AI capabilities that fall into the wrong hands and are used to generate false positives. In our scenario, three months before the crisis and start of play, US Cyber Command's 'Unified Platform' for managing and coordinating integrated cyber-, electronic- and information-warfare operations was providing statistically anomalous outputs regarding situational-awareness assessments related to the early warning of selected advanced persistent threat datasets linked to Russian cyber actors. The questionable reports appeared to be skewed by mathematical coefficients derived from large-scale metadata analysis during the beta-testing training phase of the Unified Platform's software.

A workshop background paper noted that AI programmes are driven by the data that they receive – the digital equivalent of the adages 'you are what you eat' and 'garbage in, garbage out'. This is also true of the process by which such programmes initially formulate their pattern-recognition models and evaluative procedures for use in future contexts. The malign manipulation of input data can not only pervert the output of AI functions in specific instances, but also undermine the reliability of an entire algorithm if accomplished during the 'training' phase for such programmes. Our scenario showed vividly how this could play out. Non-malign, human-design factors can also corrupt AI assessments. Because human beings define an AI system's algorithms and curate its training data, they can unintentionally insert their own biases into the system. This can cause the system to behave in unintended ways that may be undetectable to its operators due to the feedback loop created by those very biases. In addition, nuclear command-and-control personnel also faced a black-box problem in determining how or why a system came to a certain conclusion. While system inputs and outputs can be observed, the speed and scale of system processes make it difficult for personnel to isolate the logic behind any particular prediction. Once the operation of AI systems is triggered, humans are unable to monitor the systems' decision calculus in real time.

In the exercise, the US team was aware of this range of potential problems with respect to AI-driven assessments provided by Cyber Command's Unified Platform. They worried that Russian strategic-warning systems might be similarly skewed. In particular, the Americans realised that the false positives produced by Russia's strategic-warning system need not have been caused by a malign actor, as they could also have resulted from a problem intrinsic to the algorithm. To preclude Russia from perceiving any US effort to investigate as an attempt to manipulate Russia's early-warning and command-and-control systems, the US team decided not to conduct any reconnaissance. In turn, the scenario in round two had Kremlin officials learning of a prior intelligence operation by the Main Directorate of the General Staff of the Russian Armed Forces (GRU), Russia's military-intelligence agency, injecting skewed training data into AI-driven situational-awareness algorithms of the US military during their developmental phase. The objective was to prevent American AI systems from being able to recognise Russia as an aggressor.

The background papers for the exercise had noted how data-poisoning attacks introducing skewed inputs into the training dataset for an AI machine-learning process can distort an AI system's output by degrading its ability to distinguish between good data and bad data. These types of operations are usually carried out through techniques known as content generation, feedback weaponisation, perturbation injection and man-in-the-middle attacks. However, an attacker usually will not have direct access to the actual training data. To overcome this obstacle, the attacker will target the actors or methods used to collect and store machine-learning training data, such as cloud graphics-processing units, web-based repositories, and contractors or third-party service providers.

Understanding that early-warning assessments from its own AI-driven software could be skewed, the Russian team chose largely to ignore the AI algorithms that were producing results so disparate from the reality they otherwise perceived, while also deciding not to reveal any analytic problems they were encountering to their adversaries. Unaware that the Russians had, in effect, pulled the plug on the AI-driven early-warning system, the US team spent considerable time trying to persuade their counterparts to investigate its flaws. The US team also considered offering to work with Russia to neutralise any malicious third-party-introduced software problems. They recognised, however, that any such effort might itself be seen as an attempt to compromise the Russian command-and-control system. Indeed, the Russians reacted defensively. With team members playing to stereotype, trilateral meetings and a session of the United Nations Security Council ended inconclusively amid mutual recriminations.

False-positive safety alerts

In the notional ten months leading up to our crisis scenario, four civilian nuclear power plants operating in densely populated Chinese provinces began registering false-positive safety alerts by their AI-driven management software. In each case, sensors reported structural concerns in the facility that led supervising authorities to enact emergency-management procedures that stopped operations, although engineering tests revealed that no structural damage or harm to humans had actually occurred. Even so, the repeated stoppages in electricity production by these important power plants were having adverse economic effects. The operating authorities accordingly requested that the AI software provider, named GaiaForce, adjust the sensing functions to require a much higher threshold of structural-integrity damage before triggering automatic shutdown protocols. This allowed all of the power plants in question to operate at or near full capacity. GaiaForce was unable to find any defects in the functionality of its code.

Left unclear during the initial rounds was whether the false positives resulted from malicious activities. The workshop background paper explained how 'raising the noise floor' – launching a cyber attack perpetrated via digital noise and extraneous inputs containing minor elements of an actual threat – can cause an AI system to generate a stream of false positives. These false positives can lead operators to reconfigure the AI's machine-learning algorithm to avoid this error in the future. At that point, the adversary can launch an attack through the same method that the system was reconfigured to ignore. This type of attack involves social engineering in that, unlike other technical-intelligence operations, it targets the human operators and induces them to effect a change that favours the offensive adversary. While the AI system faithfully does what it has been re-instructed to do, the parameters no longer successfully serve their original defensive purposes. Thus, in round two, a nuclear power plant in Hubei province suffered structural damage as a result of operating beyond engineering parameters due to the loosening of the security indicators contained in the GaiaForce management software. Although the situation was contained in time, safety experts claimed that they were 'minutes away from the next Chernobyl or Fukushima'.

In round three, China provided detailed technical data of operational anomalies to the International Atomic Energy Agency (IAEA), along with portions of the GaiaForce source code. After obtaining this information, the US National Security Agency (NSA) assessed that the GaiaForce source code identified the potential for additional 'remote administration features' that could arise if that software were run on systems that were also infected by a malware exploit that the NSA determined was devised by the GRU. The NSA further judged that the GRU had created the GaiaForce source code and used it in its most sensitive cyber operations. According to the NSA director, the combination of GaiaForce and the malware could be used to 'weaponise' civilian nuclear reactors. That this did not occur in the exercise was down to a combination of luck and Chinese willingness to cooperate with other concerned actors.

Hijacking private-sector technology

Among the most revealing vulnerabilities exposed in the exercise was the way in which private-sector technological breakthroughs might be expropriated by another non-state actor for malevolent purposes, with dire consequences for strategic stability. In the hypothetical two months before the exercise started, a US technology company called QuantumAI, which received significant seed funding from the CIA and won Defense Advanced Research Projects Agency contracts for its advanced magnetometers and gravimeters, partnered with another company to launch four open-source, quantum-sensing satellites that used AI to measure infinitesimal changes in magnetic and gravitational fields on the earth. Subscribers began using the new system to identify new mining opportunities, sunken shipwrecks and toxic metallic effluents from industrial sites. QuantumAI only marketed its product to government-approved researchers from NATO countries, and its technology was export-controlled under both US International Traffic in Arms Regulations restrictions and the Wassenaar Arrangement.

In round one, satellite imagery of the South China Sea that rendered the water transparent and revealed the location of three Chinese submarines was put online, allegedly from sources linked to QuantumAI. While the Chinese team suspected that the US government was responsible, the US team worried that whoever put this information online might similarly reveal the location of US submarines. Exactly that transpired in round two. The same website posting locational data regarding Chinese submarines expanded its coverage to include a global map with additional markers for Russian and US nuclear submarines. This posed a clear risk to strategic stability in compromising the second-strike capability that stealthy nuclear-armed submarines provide.

Adding the markers for US submarines made it clear that the revelatory website was not affiliated with the US government. Its registration history and hosting service provider in Switzerland suggested it was actually linked to the World Peace Guardians. When US Department of Homeland Security and FBI officials approached large US social-media firms for information regarding World Peace Guardians accounts, the companies replied that they would 'share relevant information with the government when it becomes available'. The US president did decide that QuantumAI hard drives could be seized, although the CEO of QuantumAI was not fully cooperative. The idea of trying to seize World Peace Guardians servers in Switzerland was discussed, but rejected.

The QuantumAI aspect of the exercise was one manifestation of what the background paper described as a 'black box model extraction' vulnerability. Such an extraction reverse-engineers an AI system to determine its parameters. An adversary may be able to use this information to enhance the effectiveness of future operations against the system by stealing intellectual property; identifying sensitive or proprietary information related to the system's training data or objectives; or developing 'adversarial inputs' to be covertly introduced into the original AI system. Such inputs confuse the system's classifiers or its pattern-recognition function, thereby causing it to miscalculate, misclassify or misinterpret elements in its operational environment.

Malfunctioning navigational systems

Malfunctioning sensors of a different kind could have contributed to major-power conflict had the game played out a little differently. In the fictional lead-up to the June crisis scenario, a US Navy destroyer conducting a freedom-of-navigation exercise in waters claimed by China in the South China Sea came within 50 metres of colliding with a People's Liberation Army Navy vessel when its automated navigational systems were experiencing serious malfunctions. While their origin was unclear, adversarial inputs may have been injected into the ship's AI system. Attacks employing them can bypass system classifiers used for cyber security, such as worm-signature generation, spam filters, distributed denial-of-service attack detection and portable-document-format malware classification. By slightly altering an image's pixels or patterns – changes that might be undetectable to the human eye – these inputs can also cause an AI system to mislabel an image.

*   *   *

The tabletop exercise was intended to identify potential vulnerabilities created by artificial intelligence for nuclear command and control, including strategic-warning capabilities, which could then feed into a broader policy discussion. Five lessons emerged as the basis for future policy-relevant work.

Firstly, AI cannot be fully trusted. In particular, it can be risky to rely heavily on situational awareness generated by AI outputs. In the hypothetical scenario, both the US and Russian teams discounted the AI warnings that appeared inconsistent with human observations and were later found to have been generated by false data. This raises the possibility that resilient doubts about the reliability of AI could significantly attenuate its operational and strategic impact.

Secondly, regarding emerging technology and nuclear strategy, the roll-out of new technologies – in the case at hand, sensor technology for detecting submarines – affects states differently depending on their strategic force structure. The Chinese team was most alarmed about the technology because, among the major players, it has the smallest submarine fleet and one that so far does not range far beyond China's adjacent waters. Once identified, its submarines can thus be more easily neutralised. The exposure of China's submarines before those of other players reinforced Beijing's concerns that it was being targeted.

Thirdly, shared concerns about AI-generated disinformation could foster collaboration among states to address the problem via confidence-building mechanisms. In the exercise, when the operating systems of Chinese nuclear power plants 'raised the warning noise floor' in ways that appeared intended to weaponise them, the US team shared information it had about similar noise warnings in American plants. The IAEA became the forum of choice for cooperative efforts towards a solution. More broadly, the potentially destabilising risks inherent in emerging technologies, as demonstrated in the Chinese nuclear-power example, could push states to proactively promote arms control. In our scenario, this prospect loomed only as the world stood on the brink of disaster. The takeaway is that policymakers can be educated in advance about such risks before they actually arise in a crisis and work to mitigate them.

Fourthly, the role of the private sector differs among the major powers. In the exercise, the US government had limited means of persuading the developer of the ocean-see-through sensor technology to share its data. If the company in question had been Chinese or Russian, those governments could have compelled cooperation fully and immediately. In any case, the exercise illuminated the need for governments to appoint senior officials conversant with science and technology who either fully understand and appreciate the effects and ramifications of technological development, or cultivate regular access to experts who do.

Finally, while disinformation is a long-standing intelligence and strategic problem that pre-dates the cyber age, the integrity of AI systems is especially vulnerable to it. The combination of reliance on AI and its appropriation by malevolent actors could seriously amplify the disruptive effects of disinformation campaigns. Governments could play a key role in establishing regulatory frameworks that shape how new technology interfaces with the current suite of disinformation tools, such as social media. Although time limitations precluded further exploration of an AI system's vulnerability, hints and suspicions of AI-linked espionage permeated the tabletop exercise. They are likely to persist in the real world as well.

Acknowledgements

This article draws on background materials prepared by Sean Kanuck, then-director of the IISS Cyber, Space and Future Conflict Programme, who led the tabletop exercise and subsequently discussed with the author lessons that emerged from it.

Notes

[1] See generally Kenneth Payne, 'Artificial Intelligence: A Revolution in Strategic Affairs?', *Survival*, vol. 60, no. 5, October–November 2018, pp. 7–32.

Russia's Search for a Place in Europe

William H. Hill

As the Cold War ended, three major geopolitical events created a new and fundamentally different strategic context in which the post-Cold War order was constructed. Firstly, the United States decided to retain a physical presence in Europe and to remain actively involved in European security and political affairs, with NATO as its primary vehicle. Secondly, the emergence of a united German state revived the question of how to assimilate this major Central European power into the European state system. Thirdly, the collapse of the Soviet Union signalled the transformation of Russia from a multinational empire four centuries old into a post-imperial nation-state.

The leaders of Europe and North America transformed existing institutions and built new ones while these changes were taking place. From 1986 to 1992 they reached a series of landmark multilateral and bilateral arms-control agreements that deconstructed the old bipolar system of military confrontation and built a new one characterised by heightened transparency, confidence-building, and lower levels of conventional and strategic arms. The Soviet Union accepted on-site inspection in the 1986 Commission on Security and Cooperation in Europe (CSCE) 'Stockholm Document'. This led to the rapid conclusion of the Intermediate-Range Nuclear Forces Treaty, the Conventional Armed Forces in Europe Treaty, the Strategic

William H. Hill is a Global Fellow at the Woodrow Wilson International Center for Scholars, and served for nearly 30 years as a Foreign Service Officer in the US State Department, including as Head of the OSCE Mission to Moldova. He is author of *No Place for Russia: European Security Institutions since 1989* (Columbia University Press, 2018), from which portions of this article are drawn.

Survival | vol. 61 no. 3 | June–July 2019 | pp. 93–102   DOI 10.1080/00396338.2019.1614779

Arms Reduction Treaty (START) and the Open Skies Agreement.[1] By the end of 1992, the levels of conventional and strategic weapons in Europe were falling dramatically, the Warsaw Pact had dissolved itself and the perceived danger of war had receded dramatically.

From promise to peril

As the political and security institutions of Europe were overhauled, one major aim was to integrate Russia into the emerging European order. Soviet president Mikhail Gorbachev and many of his colleagues favoured transforming the CSCE, which embodied the Helsinki process, into an umbrella political and security organisation for an undivided post-Cold War Europe. The US and its allies decided to keep NATO in existence, but promised Gorbachev that they would transform the Alliance, a process which they began with the November 1991 Rome NATO summit.[2] Meanwhile, the countries of the European Community took a decisive step towards a more united Europe in establishing the European Union via the December 1992 Maastricht Treaty.

Both the EU and NATO then began a process of enlargement whereby, as of 2019, most of the countries on the continent have become members of one or both. Despite claims that NATO enlargement violated US secretary of state James Baker's pledge to Gorbachev not to move NATO 'one inch to the east', a careful examination of the record demonstrates that neither NATO nor EU expansion was primarily aimed at restraining or defending against Russia.[3] Instead, the growth of both NATO and the EU was largely aimed at facilitating a stable transition to democratic political systems, market economies and open societies in Central and Eastern Europe. In fact, Western policymakers at the time worried about antagonising Russia, and took steps, such as the 1997 NATO–Russia Founding Act, to mitigate any destabilising effects.[4]

For most of the 1990s, the US, its NATO allies, the EU, other European states and Russia worked by and large cooperatively in constructing a new post-Cold War security architecture in Europe. Russia pushed for the establishment of a European security council within the pan-European Organisation for Security and Cooperation in Europe (OSCE), arguing that it would provide a clean break with the Cold War system of alliances and divisions of Europe. The US and most of its European allies and partners supported a system of overlapping and cooperative legacy institutions, operating with divisions of tasks and responsibilities, as the best means of managing European security. The Western preference prevailed.

Meanwhile, the Balkan wars exercised a decisive influence on the manner of NATO's transformation and use, and thus on key military aspects of Europe's security architecture. As Yugoslavia disintegrated, the emerging EU, a coalition of the willing (the Contact Group) and the United Nations all unsuccessfully addressed the wars in Croatia and Bosnia. After much internal debate, NATO in 1994 went 'out of area' to help enforce the Sarajevo exclusion zone and the no-fly zones over the UN protected areas. In 1995, NATO bombing augmented the ground campaigns by Croatian forces to bring the warring parties to the Dayton peace talks. NATO then took the lead in the Implementation Force (IFOR), the peacekeeping force mandated by the Dayton Accords. It was not NATO enlargement but rather NATO's 1999 decision to go to war in Kosovo without the UN's imprimatur and over Russia's vehement opposition that caused the first serious post-Cold War rupture in relations between Russia and the West. Although NATO–Russia relations were later repaired, and cooperation was maintained for over a decade, Moscow's view of NATO as dangerously unilateralist and militarily menacing lingered, and then deepened with NATO's development of a significant expeditionary capability.

During his first term as Russia's president, Vladimir Putin attempted to overcome the damage done by NATO's 1999 war against Serbia. However, Moscow perceived little understanding from Washington, in particular in the war against separatists and militants in Chechnya. Putin's bitter reaction to the September 2004 Chechen terrorist attack in Beslan revealed the depths of his resentment.[5] Beginning in the early 2000s, Russia also found itself increasingly at odds with its Western partners over security and political issues in its 'near abroad' – the newly independent countries on Russia's borders which had been Soviet republics – in which Moscow from 1992 onward asserted special rights and influence. Western opposition to a Russia-backed settlement plan for Moldova's Transdniestrian conflict in

2003 and subsequent support for the 'Rose Revolution' in Georgia and the 'Orange Revolution' in Ukraine made the Kremlin fear that it was being pushed out of its own neighbourhood.

In turn, Putin's restoration of central authority (the 'power-vertical') in Russia prompted Western consternation and criticism. Putin moved to place the independent press and the leading oligarchs under government control, arrested Mikhail Khodorkovsky and seized his firm Yukos (Russia's largest oil company), and restricted political competition. The increasing manipulation of elections in Russia, the rising influence of security officials and restrictions on the press and civil society prompted alarm in the West.

By 2006, Russia's relationship with the West was on the rocks. At the February 2007 Munich Security Conference, Putin railed against alleged Western and, in particular, American unilateralism and hegemonism.[6] When the US and many EU and NATO countries recognised Kosovo's independence over Russia's strenuous objections, Putin vowed an appropriate response. The Kremlin answered NATO's promised membership for Ukraine and Georgia at its April 2008 summit with the August war with Georgia. To make the message crystal clear, Moscow unilaterally recognised the independence of Georgia's two separatist regions, South Ossetia and Abkhazia, and declared the near abroad a Russian sphere of 'privileged interest'.[7]

US president Barack Obama's 'reset' produced some clear successes, such as the New START treaty, a civilian nuclear-cooperation agreement and the Northern Distribution Network. However, the West paid scant attention to Russian president Dmitry Medvedev's 2008–09 proposals for an overarching pan-European security treaty, shunting the initiative into a dead-end reform process in the OSCE. NATO's bootstrapping of the 2011 UN mandate for protection of civilian populations in Benghazi into the removal of Libyan leader Muammar Gadhafi from power, culminating in his videotaped and widely broadcast murder by Libyan rebels, seemed to convince many Russians (in particular, Putin) that the US and its allies were intent on using humanitarian issues to pursue geopolitical advantage through regime change.

Putin, who became Russia's president again in 2012, responded by expanding his Eurasian integration projects, now more clearly conceived as

Russia's counterweights to the US-led integration of Western and Central Europe by way of NATO and the EU. Putin also launched his third term as president with a hardline, nationalist crackdown against Western influence and independent civil-society organisations in Russia. With the 2013–14 crisis in Ukraine, including Russia's annexation of Crimea, Russia's strained relationships with the US, NATO and the EU finally broke and the post-Cold War European security order shattered irretrievably.

The subsequent war in Ukraine ended a quarter-century of effort to integrate Russia into a Euro-Atlantic community based on Western institutions such as NATO and the EU. Since 2014, those institutions have suffered further major blows from other directions and other actors. The refugee crisis of 2015, the 2016 Brexit vote and the election of Donald Trump further shook the Euro-Atlantic order. At the present moment, Europe and the US appear to be at the dawn of a new order of highly uncertain features and direction.

Taking stock

The post-Cold War security order not only failed to prevent the outbreak of war between two of Europe's largest states, but may also have contributed to its build-up and outbreak. From the mid-1990s, both NATO and the EU maintained a policy of extending their geographic scope, mainly eastward. While these institutions expressed the aspiration and intention of forging friendly, cooperative relationships with Russia, they either implicitly or explicitly excluded the possibility of membership for Russia. Such an approach may have been workable in theory at the beginning of the post-Cold War era, when neither NATO nor the EU subsumed much more than about half of Europe. But when NATO and EU territory expanded and Russia's geographic space shrank to a point at which it appeared plausible that NATO or the EU could encompass all of Europe, it was practically inevitable that Moscow would come to fear isolation and insecurity.

Russia, of course, was hardly blameless for its isolation. It failed to complete a transition from domestic Soviet institutions to a competitive, pluralist political system and an open-market economy. Furthermore, under Gorbachev, Boris Yeltsin and Putin, Russia formally accepted the values established by the West at the heart of Europe's post-Cold War transformation, signing and accepting a series of documents and international agreements containing obligations to hold free elections; observe human rights, due process and the rule of law; and accept international scrutiny of its internal affairs and inter-state relations as to compliance with these standards. Russia, however, did not embrace and assimilate these values and practices, at least not in the manner and to the degree expected by Western interlocutors who had been encouraged by Russian reform efforts in the late 1980s and early 1990s.

Since the end of the Cold War, Russian leaders and elites have taken on the appearance but not the essence of open Western societies. Materialism, and not the dialectical kind, now rules in a Russian society made selectively wealthy by both market economics and a hydrocarbon boom. Russian leaders and officials do not credit the importance that Western leaders and societies attach to the universalisation of human-rights standards and practices. They fail to comprehend how Western societies can perceive their treatment of their own citizens as offensive, and thus assume that Western criticisms must be based upon ulterior political or economic motives. The disconnect is all the more acute in the globalised, post-Cold War world, in which Russians' access to global markets and freedom to travel make them participants in a larger community that may demand respect for its norms in return for this access.

Similarly, Russians often appear baffled as to why their relations with their neighbours should concern distant European or North American countries, especially when some of these countries themselves have historically mistreated their own neighbours. When relations were less tense and the European and American presence more distant, the disparity was not so important. With the EU and the United States now on Ukraine's doorstep, and Moscow's actions under constant scrutiny, it has assumed much greater salience and is much more likely to cause disputes or conflict.

Some pundits and policymakers have labelled the renewed division of Europe into opposing camps, with significant qualifications, a 'new Cold War'.[8] Although the current antagonisms between Russia and the West run deep indeed, the present situation in Europe differs from the prolonged

NATO–Soviet Union stand-off in a number of crucial respects. First of all, there is no true ideological competition between Russia and the West. Although Putin and his cronies may claim to promote different values from the contemporary, decadent West, the Kremlin is not offering any comprehensive, internally cohesive ideology in opposition to its rivals. Secondly, Russia is not as rich and powerful in comparison to today's EU and NATO as the Soviet Union was vis-à-vis its adversaries. The Russian nuclear arsenal is still formidable, but US and European conventional military capabilities in the aggregate significantly exceed those available to Moscow, and constitute a considerable deterrent against Russian adventurism. Thirdly, today's global strategic context is strikingly different given the economic, political and military rise of Asia, in particular China.

Although Europe is not back to where it started at the end of the Cold War, it is also not in the optimistic place that it occupied on 10 November 1989, when the East German government opened the border. Some things have improved. Despite all their shortcomings and problems, NATO, the EU and the OSCE are now fuller, more capable institutions, with demonstrated capacities to marshal and deploy resources and to address and resolve complex problems. Some things have gotten worse, after they had gotten better. Most Central and Eastern European states have successfully integrated into European political and security structures, but integration failed with Russia, and some of those European states now seem to be backsliding. Although Russia has undergone extensive internal changes, some of them salutary, the process of domestic reform in Russia appears, on balance, to have failed. Russia's internal development and reform may well depend on the Russians themselves. External efforts to direct or hasten internal transformation may seem to help, but the post-Cold War experience suggests that there is a roughly equal chance that they will prompt a counterproductive backlash.

*   *   *

Any consideration of the failures of the post-Cold War order leads almost inevitably to the question of what should be done now. The issue seems more complex than simply asking whether existing institutions such as NATO, the EU and the OSCE should survive, change or be replaced. The US and its Western allies clearly need a new understanding, both among themselves and with Russia, about what the structure and rules of the road of a new order should be. The US is not a declining power, but it is no longer far wealthier and more powerful than other major powers, especially China. Together with like-minded allied states, Washington needs to focus on preserving those elements of the rules-based international order that are most important to US security and prosperity. With regard to Russia, this probably means concentrating on existential common interests, such as nuclear arms control, non-proliferation and climate change.

For Russia to advance a rapprochement with the West, it must first and foremost change its attitude towards its neighbours. Although Russian leaders may believe they have legitimate grievances, they need to recognise and appreciate the overwhelmingly negative Western perceptions that the invasion of two neighbours, the annexation of territory, an ongoing war and an apparent assassination in Western Europe have raised over the past decade. Russia also needs to come up with policies and actions that demonstrate its clear recognition and acceptance of the full independence and sovereignty of the former Soviet states on its borders. This will not quickly or completely eradicate years (in some cases centuries) of those states' mistrust of Russia. But it would demonstrate Russia's interest in mending its relations with Europe and North America.

Given Russia and Europe's post-Cold War arc, the US and its Western allies should tamp down their hopes of changing Russia's domestic systems and practices. This does not mean abandoning the core values of institutions like NATO, the EU and the OSCE, nor jettisoning the aspiration to promote wider international acceptance and observance of these values. Given the currently fractious state of US domestic politics and international relations, however, Washington's best approach would be to rededicate American institutions and politics to affirming and living up to American ideals, especially in domestic affairs. For the time being, the US and its closest allies seem to be entering a period in which they can most effectively promote their values and ideals by example rather than instruction or imposition.

Notes

1   See OSCE, 'Document of the Stockholm Conference on Confidence- and Security-Building Measures and Disarmament in Europe Convened in Accordance with the Relevant Provisions of the Concluding Document of the Madrid Meeting of the Conference on Security and Co-operation in Europe', 19 September 1986, http://www.osce.org/fsc/41238?download=true. On the breakthrough for on-site inspections, see the interview with Ambassador Robert L. Barry, Association for Diplomatic Studies and Training Foreign Affairs History Project, http://www.adst.org/OH%20TOCs/Barry,%20Robert%20L.toc.pdf. See also Oleg Grinevsky and Lynn M. Hansen, *Making Peace: Confidence and Security in a New Europe* (New York: Eloquent Books, 2009); and Michael Mandelbaum, *The Dawn of Peace in Europe* (Washington DC: Twentieth Century Fund, 1996).

2   NATO, 'Declaration on Peace and Cooperation Issued by the Heads of State and Government Participating in the Meeting of the North Atlantic Council' (The Rome Declaration), 8 November 1991, http://www.nato.int/cps/en/natolive/official_texts_23846.htm?mode=pressrelease. See also NATO, 'The Alliance's New Strategic Concept Agreed by the Heads of State and Government Participating in the Meeting of the North Atlantic Council', 8 November 1991, http://www.nato.int/cps/en/natolive/official_texts_23847.htm?.

3   On the Baker 'promise' and NATO enlargement, see William H. Hill, *No Place for Russia: European Security Institutions Since 1989* (New York: Columbia University Press, 2018), pp. 44–6, 109–66, 405–6.

4   NATO, 'Founding Act on Mutual Relations, Cooperation and Security Between NATO and the Russian Federation', 27 May 1997, http://www.nato.int/cps/en/natohq/official_texts_25468.htm?selectedLocale=en.

5   See Vladimir Putin, 'Speech to the Nation', 4 September 2004, http://archive.kremlin.ru/eng/speeches/2004/09/04/1958_type82912_76332.shtml.

6   See Vladimir Putin, 'Speech and Following Discussion at the Munich Conference on Security Policy', 10 February 2007, http://archive.kremlin.ru/eng/speeches/2007/02/10/0138_type82912type82914type82917type84779_118123.shtml. For an analysis of Russia's growing disaffection with the West at this time, see Dmitri Trenin, 'Russia Leaves the West', *Foreign Affairs*, vol. 85, no. 4, July/August 2006.

7   'Interview Given by Dmitry Medvedev to Television Channel One, Russia, NTV', 31 August 2008, http://archive.kremlin.ru/eng/speeches/2008/08/31/1850_type82912type82916_206003.shtml.

8   See, for example, Lawrence Freedman, 'Putin's New Cold War', *New Statesman*, 14 March 2018, https://www.newstatesman.com/politics/uk/2018/03/putin-s-new-cold-war.

Brexit and Nostalgia

Edoardo Campanella and Marta Dassù

Brexit is an inflated topic. Since the United Kingdom's 2016 referendum vote in favour of the country's leaving the European Union, innumerable books, editorials and academic papers have tried to rationalise what looks like a masochistic decision in a country renowned for its pragmatism and stability. But prevalent explanations such as widening income inequalities, rising immigration fears and growing political polarisation, while certainly valid, are insufficient to justify a decision that defies any rational cost–benefit analysis. The messy negotiations between London and Brussels, coupled with Westminster's inability to constructively trace a way forward, only confirm Brexit's fundamentally irrational nature. Standard analyses are unilluminating because they implicitly neglect the true essence of Brexit. Even the most informed and politically aware citizens vote with their hearts as much as, if not more than, their minds. And voting to leave the EU, albeit by a slim majority, was primarily an emotional choice motivated by a desire to turn the clock back to a time when London was fully in charge of its domestic affairs – in a word, nostalgia. The anti-EU leaders took advantage of this emotional wave, reinforcing it in a nostalgic narrative.

To varying degrees, the 52% of Britons who opted for a divorce from Brussels were prey to nostalgic fantasies. For most Leavers, the ideal

Edoardo Campanella is a Future World Fellow at IE University, Madrid. **Marta Dassù** is Senior Advisor for European Affairs at the Aspen Institute, and was Italy's Deputy Minister of Foreign Affairs from 2011 to 2014. This article is based on their book *Anglo Nostalgia: The Politics of Emotion in a Fractured West* (Hurst, 2019).

Survival | vol. 61 no. 3 | June–July 2019 | pp. 103–111   DOI 10.1080/00396338.2019.1614781

chronological destination was 1973, just a moment before the UK joined the European Economic Community. Hard-core Brexiteers would have preferred to go further back to the Edwardian era, thus restoring the country's lost imperial greatness. The ominous uncertainty surrounding the future of the UK outside the EU, however, reveals the gap between wistful restorative aspirations and harsh political reality, and helps explain London's struggle to agree on its future relationship with Brussels.

A potent political weapon

The British did not go mad all of a sudden or all by themselves. Nostalgia for a time that no longer exists – in some cases, never existed – has become a global trend. It has infested the socio-political fabric of several nations, from the United States and continental Europe to Russia and Turkey. Ordinary citizens no longer project their aspirations onto utopian visions of an ideal-ised future. They prefer to look back to a time when national borders were less porous and governments supposedly did a better job of protecting their citizens. Fuelling this wave of nostalgia is the supposed loss of global status, economic prosperity and cultural integrity. In the twenty-first century, unlike the twentieth, yesterday tends to be associated with progress, today and tomorrow with stasis or regression.

With the world on the cusp of massive geopolitical, demographic and technological transformations, there is no shortage of reasons to be nostal-gic. The denouement of American liberal hegemony is creating seeming opportunities for post-imperial powers to reassert their lost status on the world stage. At the same time, the threats to employment posed by glo-balisation and disruptive technological change are making workers yearn for the economic security and the social mobility enjoyed by their parents. The ageing of the population psychologically compounds all these factors. Older people, unsurprisingly, are the most vulnerable to nostalgia.

From a purely psychological point of view, nostalgia is a coping strategy for dealing with moments of deep uncertainty and discomfiting discontinuity. It removes its victims from an unpleasant present and throws them into a familiar past, reinforcing their self-esteem and the self-confidence needed to navigate stressful times. Despite its romantic connotation, the word 'nostalgia' comes from medicine. In 1688, the Swiss physician Johannes Hofer coined the term by merging the Greek word *nostos* (homecoming) with *algos* (pain) to describe a medical condition that combined paranoia and melancholy so as to idealise the past while denigrating the present.

Indeed, emotions naturally shape the way people see the world, and can cause individuals with similar backgrounds to make radically different choices depending on where they fall on the emotional spectrum. Nostalgia is an especially peculiar and potent form of emotion, in that it psychologically transports those it affects two or three generations back and two or three generations ahead, heavily discounting short-term costs and massively overstating long-term benefits. This characteristic inevitably skews any purportedly rational cost–benefit analysis. But it is also a key reason why unscrupulous and misguided politicians find nostalgia such a useful propaganda tool.

Nostalgia and nationalism

Though perhaps innocuous on an individual level, collective infatuation with a mythologised past can in fact shape politics. Not only does nostalgia blur the past, present and future; it also induces citizens and governments to find comfort in a time when national borders were still rigid – a pre-globalisation era in which each nation was supposedly in control of its fate. Moreover, it strengthens bonds among those who reminisce about the same idealised time, and severs connections between them and those who do not share the vaunted ancestral experience, such as immigrants and other newcomers. Thus, nostalgia and nationalism become intimately linked.

For the UK, that linkage may be uniquely elaborate. It comprises three distinct elements of a nostalgic narrative: the golden days, the great rupture and the present discontent. The golden age consists of the imperial era during which the UK held sway over 'one continent, a hundred peninsulas, five hundred promontories, a thousand lakes, two thousand rivers, ten thousand islands'.[1] It was a multifaith, multilingual and multi-ethnic maritime imperium, with no rivals in terms of vastness and richness. The rupture came not only with the slow demise of the British Empire but also with London's decision to join the European Economic Community in 1973, a move that implicitly challenged the idea of British exceptionalism.

The present discontent has clear socio-economic roots, but it also reveals the unwillingness of many Britons to come to terms with the UK's demotion to a middle power. In the eyes of a hard-core eurosceptic, the EU represents an abrupt break from an uninterrupted history of British progress and glory starting with the introduction of the Magna Carta in 1215. From the perspective of the Leave camp, Brexit freed the UK of its European constraints and allowed it to regain control of its national past and future. But, as Liberal Democrat leader Vince Cable has put it, 'Too many were driven by nostalgia for a world where passports were blue, faces were white and the map was coloured imperial pink.'[2]

Hard-core Brexiteers' persistent references to imperial history during the referendum campaign extolled the lasting greatness of the UK, which would allow the nation to easily withstand the uncertainty and cost of its separation from Brussels. However circularly, the very motive for Brexit also served as validation of its feasibility. The 'now and here' strategy adopted by the Remain camp was too rational for a highly emotional moment caused by the last financial crisis, burgeoning immigration and globalisation. Better geared to that moment was a Leave narrative so rife with nostalgic arguments and historical references that at times it seemed completely removed from the present. Even Donald Trump went no farther back than the 1950s in depicting his ideal of America; in reminiscing about the British past, Brexiteers reached all the way to 1215. Throughout the 2016 campaign, Boris Johnson, the former mayor of London who would become foreign secretary, continually weaponised his political hero Winston Churchill; Nigel Farage, leader of the UK Independence Party, celebrated military victories that only professional historians recognise; and Member of Parliament Jacob Rees-Mogg revived the archaic notion of pure Englishness.

Their storyline conceptually centred on an atavistic and existential conflict between the United Kingdom and the European continent. It incorporated four key components: imperial pride, the discomfort of being ruled by others, an unparalleled sense of trust among Anglo-Saxon countries and the fecklessness of potential foreign invaders. Brexit was a re-situated

Battle of Britain. Having defeated the French and the Spaniards through-out the centuries, having stopped Wilhelm II, Adolf Hitler, Joseph Stalin and Leonid Brezhnev from permanently disrupting global order, London was now primed to roll back Brussels' technocrats. Of course, much of the British electorate had long been susceptible to nostalgic arguments. Events like royal weddings, the Queen's Diamond Jubilee, the 2012 Olympics, and remembrances of the Magna Carta, Shakespeare's death and the two world wars bolstered a standing if often jingoistic sense of national pride and belonging. The British culture and entertainment industry even lent a hand to the cause of Brexit by reinvigorating the 'Blitz spirit'.

Global Britain vs Little England

Notwithstanding presumptions of unbroken progress until the 1970s, the UK's global role has actually been at issue since the late Victorian era, when the British Empire's global pre-eminence was slipping as a result of combined internal and external fractures. It started in 1873 at the Oxford Union with a debate on how to reorganise and modernise Pax Britannica. Since then, plans have differed in detail, but they have all sought to unite the Anglosphere behind a common purpose and had nostalgic and utopian qualities. And they all purported to preserve a past that was falling apart by promoting London's political and economic interests to the detriment of increasingly assertive colonies. These proposals oversimplified reality, and none was ever implemented. Hard-core Brexiteers essentially revived the debate.

While the 'Global Britain' element of Brexit was meant to strengthen the UK's relationships with the United States and the Commonwealth, and establish new trade ties with countries in the Far East, hard-core Brexiteers went farther and contemplated a renewed Anglosphere consisting of Australia, New Zealand, Canada, the United Kingdom and the United States. In this context, Leavers exaggerated the degree to which London's customary 'special relationship' with Washington could overcome any post-Brexit adversity. In practice, the specialness, which elided an enormous imbalance in terms of power and influence between the two countries, has been more keenly felt in London than in Washington.

According to a survey conducted by Lord Ashcroft Polls, only 6% of Leavers wanted to expand British economic and trade opportunities outside the EU.[3] But even if knitting together the English-speaking world was not the chief practical objective of a dissatisfied British electorate, the legacy of a globe-spanning empire, as an aspirational construct, increased Brexit's cathartic political force. The notional Anglosphere, in turn, cast the illusion of preferential access to a trading area that was expected to provide alternative commercial opportunities to Europe's even though the continent remained London's largest export market. Most Brexiteers were more realistic and less grandiose, and sought mainly to regain control of borders, laws and immigrant flows.

Yet this more defensive nostalgia, raised against both Brussels and globalisation more broadly, corresponds to the idea of a Little England, which incorporates the myth of the island nation – an insular geography that shapes the character of its people. Global Britain, the Brexiteers' principal form of offensive nostalgia, is resolutely outward-looking and therefore quite inconsistent with Little England. The former depicts the ambitions of elements of the Oxbridge elite that oppose the EU, while the latter embodies the frustrations of a low-skilled working class. As shown by Brexiteers' inability to agree on a shared post-Brexit plan during the negotiations with Brussels, reconciling global and insular aspirations is a Herculean challenge that may be impossible to meet.

The Brexiteers' emotions obscured that contradiction and neutralised the initially consternating messages of the Remain camp's 'Project Fear', denigrating the experts, deriding their gloomy predictions and buoying morale with reveries of a past that they promised to restore. The brooding post-Empire anger of their rhetoric overwhelmed any rational compulsion to calmly assess the economic consequences of the UK's leaving the EU. But that is how nostalgia works. It is selective by nature. We are more likely to remember the good things from our distant past than the bad ones, and our past constantly shifts to accommodate our present, reframing personal histories to fit into a greater notional life. Social psychologists, who tend to see this phenomenon as positive at the individual level, call it 'fading affect bias'.[4]

In the end, an infatuation with a distorted past deluded millions of British citizens, as well as hundreds of pro-Brexit politicians, about the future of their country outside Europe. Thus, the UK initially entered Brexit negotiations convinced that it enjoyed global status and prestige that had actually vanished decades earlier, if not before. Reality eventually took hold: if nostalgia called for being fully out, pragmatism meant remaining partially in.

*   *   *

The Leavers, though objectively delusional, probably understood the character of their nation better than the Remainers. Englishness itself has a distinctively nostalgic feature that sets it apart from other national identities. Perhaps the UK has produced such a surplus of history that it can still nourish its citizens centuries later. Nevertheless, the Leavers leveraged their country's glorious history in an irresponsible way. They did not look to their past to inspire a virtuous future, but rather to impose an irrational political decision about the present.

The UK probably won't be the last country to experience nostalgic nationalism that results in a retrograde decision. Before other countries fall victim to the same syndrome, however, the politics of nostalgia and the grave risks it poses to the global liberal order warrant serious examination. In particular, it is important to understand how a nostalgic narrative takes root and gives rise to false myths, political miscalculations and rising tensions among nations. Ignoring the emotional dimension means failing to understand a key feature of the contemporary political debate. Of course, emotional choices are not necessarily wrong. In the end, what really matters is how emotions are orchestrated and towards what goal they are mobilised. It is also worth considering how members of the political mainstream seeking moderation and relief from incendiary nostalgic narratives could better defuse them. Instead of merely denigrating retrospective attitudes as a form of sentimentality and psychological weakness, they might recognise nostalgia's relevance and devise ways to constructively leverage the past themselves, preventing nationalists from monopolising history.

Notes

[1] See John Finch, *The Natural Boundaries of Empires and a New View of Colonization* (London: Longman, Brown, Green and Longmans, 1844), p. 203.

[2] Quoted in, for example, Tony Barber, 'Nostalgia and the Promise of Brexit', *Financial Times*, 19 July 2018, https://www.ft.com/content/bf70b80e-8b39-11e8-bf9e-8771d5404543.

[3] Lord Ashcroft, 'How the UK Voted on Brexit, and Why – A Refresher', Lord Ashcroft Polls, 4 February 2019, https://lordashcroftpolls.com/2019/02/how-the-uk-voted-on-brexit-and-why-a-refresher/.

[4] See, for example, Andrew J. Corsa and W. Richard Walker, 'Moral Psychology of the Fading Affect Bias', *Philosophical Psychology*, vol. 31, no. 7, July 2018, pp. 1,097–113.

Noteworthy

Excerpts from the Mueller Report, Vol. I

The Russian government interfered in the 2016 presidential election in sweeping and systematic fashion. Evidence of Russian government operations began to surface in mid-2016. In June, the Democratic National Committee and its cyber response team publicly announced that Russian hackers had compromised its computer network. Releases of hacked materials – hacks that public reporting soon attributed to the Russian government – began that same month. Additional releases followed in July through the organization WikiLeaks, with further releases in October and November.

In late July 2016, soon after WikiLeaks's first release of stolen documents, a foreign government contacted the FBI about a May 2016 encounter with Trump Campaign foreign policy advisor George Papadopoulos. Papadopoulos had suggested to a representative of that foreign government that the Trump Campaign had received indications from the Russian government that it could assist the Campaign through the anonymous release of information damaging to Democratic presidential candidate Hillary Clinton. That information prompted the FBI on July 31, 2016, to open an investigation into whether individuals associated with the Trump Campaign were coordinating with the Russian government in its interference activities.[1]

[...]

As set forth in detail in this report, the Special Counsel's investigation established that Russia interfered in the 2016 presidential election principally through two operations. First, a Russian entity carried out a social media campaign that favored presidential candidate Donald J. Trump and disparaged presidential candidate Hillary Clinton. Second, a Russian intelligence service conducted computer-intrusion operations against entities, employees, and volunteers working on the Clinton Campaign and then released stolen documents. The investigation also identified numerous links between the Russian government and the Trump Campaign. Although the investigation established that the Russian government perceived it would benefit from a Trump presidency and worked to secure that outcome, and that the Campaign expected it would benefit electorally from information stolen and released through Russian efforts, the investigation did not establish that members of the Trump Campaign conspired or coordinated with the Russian government in its election interference activities.[2]

[...]

The Internet Research Agency (IRA) carried out the earliest Russian interference operations identified by the investigation – a social media campaign designed to provoke and amplify political and social discord in the United States. The IRA was based in St. Petersburg, Russia, and received funding from Russian oligarch Yevgeniy Prigozhin and companies he controlled. Prigozhin is widely reported to have ties to Russian President Vladimir Putin, **[REDACTED]**.[3]

[...]

The IRA later used social media accounts and interest groups to sow discord in the U.S. political system through what it termed 'information warfare.' The campaign evolved from a generalized program designed in 2014 and 2015 to undermine the U.S. electoral system, to a targeted operation that by early 2016 favored candidate Trump and disparaged candidate Clinton.

The IRA's operation also included the purchase of political advertisements on social media in the names of U.S. persons and entities, as well as the staging of political rallies inside the United States. To organize those rallies, IRA employees posed as U.S. grassroots entities and persons and made contact with Trump supporters and Trump Campaign officials in the United States. The investigation did not identify evidence that any U.S. persons conspired or coordinated with the IRA. Section II of this report details the Office's investigation of the Russian social media campaign.

Russian Hacking Operations
At the same time that the IRA operation began to focus on supporting candidate Trump in early 2016, the Russian government employed a second form of interference: cyber intrusions (hacking) and releases of hacked materials damaging to the Clinton Campaign. The Russian intelligence service known as the Main Intelligence Directorate of the General Staff of the Russian Army (GRU) carried out these operations.

In March 2016, the GRU began hacking the email accounts of Clinton Campaign volunteers and employees, including campaign chairman John Podesta. In April 2016, the GRU hacked into the computer networks of the Democratic Congressional Campaign Committee (DCCC) and the Democratic National Committee (DNC). The GRU stole hundreds of thousands of documents from the compromised email accounts and networks. Around the time that the DNC announced in mid-June 2016 the Russian government's role in hacking its network, the GRU began disseminating stolen materials through the fictitious online personas 'DCLeaks' and 'Guccifer 2.0.' The GRU later released additional materials through the organization WikiLeaks.

The presidential campaign of Donald J. Trump ('Trump Campaign' or 'Campaign') showed interest in WikiLeaks's releases of documents and welcomed their potential to damage candidate Clinton. Beginning in June 2016, **[REDACTED]** forecast to senior Campaign officials that WikiLeaks would release information damaging to candidate Clinton. WikiLeaks's first release came in July 2016. Around the same time, candidate Trump announced that he hoped Russia would recover emails described as missing from a private server used by Clinton when she was Secretary of State (he later said that he was speaking sarcastically). **[REDACTED]**. WikiLeaks began releasing Podesta's stolen emails on October 7, 2016, less than one hour after a U.S. media outlet released video considered damaging to candidate Trump. Section III of this Report details the Office's investigation into the Russian hacking operations, as well as other efforts by Trump Campaign supporters to obtain Clinton-related emails.[4]

[…]

In sum, the investigation established multiple links between Trump Campaign officials and individuals tied to the Russian government. Those links included Russian offers of assistance to the Campaign. In some instances, the Campaign was receptive to the offer, while in other instances the Campaign officials shied away. Ultimately, the investigation did not establish that the Campaign coordinated or conspired with the Russian government in its election-interference activities.[5]

Excerpts from the Mueller Report, Vol. II

Third, we considered whether to evaluate the conduct we investigated under the Justice Manual standards governing prosecution and declination decisions, but we determined not to apply an approach that could potentially result in a judgment that the President committed crimes. The threshold step under the Justice Manual standards is to assess whether a person's conduct 'constitutes a federal offense.' U.S. Dep't of Justice, Justice Manual § 9-27.220 (2018) (Justice Manual). Fairness concerns counseled against potentially reaching that judgment when no charges can be brought. The ordinary means for an individual to respond to an accusation is through a speedy and public trial, with all the procedural protections that surround a criminal case. An individual who believes he was wrongly accused can use that process to seek to clear his name. In contrast, a prosecutor's judgment that crimes were committed, but that no charges will be brought, affords no such adversarial opportunity for public name-clearing before an impartial adjudicator.

The concerns about the fairness of such a determination would be heightened in the case of a sitting President, where a federal prosecutor's accusation of a crime, even in an internal report, could carry consequences that extend beyond the realm of criminal justice. OLC noted similar concerns about sealed indictments. Even if an indictment were sealed during the President's term, OLC reasoned, "'it would be very difficult to preserve [an indictment's] secrecy," and if an indictment became public, "[t]he stigma and opprobrium" could imperil the President's ability to govern.' Although a prosecutor's internal report would not represent a formal public accusation akin to an indictment, the possibility of the report's public disclosure and the absence of a neutral adjudicatory forum to review its findings counseled against potentially determining 'that the person's conduct constitutes a federal offense.' Justice Manual § 9-27.220.

Fourth, if we had confidence after a thorough investigation of the facts that the President clearly did not commit obstruction of justice, we would so state. Based on the facts and the applicable legal standards, however, we are unable to reach that judgment. The evidence we obtained about the President's actions and intent presents difficult issues that prevent us from conclusively determining that no criminal conduct occurred. Accordingly, while this report does not conclude that the President committed a crime, it also does not exonerate him.[6]

Sources

1 Special Counsel Robert S. Mueller, III, 'Report on the Investigation into Russian Interference in the 2016 Presidential Election', Volume I (Washington DC: US Department of Justice, 2019), p. 1.
2 *Ibid.*, pp. 1–2.
3 *Ibid.*, p. 4.

4 *Ibid.*, pp. 4–5.
5 *Ibid.*, p. 173.
6 Special Counsel Robert S. Mueller, III, 'Report on the Investigation into Russian Interference in the 2016 Presidential Election', Volume II (Washington DC: US Department of Justice, 2019), p. 2.

A Near-consensus: Israel's Security Establishment and the Two-state Solution

Benjamin L. Shaver and Guy Ziv

Veterans of Israel's security establishment have been engaged in the country's national-security debates since its founding. Upon their retirement, generals have often entered politics, becoming members of the Knesset, government ministers and, on occasion, prime ministers. Indeed, three of Israel's 12 prime ministers – Yitzhak Rabin, Ehud Barak and Ariel Sharon – were retired generals. In Israel's most recent election, on 9 April 2019, three former Israel Defense Forces (IDF) chiefs of staff teamed up with a prominent politician to form a new centrist list in an unsuccessful effort to defeat Prime Minister Benjamin Netanyahu. Other retired security-establishment figures have been vocal outside of the formal political process – joining, for example, extra-parliamentary groups as active members of Israeli civil society.

In light of the country's famously hawkish security culture, this establishment's view on the conflict with the Palestinians is striking. Notwithstanding the vicissitudes of the on-again, off-again peace process and mixed assessments about Israel's negotiating partner, retired senior security officials have consistently stressed their support for a deal with the Palestinians based on the two-state solution. Given demographic realities, they have said, the establishment of a separate Palestinian state would secure Israel as a Jewish and democratic state. Crucially, a clear majority of high-ranking former IDF

Guy Ziv, the lead author of this article, is an assistant professor at American University's School of International Service and author of *Why Hawks Become Doves: Shimon Peres and Foreign Policy Change in Israel* (SUNY Press, 2014). **Benjamin L. Shaver** is a master's student at the University of Chicago's Committee on International Relations.

Survival | vol. 61 no. 3 | June–July 2019 | pp. 115–138   DOI 10.1080/00396338.2019.1614790

officials and former heads of the Mossad and Shin Bet intelligence services support the two-state solution.

The near-consensus among Israel's top security officials is significant because it challenges claims by the ruling right-wing coalition that the two-state solution is neither desirable nor feasible. Furthermore, the intensified activism of these former senior security officials in the last decade can be seen as a rebuke to Netanyahu. He has cultivated an image as 'Mr Security' – that is, as the one responsible adult in Israel who can be trusted to keep the country safe – and distanced himself from his public endorsement in 2009 of a two-state solution whereby 'a demilitarized Palestinian state exists alongside the Jewish state'.[1] Instead, he has chosen to align with right-wing coalition partners who explicitly reject this vision. Indeed, in an eleventh-hour gambit aimed at clinching re-election in April, Netanyahu pledged to annex Jewish settlements in the West Bank. Yet hundreds of security-establishment veterans have spoken out against his government's extant policy of 'creeping annexation' of the West Bank via settlements, emphasising a sense of urgency in working toward the establishment of a Palestinian state. The security community's motivation for supporting the two-state solution is straightforwardly a central tenet of mainstream Zionism: that Israel must remain a democratic Jewish state with equal rights for all.

Despite a moribund peace process and growing scepticism about the viability of a sovereign Palestinian state, the two-state solution remains the dominant paradigm and frame of reference for resolving the Israeli–Palestinian conflict. The idea of partitioning the land claimed by both Jews and Arabs is an old one, dating back to the 1930s Mandatory Palestine period, proposed first by the United Kingdom in 1937 and later by the United Nations Special Committee on Palestine in 1947. Partition became relevant again following Israel's capture of the West Bank, East Jerusalem and the Gaza Strip – territories inhabited by the Palestinians – in the 1967 Arab–Israeli War. Even as the war was being waged, members of the security establishment proposed variations of a Palestinian state, all of which were rejected by the political establishment. As we show, the majority of security-establishment veterans believe that time is running out for the two-state solution, which they view as paramount to Israeli interests.

Study design

This project employed a mixed-methods design in an attempt to ascertain the views of veterans of Israel's security establishment concerning the two-state solution. We analysed published statements by senior security-establishment figures and statements gleaned in nearly two dozen interviews that we conducted from December 2015 through December 2018 with retired generals, former heads of the Mossad and Shin Bet intelligence services, and ex-national security advisers to Prime Minister Netanyahu. To try to disconfirm our thesis – that a majority of these retired high-ranking security officials support the two-state solution – we drew on content analysis of newspaper sources, covering the period from January 2001 through May 2018, yielding a rich dataset on these individuals' views on the two-state solution.

Testing two-state support with text sources

We compiled an original dataset of retired senior officers from Israel's security services who have publicly expressed an opinion on the two-state solution. To capture a range of source material, we used two distinct Boolean searches to generate a pool of more than 5,000 articles from LexisNexis that were published between January 2001 and May 2018. We assessed January 2001 as a logical starting place for testing the security community's support for the two-state solution because the December 2000 'Clinton Parameters' are widely regarded as having established the political saliency of the two-state solution. To avoid sampling too heavily from any one news source and thus potentially biasing our data, our sampling design ensured that the articles we analysed came from diverse sources.

Coding rule

We applied the following coding rule when analysing quotations drawn from news-paper articles to assess a security official's stance on the two-state solution: to be coded as *for* or *against* the two-state solution, a quotation must come directly from a former senior security official and it must unambiguously indicate whether he or she supports the two-state solution. In cases in which an individual appeared to merely imply support or opposition, his or her comments were coded as 'inconclusive'. Even with a coding rule, however, generating a dataset from text sources relies on a certain degree of subjective judgement by those doing the coding.[2] To minimise this unavoidable hitch in our investigation, we conducted a series of inter-coder reliability checks.

Our dataset included only retired senior security officials in order to more accurately capture the sentiment of those individuals with the greatest amount of experience in a combat or other national-security setting. Our strict definition of 'retired senior security officials' refers to officers whose rank upon retirement is higher than a colonel in the IDF or who served as a chief or deputy chief of the Shin Bet or Mossad intelligence agencies. We also included former heads of the National Security Council (NSC), a position created in 1999 to coordinate information from the various intelligence agencies and provide foreign-policy advice based on guidelines provided by the prime minister.

Dataset construction

To understand how we have applied the coding rule, consider the following excerpt from an op-ed written by former Shin Bet director Admiral (Retd) Ami Ayalon in 2003:

> All of which returns us, by dint of contradistinction, to the 'Peoples' Voice' peace petition I have been promoting along with my Palestinian partner, Prof. Sari Nusseibeh. Unlike Geneva, our initiative is a simple declaration of principles, one page in length. Both call for an end to the conflict and borders along the 1967 lines, with Israel as a state of the Jews and the Palestinian state demilitarized. But the Peoples' Voice explicitly limits the right of return to the future Palestine, and rules out Palestinian sovereignty on the Temple Mount.[3]

This excerpt demonstrates Ayalon's support for the two-state solution. The People's Voice petition he references, which he drafted in 2002 with Professor Sari Nusseibeh, a prominent Palestinian scholar, calls for the establishment of two states. In addition to referencing the petition, he also states that he is calling for an end to the conflict between Israelis and Palestinians and the establishment of a state for Palestinians and a state for Jews. A counterexample comes from former national security advisor Major-General (Retd) Giora Eiland: 'What remains certain is that the disadvantages of the currently envisioned two-state paradigm outweigh its advantages in the eyes of the combatants. As thus, it has run its course.'[4] This excerpt clearly demonstrates Eiland's opposition to a two-state solution.

Applying the coding rule resulted in a dataset of 520 comments that indicate a position on the two-state solution by 62 individuals made over a 17-year period. For each quotation, we recorded the following information: name, position as cited in the article, organisation, whether the quoted individual is retired, his or her stance on the two-state solution, his or her quotation and whether an alternative solution is proposed by this individual. Unsurprisingly, the 520 comments are not uniformly distributed across the 62 individuals. Some individuals included in the dataset appeared numerous times, while others appeared far less frequently. Due to this variance, analysing the data at the comment level produced results heavily skewed toward the opinions held by the most frequently quoted individuals. To correct for this distortion, rather than examining the dataset at the level of the individual comment, we analysed the data at the level of individual official by collapsing individual comments into a single entry for each of the 62 officials who appeared in the articles. We applied a 'majority rule' to the collapsing process, coding these officials on the opinions they expressed the majority of times.

Coder training and oversight

We tasked three students to aid in the creation of our LexisNexis dataset. To ensure the highest possible level of accuracy and replicability in the data, the coders were trained before they began coding on their own and were subject to a series of inter-coder reliability checks. The training began when we introduced the coders to the coding rule. We subsequently went through a 'story norming' process to acclimate the coders to the coding process, which entailed coding articles as a group and pointing out errors as they occurred. Coders later received a batch of ten test articles to code on their own. Once they completed that test batch, we met to compare their results with a master set of results that we had coded. At that point, any errors were pointed out to the coder. If the coder's results did not match the master results for more than 80% of the coding, they were given additional sets of test articles to complete. This process continued until they had achieved a score of 80% or above for a set of test articles. After completing the training, coders received batches of 75 articles to read and code each week. To ensure high-quality coding, we frequently checked the coders' work and provided feedback as necessary. In cases where quotations were unclear, we provided a second opinion.

Inter-coder reliability

Reliability, defined by Andrew Hayes and Klaus Krippendorff as 'whether a coding instrument, serving as common instructions to different observers of the same set of phenomena, yields the same data within a tolerable margin of error', is a necessary component of originally created datasets because it ensures that the data collection is replicable.[5] To verify that our coders achieved the level of reliability necessary for future replication, we computed two measures of inter-coder reliability. This was accomplished by having the coders overlap on their coding assignments for 50 articles. The coding for these articles was then used to calculate the percent agreement – the number of articles in which two coders agreed on the coding divided by the number of articles in the sub-sample on which they overlapped – and Fleiss' κ, which accounts for agreement due to chance.

For both statistics, a result of .00 is equivalent to no agreement, and a result of 1.00 is equivalent to perfect agreement; however, perfect agreement is never expected. Of the two tests, percent agreement is the least conservative method because it is simply the percentage of coding decisions that a pair of coders agrees on out of a sample of coding in which the pair overlaps.[6] In comparison, because Fleiss' also accounts for agreement due to chance, a lower value is expected.

After completing the coding process, we computed each pair of coders' percent agreement. The results appear in the table below. Although there is no universally agreed cut-off for acceptable results, each pair of coders' percent agreement exceeded .80, which scholars consider acceptable.[7]

In comparison to percent agreement, which is computed for pairs of coders, Fleiss' is computed for multiple coders at once. Because Fleiss' is the more conservative statistic, a > 0.80 is considered to be 'almost perfect agreement'.[8] The Fleiss' generated for our three coders was .78. This places us right below the cut-off for 'almost perfect agreement' and on the very high end of 'substantial agreement', according to Landis and Koch's scale.

Percent Agreement		
C1 vs C2	C2 vs C3	C1 vs C3
0.88	0.82	1.00

A near-consensus

In the last two decades, the question of a future Palestinian state has dominated the political discourse, with the centre and left-of-centre portions of
the electorate – and some self-identified right-wing voters – supporting the
two-state solution. The views of the Israeli security community have traditionally been aligned with the centre-left – the so-called 'peace camp' – on this
issue. This faction has supported territorial compromise and today opposes
the expansion of Jewish settlements in the West Bank, seeing them as an
obstacle to an eventual peace agreement. The right-wing 'national camp'
has consistently advocated Israel's annexation of the West Bank – which it
references by its biblical names, Judea and Samaria – and the construction of
Jewish settlements there. In recent years, there has also been some support
in right-wing circles for recapturing the Gaza Strip, from which Israel withdrew in 2005, in response to recurring violence along the border.

Our research indicates that a disproportionate number of senior veterans of Israel's security establishment who have held forth on this issue
publicly have voiced their support for the creation of a Palestinian state
in op-eds, published interviews and social media. Many of these former
security officials have entered the political arena; others have joined one
or more non-partisan organisations of security veterans advocating two-
state diplomacy. Those entering the political fray have traditionally run
with centrist or left-of-centre parties. Recent exceptions to this practice
include Major-General (Retd) Yoav Galant and former Shin Bet head Avi
Dichter, who joined the right-wing Likud party despite being at odds
with their party colleagues over the two-state solution, which they had
endorsed in the past.[9] Both of the IDF chiefs of staff who went on to
become prime ministers, Yitzhak Rabin and Ehud Barak, ran as leaders of
the Labor Party, and the only other general to have assumed the highest
office – Ariel Sharon – broke from the Likud party over his decision to dis-
engage unilaterally from Gaza, forming the new centrist Kadima party,
which supported the two-state solution. In the 2019 elections, Benny
Gantz and Gabi Ashkenazi, two former IDF chiefs, formed a centrist ticket
opposing the Netanyahu-led right bloc and advocating a two-state solution. Although Moshe Ya'alon, another retired IDF chief, publicly opposes

Palestinian statehood, he nevertheless joined his two fellow ex-generals on the ticket opposing Netanyahu.

The relatively dovish politics of retired security officials has been an enduring source of frustration for right-wing politicians who oppose Palestinian statehood. Netanyahu, having spent years cultivating his tough-guy image, has long tried to discredit his critics in the security establishment by disparagingly labelling them 'leftists'.[10] In the mid-2000s, to stave off challenges from recently retired IDF generals, he encouraged passage of the so-called 'Halutz Law', named for then-IDF chief of staff Dan Halutz, who was expected to run for the top office upon retirement.[11] The law, which was passed in 2007, increased the cooling-off period before former senior defence officials could enter politics from six months to three years after their retirement.[12]

More recently, a number of right-wing politicians have shattered a long-standing norm by openly attacking sitting members of the security establishment, as when Education Minister Naftali Bennett called on the then-IDF chief of staff Gadi Eizenkot to escalate the army's response to Hamas's rocket attacks from Gaza into Israel. 'I don't think shooting children who are launching rockets is right', Eizenkot responded, saying that 'this contradicts my operational and ethical position'.[13] Several months later, the two men clashed again when Bennett suggested that the army's Military Advocate General was imposing 'legal and conceptual hoops' that prevented soldiers from carrying out their fighting duties.[14] A populist former defence minister likened the IDF top brass to the left-wing non-governmental organisation Peace Now.[15] Another right-wing politician argued that there was 'a problem' with those heading Israel's security agencies because 'over the years the heads of Shin Bet and Mossad become leftists'.[16]

Retired members of the security establishment, who are finally free to express their political opinions, openly acknowledge that their views on Israel's conflict with the Palestinians reflect those of a clear majority of their colleagues. 'For every 50 [who think like me], there are just a few who don't think like that', says Major-General (Retd) Gadi Shamni.[17] Ehud Barak has made a similar point, stating that 'if you put in one room all the living former heads of the Mossad, the Shin Bet, and the Israel Defense Forces,

Table 1: **Overall Support for the Two-state Solution**

Total	Support	Oppose	Inconclusive
Sum	53	7	2
Percentage	85%	11%	3%

more than 90 per cent of them would say that it's simpler to protect Israel from a border that assures our security interests next to a Palestinian state, than to protect a "greater Israel" with millions of Palestinians living under its control'.[18] Our study supports these claims. In our interviews with former IDF top brass, retired generals offered similar appraisals of their peers, with estimates of those who supported the two-state solution ranging between 70% and 95%.[19]

The coded statements in our original dataset back these estimates, indicating that a clear majority of former high-ranking security officials in Israel who have publicly expressed a view on the Israeli–Palestinian conflict support the two-state solution. Of the 62 individuals in our dataset, 53, or 85%, support the two-state solution, compared to seven, or 11%, who do not.

These findings put veterans of the Israeli security establishment starkly at odds with the nation's right-wing political establishment. While the sample from which our data is generated does not include a comprehensive list of retired security officials – such a list is not available – it serves as a representative sample of the larger population of interest. By including former officials from the entire range of senior ranks, the dataset provides a robust check for the conclusions drawn from our analysis of our interviews and published articles.

A security and moral imperative

What explains the overwhelming support for the two-state solution in the Israeli security community? The recurring explanation offered in our interviews with retired senior officials is twofold: security and values, as summed up by Major-General (Retd) Elazar Stern of the centrist Yesh Atid party and a member of the Knesset (MK).[20] They view themselves as working to safeguard Israel as both a Jewish state and a democracy, two persistent aspects of mainstream Zionism.[21] Given the demographic realities, they perceive

Israel's Jewish majority to be in danger, and are increasingly concerned about political developments they see as imperilling the nation's democratic standing. Israeli demographers and political geographers have long warned that it is only a matter of time before Israel, as presently constituted, ceases to be a Jewish state.[22] On 26 March 2018, Colonel Uri Mendes, the deputy head of the Civil Administration, told the Knesset's Foreign Affairs and Defense Committee that demographic parity between Jews and Muslims between the Mediterranean Sea and the Jordan River already existed.[23] A high-ranking general interviewed for this project echoed the sentiment of many interviewees in saying that 'seeking to end control over the lives of 2.4 million Palestinians in the West Bank is both a moral and practical imperative' for Israel.[24] 'Jewish values, as I see them, don't go with inequality', says a former Mossad chief, who believes that a two-state solution is essential to fulfilling 'the Zionist dream'.[25] Even some ex-generals who are sceptical of the viability of an independent Palestinian state given internal Palestinian dynamics want to see Israel safeguarding its security while working toward a future in which it does not exert control over the Palestinians.[26]

Israeli right-wing ideologues embrace variations of the so-called 'one-state solution' – a single state from the Mediterranean Sea to the Jordan River. Some one-state proponents, such as President Reuven Rivlin and Likud MK Tzipi Hotovely, support the notion of equal rights for both nations and would thus extend citizenship to the Palestinians. For Hotovely, a Palestinian state would pose a far greater danger to Israel than a binational state because in the latter scenario, 'we have a degree of control, but the moment you abandon the area to the Palestinian entity, what control do you have over what will happen there?'[27] Others on the right would deny citizenship to the Palestinians in a one-state scenario. MK Bezalel Smotrich, a leader of the far-right Tkuma faction, has said that if he had to choose between a Jewish state and a democratic one, he would forgo the latter.[28] A number of annexation bills have been proposed in the Knesset in recent years, including one by the former justice minister, that would annex 'Area C', which comprises approximately 60% of the West Bank.[29] Yuli Edelstein, a senior politician in Netanyahu's Likud party, has said that 'the 21st Knesset will apply Israeli sovereignty in Judea and Samaria'.[30]

In repudiation of claims on the right that a Palestinian state would represent a formidable security threat to Israel, Police Major-General (Retd) Shaul Givoli, a former commander of the Civil Guard and IDF deputy brigade commander, has written that a two-state solution 'solves the security problem' and that 'retaining occupied territory is not only a moral, social and foreign-affairs disaster, but also a significant security risk'.[31] Givoli is one of hundreds of former high-ranking IDF officers who have been active in the Peace and Security Association (formerly the Council for Peace and Security), a non-partisan organisation established in 1988 that has been unabashedly supportive of the two-state solution. To Givoli's colleagues in the security community, any 'one-state' proposal is a non-starter because the prospect of an illiberal apartheid state – a Jewish minority ruling over a Palestinian majority – or, alternatively, a binational state in which Israel ceases to be Jewish, is regarded as a far greater danger than relinquishing territories to the Palestinians for a separate state. In short, to senior security-establishment veterans, the two-state solution is seen as the one resolution to the intractable conflict that would enable Israel to realise the Zionist vision while retaining its democratic character.

Table 2: **Position on the Two-state Solution by Individual**

Title	Name	Organisation	Opinion
Brig.-Gen. (Retd), Division Head in Shin Bet	Lior Akerman	Shin Bet	Yes
Maj.-Gen. (Retd), National Security Adviser	Yaakov Amidror	IDF	No
National Security Adviser	Uzi Arad	NSC	Yes
Brig.-Gen. (Retd), National Security Adviser	Dani Arditi	IDF	Yes
Lt-Gen. (Retd), IDF Chief of Staff	Gabi Ashkenazi	IDF	Yes
Shin Bet Director, Admiral (Retd)	Ami Ayalon	IDF	Yes
Lt-Gen. (Retd), IDF Chief of Staff	Ehud Barak	IDF	Yes
Deputy Chief of Mossad	Ram Ben-Barak	IDF	Inconclusive
Brig.-Gen. (Retd)	Binyamin Ben-Eliezer	IDF	Yes
Maj.-Gen. (Retd)	Avihu Ben-Nun	IDF	Yes
Brig.-Gen. (Retd)	Eyal Ben-Reuven	IDF	Yes
Brig.-Gen. (Retd), Director of IDF Strategic Planning Division	Shlomo Brom	IDF	Yes
Brig.-Gen. (Retd), Shin Bet Director	Yoram Cohen	Shin Bet	Inconclusive
Mossad Director	Meir Dagan	IDF	Yes
Maj.-Gen. (Retd), Head of the IDF Central Command, National Security Adviser	Uzi Dayan	IDF	Yes
Brig.-Gen. (Retd)	Udi Dekel	IDF	Yes
Shin Bet Director	Avi Dichter	Shin Bet	Yes

Shin Bet Director	Yuval Diskin	Shin Bet	Yes
Maj.-Gen. (Retd)	Giora Eiland	IDF	No
Brig.-Gen. (Retd)	Effi Eitam	IDF	No
Maj.-Gen. (Retd)	Itzik Eitan	IDF	Yes
Brig.-Gen. (Retd)	Arieh Eldad	IDF	No
Deputy Chief of National Security Council	Chuck Freilich	NSC	Yes
Maj.-Gen. (Retd)	Shlomo Gazit	IDF	Yes
Shin Bet Director	Carmi Gillon	Shin Bet	Yes
Brig.-Gen. (Retd), Police Maj.-Gen. (Retd)	Shaul Givoli	IDF	Yes
Maj.-Gen. (Retd), Senior Mossad Official	Rolly Gueron	Mossad	Yes
Maj.-Gen. (Retd)	Gershon Hacohen	IDF	No
Mossad Director	Efraim Halevy	Mossad	Yes
Lt-Gen. (Retd), IDF Chief of Staff	Dan Halutz	IDF	Yes
Deputy Shin Bet Director	Yisrael Hasson	Shin Bet	Yes
Brig.-Gen. (Retd)	Michael Herzog	IDF	Yes
Brig.-Gen. (Retd)	Giora Inbar	IDF	Yes
Brig.-Gen. (Retd)	Uzi Keren	IDF	Yes
Deputy Mossad Chief	David Kimche	Mossad	Yes
Maj.-Gen. (Retd)	Shlomo Lahat	IDF	Yes
Maj.-Gen. (Retd)	Amos Lapidot	IDF	Yes
Maj.-Gen. (Retd), Commander of IDF Northern Command, Deputy Mossad Director	Amiram Levin	IDF	Yes
Lt-Gen. (Retd), IDF Chief of Staff, Director of Military Intelligence	Amnon Lipkin-Shahak	IDF	Yes
Maj.-Gen. (Retd)	Amos Malka	IDF	Yes
Maj.-Gen. (Retd), IDF Director of Military Intelligence	Amram Mitzna	IDF	Yes
Lt-Gen. (Retd), IDF Chief of Staff	Shaul Mofaz	IDF	Yes
Mossad Director	Tamir Pardo	Mossad	Yes
Brig.-Gen. (Retd)	Ilan Paz	IDF	Yes
Shin Bet Director	Yaakov Peri	Shin Bet	Yes
Maj.-Gen. (Retd)	Amnon Reshef	IDF	Yes
Maj.-Gen. (Retd)	Danny Rothschild	IDF	Yes
Maj.-Gen. (Retd)	Oren Shachor	IDF	Yes
Shin Bet Director	Avraham Shalom	Shin Bet	Yes
Maj.-Gen. (Retd)	Gadi Shamni	IDF	Yes
Maj.-Gen. (Retd)	Ariel Sharon	IDF	Yes
Maj.-Gen. (Retd)	Nathan Sharony	IDF	Yes
Mossad Director	Shabtai Shavit	Mossad	Yes
Brig.-Gen. (Retd)	Efraim Sneh	IDF	Yes
Brig.-Gen. (Retd)	Moshe Tamir	IDF	Yes
Lt-Gen. (Retd), IDF Chief of Staff	Moshe Ya'alon	IDF	No
Maj.-Gen. (Retd), IDF Chief of Defense Intelligence	Amos Yadlin	IDF	Yes
Maj.-Gen. (Retd)	Amos Yaron	IDF	Yes
Mossad Director	Danny Yatom	Mossad	Yes
Mossad Director	Zvi Zamir	Mossad	Yes
Maj.-Gen. (Retd)	Rehavam Ze'evi	IDF	No
Brig.-Gen. (Retd)	Gadi Zohar	IDF	Yes

Partition

Uzi Arad, a former national security adviser to Netanyahu, points out that the two-state solution has its origins in the idea of partition, which had always been 'the preferred formula' to Zionists.[32] Indeed, the mainstream Zionist leadership had accepted the principle of partition, as enunciated in the British Partition Plan of 1937 and, subsequently, the United Nations Partition Plan of 1947.[33] But the Arab leadership rejected the idea of apportioning the land. Ultimately, the state of Israel was established in British Mandate Palestine in addition to territory it gained following its victory in the 1948–49 Arab–Israeli war, while Jordan took over the West Bank and East Jerusalem in that war. Partition would not become conceptually relevant again until the next Arab–Israeli War, nearly two decades later.

The 1967 Arab–Israeli War resulted in the threefold increase of Israel's territory, with the Sinai, the Gaza Strip, the West Bank, East Jerusalem and the Golan Heights no longer in Arab hands. The future of these territories and the fate of their inhabitants preoccupied the Israeli government, which hoped to transform Israel's astounding military victory into a diplomatic one. Even before the war was over, prime minister Levi Eshkol called for 'changing the nature of Israeli–Arab relations as they have existed since 1948' while forming a plan aimed at 'achieving permanent peace and border security'.[34]

The notion that Israel should work toward the establishment of a Palestinian state encompassing at least parts of the newly occupied territories enjoyed greater support in the military than it did among members of Eshkol's cabinet. IDF chief of staff Yitzhak Rabin advised Eshkol to accept a demilitarised Palestinian state in the West Bank that would be connected to Israel via the Jordan River, which would serve as Israel's security border.[35] Other senior military officers then supporting the creation of a Palestinian state, in one form or another, included Yisrael Tal, an Armoured Corps general; Mati Peled, the IDF's supply chief; Rehavam Ze'evi, deputy head of Military Operations; and Shlomo Gazit, head of the IDF intelligence branch assessment department.[36]

Various diplomatic proposals from the IDF and intelligence services swiftly made their way to the government. On 9 June, the IDF intelligence branch proposed a set of guidelines for Israel's policy. Writes Gazit:

> Our proposal was based on the assumption that Israel would exploit the military developments to establish a new relationship with its Arab neighbors. The goal was a formal and comprehensive peace with all the Arab States, based on a nearly full withdrawal to the 4 June lines or, at the very least, stabilizing a *de-facto* Israeli–Arab co-existence, while finding agreed solutions to the main problems that separated the parties.[37]

The plan included the establishment of a demilitarised but independent Palestinian state in the West Bank and Gaza Strip, with border modifications reflecting the changes effectuated in the two decades prior to the war. Additional proposals for relinquishing parts of the West Bank to the Palestinians were submitted by a number of generals and officers serving in specialised units.[38] Israel's intelligence organisations, the Mossad and the Shin Bet, likewise recommended that the Eshkol government consider the creation of a Palestinian state.[39]

The Eshkol government declined to adopt any of these proposals for facilitating Palestinian statehood. Instead, the political establishment promoted the 'Jordanian option', which entailed returning most of the West Bank to Jordan's King Hussein.[40] Eshkol was clearly concerned about the political risks he faced were he to launch a diplomatic initiative with the Palestinians. Some 71% of Israelis opposed relinquishing the West Bank by way of a peace agreement, one survey found.[41] Moreover, Eshkol was overshadowed by Moshe Dayan, the charismatic general who had become minister of defence and was widely seen as the hero of Israel's audacious victory. 'If I reach out a hand, and no hand is returned in peace, then Abu Jildah [his nickname for Dayan] and the terrorist [his nickname for former leader of the Zionist militant group Irgun and future prime minister Menachem Begin] will give me a *petsale* [Yiddish for slap] that will knock me off my chair', he confided to a friend.[42] Domestic constraints – real or perceived – thus stymied any bold moves the prime minister may have earlier considered.

Security community vs political establishment

A decade later, Yehoshafat Harkabi, a retired major-general and a former head of IDF military intelligence, abandoned his own hardline positions and advocated talks with the Palestine Liberation Organisation (PLO), dismantling existing settlements and establishing a Palestinian state based on Israel's pre-1967 borders.[43] Acknowledging that there would be serious security problems with which Israel would need to contend if the West Bank were no longer under Israeli control, he nevertheless concluded that 'our choice is not between good and bad, but between bad and worse'.[44] Harkabi warned that 'the demographic trend will work against us' and that 'a binational state would be a very uneasy state'.[45] He rejected the idea advanced by Begin and others on the right that Jewish immigration to Israel would offset the growth of the Palestinian population within post-1967 borders. In his book *Israel's Fateful Hour*, he writes:

> Some Israelis believe that annexation will bring about a new flourishing of Zionism and awaken a fresh wave of Jewish immigration to offset the increase in the Arab population. But increased Jewish immigration would not affect the presence of a large Arab population, even if its relative proportion in the country was thereby decreased. Nor is there any reason to assume that Jewish immigration will increase. Jews may be attracted to a *Jewish* state, but not to a country with a mixed and unsettled population. No preaching about their obligation to move to Israel will help. Jews will prefer to continue to live with their peaceable Christian neighbors in America or Europe rather than to live alongside an angry Muslim population.[46]

Harkabi's conclusions, set forth a decade before the first Palestinian intifada broke out and more than two decades before the two-state solution emerged as a mainstream approach, appear prophetic in retrospect.

It took another former general, Yitzhak Rabin, to adopt Harkabi's call for engaging the PLO. Rabin's tough tactics as the minister of defence during the first intifada, which began in December 1987, proved ineffective in putting an end to the Palestinian uprising. Israel had always defeated Arab armies on the battlefield, but suppressing demonstrating Palestinian teens and young adults, armed only with stones and the occasional Molotov cocktail, was a challenge Israel had never faced. Rabin became convinced that the solution lay in diplomacy rather than military force.[47] As the Labor

Party candidate, he defeated Yitzhak Shamir, the Likud's hardline prime minister, in the June 1992 elections and, a year later, gave Shimon Peres, the foreign minister, the green light to engage in the back-channel talks with the PLO that spawned the Oslo process.[48] That process did not produce a final peace agreement, but it did effectively end the intifada, led to mutual recognition between Israel and the PLO, gave the Palestinians self-rule in parts of the occupied territories, instituted security coordination and ushered in an era of hope. Although Rabin never publicly endorsed Palestinian statehood, it was clear to him that the logical extension of the Oslo process was a Palestinian state.[49]

The assassination of Rabin by a far-right Israeli extremist on 4 November 1995, and the broader rise of the right with the election of Benjamin Netanyahu six months later, constituted the beginning of the end of the Oslo peace process. Netanyahu was emphatically opposed to a Palestinian state and only reluctantly carried out Israel's obligations under the Oslo agreements. These included the Hebron Protocol, which required that Israeli troops withdraw from 80% of Hebron, and the Wye River Memorandum, which dictated that they pull out of an additional 13% of the West Bank. Ehud Barak, Netanyahu's former military commander and his successor as prime minister, was a former IDF chief of staff who, like Rabin, joined the centre-left Labor Party and led it to victory. In contrast to Netanyahu, Barak publicly endorsed the establishment of a Palestinian state in January 1997.[50] Four months later, Barak's Labor Party adopted the platform plan recognising the Palestinian people's right to self-determination in a state with limited sovereignty.[51]

In the summer of 2000, Barak convinced US president Bill Clinton to convene a summit at Camp David in an effort to reach a comprehensive peace agreement, based on the two-state solution. Following 14 days of difficult negotiations, the participants left empty-handed. Barak had offered unprecedented concessions, agreeing to part with more than 90% of the West Bank and all of the Gaza Strip; to dismantle most of the settlements; and to divide Jerusalem by offering the Palestinians sovereignty over the Muslim and Christian quarters of the Old City and custodianship of the Temple Mount/Haram al-Sharif. These compromises fell short of PLO chairman and Palestinian National Authority president Yasser Arafat's demands. A mutual blame game ensued. Ariel Sharon's provocative visit to the Temple Mount/Haram al-Sharif sparked the violent second intifada, known as the Al-Aqsa intifada, and soured the atmosphere. The Taba Summit, which took place on 21–27 January 2001, was a last-ditch effort to bridge the gaps between the two sides. Despite progress, the negotiators ran out of time. Clinton was no longer president, while Israeli elections on 6 February 2001 made Sharon prime minister.

In September 2002, as the Sharon government was confronting continuous violence stemming from the second intifada, Ami Ayalon, a former Shin Bet chief and ex-commander of Israel's navy, held a joint press conference with Palestinian philosopher Sari Nusseibeh in which they unveiled 'The People's Voice', a blueprint for peace. The two men noted their intention to collect Israeli and Palestinian signatures to help leaders conduct negotiations toward the establishment of a Palestinian state based on the pre-1967 borders, with 1:1 territorial modifications in accordance with the vital needs of both sides.[52] Asher Susser notes that Ayalon and Nusseibeh succeeded where everyone else had failed in covering all the critical issues concerning the two-state solution – permanent borders; Jerusalem ('an open city, the capital of two states'); and the refugee issue (Palestinian refugees would 'return only to the State of Palestine' while Jews would 'return only to the State of Israel').[53]

The following year, on 14 November 2003, Israel's then-largest-circulation daily, *Yedioth Ahronoth*, published a joint interview with Ayalon and three other former Shin Bet chiefs – Carmi Gillon, Yaakov Peri and Avraham Shalom – who warned that Israel would be in grave danger if the Sharon government did not work toward a political arrangement with the Palestinians.[54] They called on the government to withdraw from the West Bank and Gaza Strip, even at the risk of clashing with some of the settlers.[55] Sharon was well acquainted with these retired intelligence chiefs, and their interview reportedly influenced his decision to change course.[56] On 18 December, in a historic address at the Herzliya Conference, Sharon announced his unilateral disengagement plan, entailing 'the redeployment of IDF forces along new security lines and a change in the deployment of settlements, which will reduce as much as possible the number of Israelis located in the heart of the Palestinian population'. The end goal, he emphasised, would be the establishment of 'a democratic Palestinian state with territorial contiguity in Judea and Samaria and economic viability, which would conduct normal relations of tranquillity, security and peace with Israel'.[57] In August 2005, the Sharon government withdrew the IDF and dismantled all Israeli settlements in the Gaza Strip, as well as four in the West Bank. The Palestinian Islamist militant group Hamas, however, defeated Fatah, the main secular Palestinian party, in the 2006 Palestinian legislative elections and took over the Gaza Strip by force the following year, lowering prospects for serious diplomatic headway.

Nine years later, the four ex-Shin Bet directors were joined by two others in an Israeli documentary, *The Gatekeepers*, which received international critical acclaim and an Academy Award nomination. The filmmaker, Dror Moreh, was inspired to make the film after Dov Weisglass, Sharon's chief of staff, told him about the profound impact the Shin Bet heads had made on his boss.[58] In Moreh's film, the former spymasters spoke honestly and bluntly about their experiences in fighting terrorism. 'After retiring from this job, you become a bit of a leftist', said Peri, who ran the agency from 1988 to 1994.

An urgent matter of security

Although the experiences of the former Shin Bet chiefs, as documented in *The Gatekeepers*, may not mirror those of every retired security official, our research shows that the vast majority of senior security veterans have reached the same conclusion: that it is in Israel's national interest to work toward a two-state solution. These calls have taken on greater urgency in the Netanyahu era, as Israel appears to be inching toward a binational reality given the country's demographic trends coupled with settlement growth throughout the West Bank, including in densely populated Palestinian areas. Netanyahu's government has built new settlements at a frenetic pace while retroactively authorising thousands of illegally built units in heavily populated Palestinian areas that would likely be included in a future Palestinian state.[59] 'We're here to stay, forever', Netanyahu told settlers at an event marking 50 years of Israel's occupation of the West Bank.[60] His Likud party opposes the two-state solution, as do the other right-wing factions. In his 2015 re-election campaign, he vowed that there would never be a Palestinian state formed as long as he were prime minister.[61] In his 2019 re-election campaign, Netanyahu accused rivals who have spoken of the need to reach an arrangement with the Palestinians of being 'leftists'.[62] He warned that if the centrist Blue and White party formed the next government, it would usher in a Palestinian state that would threaten Israel's existence.[63] And three days before he was re-elected to a fifth term in the 9 April 2019 elections, Netanyahu vowed to extend sovereignty over the West Bank, a declaration aimed at consolidating his base.[64]

In the absence of peace talks, veterans of the security establishment, convinced that time is running out for the two-state solution, would like to see Israel undertake measures to preserve the option. Major-General (Retd) Amos Yadlin, a former chief of Israeli military intelligence, and former Israeli peace negotiator Gilead Sher have argued, for example, that even with continued Palestinian intransigence Israel could 'proactively take constructive, unilateral, internationally coordinated steps towards a two-state reality, meaning the de facto – if not yet de jure – existence of two nation-states for two peoples'.[65] In 2009, Sher and former Shin Bet head Ami Ayalon co-founded Blue White Future, an organisation that advocates Israeli unilateral steps, such as facilitating the relocation of Jewish settlers, to keep the two-state solution alive even during a prolonged political impasse.

Highlighting the sense of urgency in the security community, a nonpartisan group of retired senior security officials founded Commanders for Israel's Security (CIS) in October 2014, six months after the collapse of the peace talks brokered by John Kerry, then the US secretary of state. CIS includes as members 300 retired IDF generals and former heads of the Mossad, Shin Bet and police services who support an Israeli security–political initiative to realise the two-state solution. Major-General (Retd) Amnon Reshef, its founder and chairman, has compared Israel's current situation to the existential peril it faced during the War of Independence in 1948–49 and in the first days of the 1973 Yom Kippur War, when Israel was caught off guard by an Arab surprise attack and almost militarily defeated.[66]

The large number of security veterans who have joined such non-partisan organisations share the conviction that forging a Palestinian state is a vital – and pressing – Israeli national-security interest. Many of the retired security officials see the two-state solution in existential terms. A Palestinian state is imperative 'if we want a Jewish, democratic, secure, and legitimate Israel', says Yadlin, who today heads the Institute for National Security Studies (INSS), a Tel Aviv-based think tank.[67] In October 2018, the INSS unveiled a two-state strategic framework to which numerous security veterans, including Benny Gantz, Gabi Ashkenazi and Moshe Ya'alon – the three former IDF chiefs who ran together on the joint Blue and White ticket in the April 2019 elections – contributed.[68] This otherwise heterogeneous group is united in its desire 'to improve Israel's strategic situation' and 'halt the drift toward a one-state solution'.[69] The fear of a binational state-in-the-making has impelled Israel's legacy security community to undertake a concerted effort to ensure Israel's future as a Jewish and democratic state by means of a two-state solution.

*   *   *

A clear majority of Israel's ex-generals and former spymasters – 85% – support the two-state solution to the Israeli–Palestinian conflict. Their chief rationale for the creation of a separate Palestinian state is their desire to preserve Israel as a sovereign Jewish state. Their concern that demographic trends threaten Israel's Jewish majority and thus the Zionist dream of Jewish self-determination drives their support for partitioning the land. Many veterans, including sceptics of the two-state solution, also emphasise a moral dimension: a desire to end Israel's 52-year rule over the Palestinians. These concerns have been present for decades in the security community, yet in recent years they have taken on greater urgency given the absence of a peace process, the Israeli government's policy of 'creeping annexation' of the West Bank that is threatening to transform Israel into a binational state, and, more recently, the Trump administration's unquestioning support for Netanyahu. Given their persistence, their cohesiveness, their pubic prominence and their singular credibility as assessors of Israel's security, the former generals and spymasters appear, improbably, to be indispensable to the viability of the two-state solution.

Acknowledgements

Andrew Spath was instrumental in the design of this study. We are indebted to him for his invaluable guidance from the inception of this project to its completion. We are deeply grateful to Sean O'Conner for his research assistance and for generously giving of his time and knowledge. We also wish to thank Alina Alimova, Max Lanosga and Pallavi Sengupta for their research assistance on this project.

Notes

1 'Address by Prime Minister Benjamin Netanyahu at Bar-Ilan University', 14 June 2009, http://mfa.gov.il/MFA/PressRoom/2009/Pages/Address_PM_Netanyahu_Bar-Ilan_University_14-Jun-2009.aspx.

2 Michael P. Colaresi, Karen A. Rasler and William R. Thompson, *Strategic Rivalries in World Politics: Position, Space and Conflict Escalation* (Cambridge: Cambridge University Press, 2007), p. 29.

3 Ami Ayalon, 'My Alternative to Geneva', *Jerusalem Post*, 18 November 2003.

4 David M. Weinberg, 'Know Comment: Revolutionizing the Peace Process', *Jerusalem Post*, 11 September 2014, https://www.jpost.com/Opinion/Know-Comment-Revolutionizing-the-peace-process-375131.

5 Andrew F. Hayes and Klaus Krippendorff, 'Answering the Call for a Standard Reliability Measure for Coding Data', *Communication Methods and Measures*, vol. 1, no. 1, April 2007, pp. 77–89. See also Slava Mikhaylov, Michael Laver and Kenneth R. Benoit, 'Coder Reliability and Misclassification in the Human Coding of Party Manifestos', *Political Analysis*, vol. 20, no. 1, Winter 2012, pp. 78–91.

6 Matthew Lombard, Jennifer Snyder-Duch and Cheryl Campanella Bracken, 'Content Analysis in Mass Communication: Assessment and Reporting of Intercoder Reliability', *Human Communication Research*, vol. 28, no. 4, October 2002, p. 590.

7 Kimberly A. Neuendorf, *The Content Analysis Guidebook* (Thousand Oaks, CA: SAGE Publications, 2001), p. 143. There is no agreed-upon rule for what constitutes 'good' or 'bad' agreement. The cut-off of 80% comes from Neuendorf, who writes, 'coefficients of .90 or greater would be acceptable to all, .80 acceptable in most situations, and below that there exists great disagreement'.

8 J. Richard Landis and Gary G. Koch, 'The Measurement of Observer Agreement for Categorical Data', *Biometrics*, vol. 33, no. 1, March 1977, p. 165. See also Joseph L. Fleiss, Bruce Levin and Myunghee Cho Paik, *Statistical Methods for Rates and Proportions* (Hoboken, NJ: Wiley-Interscience, 3rd edition, 2003), p. 604.

9 See Avi Dichter, 'The Regional Approach Might Get Us There Faster', *Jerusalem Post*, 9 June 2009, https://www.jpost.com/Opinion/Op-Ed-Contributors/The-regional-approach-might-get-us-there-faster;

Barak Ravid, 'Israeli Policy Is Not to Build in West Bank Settlements, Housing Minister Says', *Haaretz*, 28 May 2016, https://www.haaretz.com/israel-news/.premium-housing-minister-israeli-policy-is-not-to-build-in-west-bank-1.5388672; and 'Just One in Five Israeli Ministers Openly Back Two-state Solution', *Middle East Monitor*, 28 June 2016, https://www.middleeastmonitor.com/20160628-just-one-in-five-israeli-ministers-openly-back-two-state-solution/.

10 Yoram Peri, *Telepopulism: Media and Politics in Israel* (Palo Alto, CA: Stanford University Press, 2004), p. 196.

11 Mazal Mualem, 'Three-year IDF Cooling-off Period Targets Netanyahu's Rivals', Al-Monitor, 14 July 2015, http://www.al-monitor.com/pulse/originals/2015/07/israel-cooling-off-generals-politics-netanyahu-rivals.html.

12 *Ibid*. Ironically, by 2007 Halutz was no longer popular due to his role in the 2006 Lebanon War, which was widely viewed as a failure.

13 Tzvi Lev, 'Bennett Faces Off Against IDF Chief: Why Aren't You Shooting?', *Israel National News*, 15 July 2018, http://www.israelnationalnews.com/News/News.aspx/248973.

14 Raoul Wootliff and TOI Staff, 'In Rare Critique, Army Chief Blasts Bennett for Disparaging IDF Lawyers', *Times of Israel*, 19 November 2018, https://www.timesofisrael.com/in-rare-critique-army-chief-blasts-bennett-for-disparaging-idf-lawyers/.

15 Michael Bachner, 'Before He Quit, Liberman Said to Tell Top Brass They Sound Like Peace Now', *Times of Israel*, 6 December 2018, https://www.timesofisrael.com/before-he-quit-liberman-said-to-tell-idf-top-brass-they-sound-like-peace-now/.

16 TOI Staff, 'Coalition Chair: Security Chiefs "All Become Leftists" On the Job', *Times of Israel,* 25 June 2016, https://www.timesofisrael.com/coalition-chair-security-chiefs-all-become-leftists-on-the-job/.

17 Yaakov Katz, 'Facing Terror, Should Israel "Divorce" the Palestinians?', *Jerusalem Post*, 13 December 2018, https://www.jpost.com/Opinion/Editors-Notes-The-West-Bank-generals-speak-574309.

18 Amir Tibon, 'Netanyahu vs. the Generals', Politico, 3 July 2016, https://www.politico.com/magazine/story/2016/06/netanyahu-prime-minister-obama-president-foreign-policy-us-israeli-relations-middle-east-iran-defense-forces-idf-214004.

19 Personal interviews with Brig.-Gen. (Retd) Dani Arditi, Reut, Israel, 27 June 2017; MK Eyal Ben Reuven, Jerusalem, 27 June 2017; Brig.-Gen. (Retd) Ilan Paz, Moshav Kerem Maharal, Israel, 14 June 2016; Maj.-Gen. (Retd) Amram Mitzna, Tel Aviv, 2 July 2017; Maj.-Gen. (Retd) MK Elazar Stern, Jerusalem, 27 June 2017. Two interviewees requested their names be withheld: a senior general still in uniform, interviewed on 25 September 2017, and a former head of the Mossad, interviewed on 5 July 2017.

20 Personal interview with Major-General (Retd) MK Elazar Stern, Jerusalem, 27 June 2017.

21 Gadi Taub, 'Can Democracy and Nationalism Be Understood Apart?

The Case of Zionism and its Critics',
*Journal of Israeli History: Politics,
Society, Culture*, vol. 26, no. 2,
September 2007, pp. 157–77.

22 Shaul Arieli, 'The Dangers of
Annexing the West Bank', *Haaretz*, 27
January 2017, http://www.haaretz.
com/opinion/.premium-1.767461;
Sergio DellaPergola, 'To Be the State
of the Jews, You Need a Conspicuous
Jewish Majority', in George E. Johnson
(ed.), 'What Will the Jewish World
Look Like in 2050?', *Moment Magazine*,
13 February 2017, p. 33; and personal
interview with Sergio DellaPergola,
Hebrew University, Jerusalem, 21 June
2017; phone interview with Arnon
Soffer, 2 July 2017.

23 Moran Azulay and Elior Levy,
'Report: Equal Number of Jews,
Muslims Live from River to the
Sea', Ynet News, 26 March 2018,
https://www.ynetnews.com/
articles/0,7340,L-5198085,00.html.

24 Personal interview with a senior general still in uniform, Washington DC,
25 September 2017.

25 Personal interview with a former head
of the Mossad, Israel, 5 July 2017.

26 Personal interview with Brig.-Gen.
(Retd) Assaf Orion, Washington DC,
26 December 2018.

27 Noam Sheizaf, 'Endgame', *Haaretz*, 15
July 2010, http://www.haaretz.com/
israel-news/endgame-1.302128.

28 Hezki Baruch, 'Sovereignty Panel: A
Return to Zionism and a Response to
Terrorism', Arutz 7, 10 October 2015,
http://www.inn.co.il/News/News.
aspx/307482.

29 Raphael Ahren, 'Shaked Touts
"Confederation" of Jordan, Gaza,
and Parts of West Bank', *Times

of Israel*, 29 November 2018,
https://www.timesofisrael.com/
shaked-touts-confederation-of-jordan-
gaza-and-parts-of-west-bank/.

30 Ariel Kahana, 'The Next Knesset
Will Apply Israeli Sovereignty in
Judea and Samaria', *Israel Hayom*,
1 February 2019, https://www.
israelhayom.com/2019/02/01/
the-next-knesset-will-apply-israeli-
sovereignty-in-judea-and-samaria/.

31 Shaul Givoli, 'The Road to
Israelestine', *Haaretz*, 14 May 2009,
https://www.haaretz.com/1.5052493.

32 Personal interview with Dr Uzi Arad,
Tel Aviv, 17 June 2016.

33 Benny Morris, *One State, Two States:
Resolving the Israel/Palestine Conflict*
(New Haven, CT: Yale University
Press, 2009), pp. 61–2, 78–80.

34 Tom Segev, *1967: Israel, the War, and
the Year that Transformed the Middle
East* (New York: Metropolitan Books,
2007), p. 359.

35 See Shlomo Gazit, *Trapped Fools: Thirty
Years of Israeli Policy in the Territories*
(London: Frank Cass, 2003), p. 544;
and Avi Raz, *The Bride and the Dowry:
Israel, Jordan, and the Palestinians in the
Aftermath of the June 1967 War* (New
Haven, CT: Yale University Press), p.
187.

36 Amnon Barzilai, 'A Brief History of
the Missed Opportunity', *Haaretz*,
5 June 2002, https://www.haaretz.
com/1.5162716.

37 Gazit, *Trapped Fools*, p. 142.

38 *Ibid.*, pp. 142–3; Raz, *The Bride and the
Dowry*, p. 41.

39 Raz, *The Bride and the Dowry*, pp.
26–31, 40–1; Segev, *1967*, p. 513.

40 Gazit, *Trapped Fools*, pp. 154–7.

41 Segev, *1967*, p. 551.

42 Raz, *The Bride and the Dowry*, p. 48.

43 Yehoshafat Harkabi, *Arab Strategies and Israel's Response* (New York: Free Press, 1977).

44 Yehoshafat Harkabi, 'Striving to Attain the Possible', *Cahiers de la Méditerranée*, Année 1984, p. 171.

45 See Yehoshafat Harkabi and Salim Tamari, 'Yehoshafat Harkabi: Choosing Between Bad and Worse', *Journal of Palestine Studies*, vol. 16, no. 3, Spring 1987, pp. 46–7.

46 Yeshohafat Harkabi, *Israel's Fateful Hour* (New York: Harper & Row, 1988), p. 50.

47 Guy Ziv, *Why Hawks Become Doves: Shimon Peres and Foreign Policy Change in Israel* (Albany, NY: SUNY Press, 2014), p. 102.

48 *Ibid.*, pp. 99–100, 112.

49 See Dan Kurzman, *Soldier of Peace: The Life of Yitzhak Rabin* (New York: HarperCollins, 1998), pp. 24 and 473; and Ziv, *Why Hawks Become Doves*, pp. 103–4.

50 Eldad Beck, 'Barak Conditionally Supports Palestinian State', *Jerusalem Post*, 26 January 1997.

51 Sarah Honig, 'Labor Plank Supports Palestinian State', *Jerusalem Post*, 15 May 1997.

52 'Ayalon, Ex-PLO Official Nusseibeh Launch Joint Peace Drive', *Haaretz*, 25 June 2003, https://www.haaretz.com/1.5485750.

53 Asher Susser, *Israel, Jordan, and Palestine: The Two-state Imperative* (Waltham, MA: Brandeis University Press, 2012), p. 60.

54 Greg Myre, '4 Israeli Ex-Security Chiefs Denounce Sharon's Hard Line', *New York Times*, 15 November 2003, https://www.nytimes.com/2003/11/15/world/4-israeli-ex-security-chiefs-denounce-sharon-s-hard-line.html.

55 Jason Keyser, 'Ex-Israel Security Chiefs Push for Truce', AP, 14 November 2003.

56 Mitch Ginsburg, 'How I Persuaded Six Intelligence Chiefs to Pour Out Their Hearts', *Times of Israel*, 11 January 2013, https://www.timesofisrael.com/how-i-persuaded-six-intelligence-chiefs-to-pour-out-their-hearts/.

57 Address by Prime Minister Ariel Sharon at the fourth Herzliya conference, 18 December 2003, http://www.mfa.gov.il/mfa/pressroom/2003/pages/address%20by%20pm%20ariel%20sharon%20at%20the%20fourth%20herzliya.aspx.

58 Ginsburg, 'How I Persuaded Six Intelligence Chiefs to Pour Out Their Hearts'.

59 See Peace Now, 'Peace Now's Annual Settlement Construction Report for 2017', http://peacenow.org.il/wp-content/uploads/2018/03/Annual-Report-2017_Final.pdf; and Tovah Lazaroff, 'Day After Election Called, Netanyahu Green Lights New Settler Homes', *Jerusalem Post*, 25 December 2018, https://www.jpost.com/Israel-News/Netanyahu-fast-tracks-Palestinian-land-seizures-575418.

60 Yotam Berger, 'Netanyahu Vows to Never Remove Israeli Settlements from West Bank: "We're Here to Stay, Forever"', *Haaretz*, 29 August 2017, https://www.haaretz.com/israel-news/netanyahu-vows-to-never-remove-west-bank-settlements-we-re-here-to-stay-1.5446461.

61 Eliott C. McLaughlin, 'Israel's PM Netanyahu: No Palestinian State on My Watch', CNN, 16 March 2015, http://www.cnn.

com/2015/03/16/middleeast/
israel-netanyahu-palestinian-state/.

62 Stuart Winer and TOI Staff, 'Likud,
Right Pounce on Gantz Stump
Speech as Proof He Is a Leftist',
Times of Israel, 29 January 2019,
https://www.timesofisrael.com/
likud-right-pounce-on-gantz-stump-
speech-as-proof-he-is-a-leftist/.

63 David Rosenberg, 'Gantz–Lapid
Government Means a Palestinian
State', Israel National News,
2 February 2019, http://www.
israelnationalnews.com/News/News.
aspx/259423.

64 David M. Halbfinger, 'As Netanyahu
Seeks Re-election, the Future of the
West Bank is Now on the Ballot',
New York Times, 7 April 2019, https://
www.nytimes.com/2019/04/07/world/
middleeast/israel-election-netanyahu-
west-bank.html.

65 Amos Yadlin and Gilead Sher,
'Unilateral Peace', *Foreign Policy*,
18 March 2013, https://www.gsher-
law.com/webfiles/fck/file/articles/
Unilateral%20Peace%20-%20By%20

Amos%20Yadlin%20and%20
Gilead%20Sher%20_%20Foreign%20
Policy.pdf.

66 Major-General (Retd) Amnon Reshef,
'A Crucial Decision for Israel's
Security', *Yediot Ahronot*, 16 March
2015, http://en.cis.org.il/2015/03/16/a-
crucial-decision-for-israels-security/.

67 Trudy Rubin, 'Bold Proposals for
the Middle East', *Mercury News*,
8 February 2013, https://www.
mercurynews.com/2013/02/08/
trudy-rubin-bold-proposals-for-the-
middle-east/.

68 Judi Ari Gross, 'Proposal Would
Split Israel from Palestinians – But
Don't Call it a Peace Plan', *Times of
Israel*, 8 October 2018, https://www.
timesofisrael.com/proposal-would-
split-israel-from-palestinians-but-
dont-call-it-a-peace-plan/.

69 'The INSS Plan: A Political–Security
Framework for the Israeli–Palestinian
Arena', INSS, 8 October 2018,
http://www.inss.org.il/event/
inss-plan-political-security-frame-
work-israeli-palestinian-arena/.

Russia and the European Union: Crisis and Prospects

Vladimir Ryzhkov

In the drama of 2014 – political crisis in Ukraine, Russia's annexation of Crimea, armed conflict in eastern Ukraine – Russia–EU relations turned almost overnight into confrontation and near conflict. As Yury Borko has observed, five basic factors define that confrontation today: 1) mutual diplomatic and economic sanctions and counter-sanctions; 2) a 'freeze' in official relations and mechanisms for cooperation under existing treaties and agreements, as well as in the working relationship between the two sides; 3) a 'freeze' in both official and unofficial talks on preparing a new foundational Russia–EU agreement to replace the outdated Partnership and Cooperation Agreement of 1994 that expired in 2007, and that both parties have renewed annually since; 4) chronic military tensions and confrontational rhetoric – including accusations that, among other things, Russia supports extremist, right-wing, populist and anti-European forces within the EU, and that its intelligence agencies attempted to assassinate Sergei Skripal in the UK – accompanied by actions such as military exercises and flyovers by military aircraft; and 5) the resultant, near-complete breakdown in mutual trust. Russia–EU relations are now at their lowest point in history, having been in deep crisis for five years.[1]

Most politicians and experts are extremely pessimistic about the possibility of restoring constructive relations. They hold out little hope for resuming

Vladimir Ryzhkov is a Professor in the Department of International Relations at National Research University Higher School of Economics. He was Head of the Russian State Duma delegation to the Russia–EU Parliamentary Cooperation Committee (Russia–EU PCC) from 1997 to 2000.

Survival | vol. 61 no. 3 | June–July 2019 | pp. 139–164   DOI 10.1080/00396338.2019.1614789

institutional dialogue and multilateral cooperation, or for laying the basis for new and more positive relations. Yet some qualitative changes are in evidence that should restore hope to both sides, if not for an imminent breakthrough in relations, then at least for greater openness to dialogue and a search for solutions. Firstly, the crisis has shifted since 2015 from its acute phase to a smouldering, almost routine phase. The parties have grown tired of the confrontation, have recognised the strategic futility of its continuation and have become politically fixated on the resultant status quo (primarily in Ukraine).

Secondly, EU politicians now have a more balanced understanding of the state of affairs in Ukraine. In particular, they are starting to accept that the authorities in Kiev – and not just those in Moscow and Donetsk – bear a share of the responsibility for the failure to implement the Minsk agreements intended to settle the conflict in eastern Ukraine. One indication of this is a recent interview that EU Ambassador to Russia Markus Ederer gave to Interfax, in which he said: 'there is a lack of political will to implement these Minsk agreements … on both sides'.[2]

Sanctions have burdened the Russian economy

Thirdly, the imposition of an increasing number of sanctions and counter-sanctions has burdened both the Russian economy, which continues to be afflicted by economic stagnation, and that of the EU, which has never fully recovered from the 2008–09 crisis.[3] Russian leaders constantly emphasise the need to intensify mutually beneficial economic ties in trade, manufacturing, investment and innovation.[4]

Fourthly, the Russian president, prime minister and foreign minister have been meeting regularly with senior EU officials and the leaders of individual EU states. This testifies to both sides' continuing desire to restore the kind of normal relations they both consider obligatory and to overcome the current crisis. In the first ten months of 2018 alone, Russian President Vladimir Putin either met with or telephoned the leaders of at least 12 of the 28 EU countries (Austria, Belgium, Bulgaria, Croatia, Finland, France, Germany, Greece, Hungary, Italy, Portugal and Spain).[5] Over the same period, Russian Foreign Minister Sergei Lavrov met with his counterparts in Austria, Belgium, Croatia, Cyprus, Denmark, France, Germany,

Greece, Hungary, Italy, the Netherlands, Portugal, Slovakia, Slovenia and Spain – that is, with the foreign ministers of 15 EU countries – either in Moscow or during his travels.[6] In addition, Lavrov held talks with EU High Representative for Foreign Affairs and Security Policy Federica Mogherini, German Chancellor Angela Merkel and French President Emmanuel Macron.[7] Such frequent contact with EU officials contradicts the popular but incorrect belief that relations are frozen and testifies, if not to a trend towards a normalisation of relations, then at least to a mutual desire that they should be normalised.

Finally, the presidency of Donald Trump in the US has led to major changes in international relations, with consequences for both Russia and the EU. The Trump administration's reflexive protectionism and disruption of the existing system of international trade runs counter to the basic positions of both the EU and Russia. The same holds true of Washington's decision to withdraw from the nuclear deal with Iran and the Intermediate-Range Nuclear Forces (INF) Treaty. The fact that the EU and Russia both disagree with the White House's policies and decisions reinforces their motivation to improve their own bilateral relations. China is also a factor in this equation. Beijing remains a strategic partner for Russia, a relationship of some importance to Moscow given that the West has not only maintained, but also increased, its sanctions against Russia. At the same time, it is in Russia's national interest to avoid a one-sided foreign policy characterised by excessive dependence on its large eastern neighbour. This too is a motivation to normalise relations with the EU.

Thus, a comparatively new international and economic situation has arisen that may well offer an opportunity for the phased restoration of Russia–EU cooperation – or for such cooperation to emerge on an entirely new basis – however dubious those prospects might seem at present. The Russian expert community generally agrees on the need for Russia to normalise relations with the EU, and with the West more broadly, in order to make progress in the urgent task of national development.[8] The purpose of this article is to consider additional possible arguments in favour of restoring and, more broadly, forming new, positive relations between Russia and the EU, and to suggest several possible steps in that direction.

Finding the compatible in incompatible positions

The EU responded to the Ukraine crisis by imposing, and later expanding, a raft of political, diplomatic, economic, financial and technological sanctions against Russia beginning in 2014.[9] The EU Council has renewed these sanctions every six months since then. In addition, immediately following Russia's annexation of Crimea in March 2014, the leading EU countries of France, Germany, Italy and the United Kingdom supported excluding Russia from the G8. The EU also halted systematic meetings and working dialogues within the framework of the Partnership Cooperation Agreement (primarily regular, top-level Russia–EU summits and cooperation within other existing formats).

In March 2016, the EU Council unanimously approved the five guiding principles of its foreign policy towards Russia that are still in force today.[10] Firstly, it stated that the future of Russia–EU relations is inextricably linked to the situation in Ukraine. Full implementation of the Minsk agreements is the prerequisite for any improvement in relations. The EU also confirmed that it considers Russia's annexation of Crimea illegal, and unequivocally refused to grant it official recognition.

Secondly, the EU declared its desire for closer ties with Russia's former Soviet neighbours, particularly in Central Asia. It also declared its desire to bolster its internal resilience, particularly in terms of energy security, hybrid threats and strategic communication. Fourthly, it identified a need for selective engagement with Russia, both on fundamental foreign-policy issues (such as Iran, the Middle East, Syria, the Korean Peninsula, migration, climate change and the fight against terrorism) and on other issues where the European Union has a clear interest. Finally, the EU expressed its willingness to provide greater support to Russia's civil society, facilitate and support people-to-people contacts, and develop scientific, cultural, educational and other forms of exchange, with particular attention to young people, seeing this as a useful investment in the future of the relationship.

Moscow's official position on these issues seems at first glance to be the exact opposite of the EU's. From Russia's point of view, the annexation of Crimea is a done deal and is not up for discussion. Russia believes that the authorities in Kiev, more than anyone else, hold the key to resolving the conflict in eastern Ukraine, and perceives the EU's Eastern Partnership programme, and its stated desire to expand its cooperation and presence in Central Asia, as placing the EU in intense competition with Russia. Moscow believes that Brussels might want to undermine integration processes in the former Soviet space.[11] The EU countries' desire to strengthen their internal resilience in the fields of energy, cyber security, and hybrid and political threats – encompassing, among other things, fake news, support for radical anti-European political forces and so on – is interpreted as an implicit accusation that Russia is involved in dangerous and destructive activities in these areas. Moscow also harbours suspicions about Brussels' intention to support Russian civil society as a potentially subversive and even hostile action – a form of retaliation for the decision by Russian authorities to crack down on civil society and to limit the ability of Russian non-governmental organisations (NGOs) to accept foreign assistance. (Those that have received foreign assistance have been derided as 'foreign agents' and 'undesirable organisations', among other labels.[12]) This stance appears irreconcilable with the EU's, but is it really?

As paradoxical as it might seem, Russia and the EU share a wide range of interests and political approaches, even in areas where they appear to disagree. These might serve as the basis for overcoming specific obstacles and for gradually forming new, constructive relations. We will consider these differences in light of the five EU principles.

Ukraine

The Ukrainian crisis is the most difficult issue blocking the restoration of relations. The country's recent presidential election, however, could present an opportunity for moving towards a resolution of this long-standing dispute. New president-elect Volodymyr Zelensky was widely supported by voters in the east and centre of Ukraine. He expressed a readiness for negotiations with Putin, and his political rhetoric generally seems more moderate than that of his predecessor, Petro Poroshenko. The Kremlin has also expressed a cautious willingness to have contacts with the new Ukrainian leadership. This makes the possibility of a positive dialogue between Moscow and Kiev, though still extremely difficult, more likely.

In his speech at the Valdai Discussion Club in Sochi on 18 October 2018, Putin reaffirmed the Russian leadership's firm commitment to the Minsk agreements as the basis for resolving the conflict and as a compromise document that all sides have signed, one that takes into account the interests of all the parties to the conflict.[13] At the same time, he declared Russia's interest 'in restoring full-format relations with Ukraine' and expressed Moscow's hope that 'it will be possible to establish at least some kind of relations with the country's new leadership and to reach agreement on something'. Russia and the EU should do everything in their power to make use of the opportunity presented by the start of a new political cycle in Ukraine.

A solution concerning eastern Ukraine is attainable

It is important to note that the question of Crimea and that of eastern Ukraine should not be treated as a single issue. The difference is not that Crimea is no longer a problem as Moscow asserts, but that the disagreement is insoluble under current circumstances, whereas a solution concerning eastern Ukraine is attainable. It is understood that the EU and Kiev, regardless of who their particular leaders are, will never recognise Crimea as part of Russia, and that the EU will not lift its Crimea sanctions. Likewise, Russia's neighbouring and partner countries such as China, Belarus, Kazakhstan and Armenia have also declined to recognise the peninsula as part of Russia, something that Moscow will have to factor into its foreign policy. At the same time, the EU should accept the fact that the population of Crimea has largely shifted its allegiance to Russia. (The exception is the dissenting part of the Crimean Tatar community.) The good news is that Crimea itself is not a 'hot spot' and poses no humanitarian threat to Ukraine, the EU or its own citizens. The issue of Crimea must and will inevitably remain a major item on the Russia–EU agenda. It should not, however, be allowed to derail efforts to re-establish Russia–EU cooperation – even if a heavy shadow has fallen over those efforts.

Eastern Ukraine, which remains a flashpoint and a hotbed of tension, is another matter. The two sides frequently exchange mortar and artillery fire, and military skirmishes are common. As many as 1.5 million residents have fled the region. Economic and social ties between eastern Ukraine and the rest of the country have been severed. The humanitarian situation is so dire that the citizens who have stayed behind require constant aid. It would be impossible for Russia and the EU to normalise relations without first resolving the crisis in eastern Ukraine.

The parties involved must achieve not only a total ceasefire and a freeze in the conflict (which, by itself, would not improve Russia's relations with the EU or Ukraine), but should also strive to achieve a political settlement. The difficulty lies in trying to identify and act on the common interests and motives of the participants and arbiters of the conflict – Russia, Ukraine, the Luhansk and Donetsk people's republics (LPR and DPR), the EU and the US – that are now separated by deep divides. Presently, these motives and interests seem not only incompatible but inimical. The DPR and LPR want to break away from Ukraine and place themselves firmly in Russia's orbit – either as new states recognised by Moscow, following the model of Abkhazia and South Ossetia, or, like Crimea, as a part of Russia itself. Kiev is ready and willing to devolve control (sovereignty) to the eastern territories, but only under harsh terms that would not confer true autonomy or constitute genuine federalisation, and that would require the cleansing of all pro-Moscow politicians from the ranks of the authorities there. The US would like to retain its strong influence over Ukrainian leaders and policy, maintain the country's anti-Moscow stance, and perhaps eventually include Ukraine in NATO. The EU would like to see stabilisation and reconciliation in Ukraine, as well as seeing Moscow restore normal relations with both Kiev and Brussels (in keeping with the objectives of ensuring the stability and security of the entire European continent and the economic development of the EU). At the same time, however, the EU insists that Moscow be held culpable for the larger Ukrainian crisis, that full control over the eastern territories be restored to Kiev and that the Ukrainian people be given full freedom to determine their own political and military orientation (towards the EU and NATO) without taking Moscow's opinion into consideration.

Moscow opposes all of these positions. Recognising or incorporating the DPR and LPR into Russia would make the confrontation with the West and Ukraine even more dire, prolonging it and greatly increasing its cost to the

Russian economy and society. It would also mean losing Ukraine as a good neighbour forever. That is too high a cost for Russia to pay. As Putin has suggested, it would have been possible to freeze the conflict in eastern Ukraine with the aid of UN peacekeeping forces.[14] Over the long term, however, the freezing of the conflict and the resulting emergence of new, unrecognised and openly pro-Moscow quasi-states in eastern Ukraine would effectively mean that Russia would remain in conflict with Ukraine, the EU and the West. This would run counter to Russia's long-term interests. The conflict in eastern Ukraine does not need to be frozen, but rather resolved through a full-fledged political settlement.

Russia is seeking security guarantees

Moscow opposes any solution that restores Kiev's sovereignty over Donetsk and Luhansk but that does not guarantee their autonomy and the protection of their Russian-speaking populations; that does not guarantee them the right to choose their own regional and local authorities, and to use the Russian language; and that does not restore the economic and social structures in those regions that provide for unrestricted ties to, and open borders with, Russia. In addition, and what the EU only poorly grasps, is that Ukraine's military and political orientation is a defining issue for Russia. It would be militarily and strategically unacceptable for Russia to share a border with a Ukrainian state that was part of NATO, or that allowed Western military infrastructure to be stationed on its territory. President Putin made this clear in his 'Crimean speech' on 18 March 2014. In his remarks, he closely linked the desire of Ukraine's post-Maidan leadership to join NATO with the possible appearance of NATO military bases on Ukrainian territory, particularly a NATO naval base in Sevastopol.[15] It is possible that leaders in Kiev and Washington have precisely this outcome in mind. If so, this would render the political and strategic differences between Russia and the US plus Ukraine intractable. Moscow would like to achieve a settlement to the conflict, but only on the condition that the people of eastern Ukraine receive reliable legal and political guarantees as detailed in the Minsk agreements. Russia is also seeking reliable guarantees for its own security, including Ukraine's neutrality (which would foreclose its inclusion in NATO) and the non-deployment of Western military infrastructure on Ukrainian territory.

Furthermore, Moscow cannot agree with the EU's unilateral assessment that Russia is solely responsible for the conflict. Moscow insists that the EU acknowledge its own responsibility for taking the dangerous and reckless step of drawing Ukraine into association with the EU without considering Russia's concerns, and that Brussels acknowledge the violent and illegitimate nature of the transfer of power in Kiev in early 2014.

The differences between the sides are deep and acute. However, the strategic need to normalise relations between Russia and Ukraine, and between Russia and the EU, demands that politicians and experts search for common ground in order to ease tensions and facilitate a political settlement to the conflict. This will not be accomplished with a single political decision. But the parties do have common interests and should be able to find a basis for normalising relations, even under the extreme circumstances that now exist. The residents of the DPR and LPR want to resume normal life in a law-based democratic state – that is, with firm guarantees that their rights and freedoms will be respected; with political representation at the local, regional and national levels; and with pardons and amnesty for participants in the conflict. Moscow is interested in seeing the conflict end and relieving itself of the considerable political and economic costs associated with it; in restoring normal relations and cooperation with Kiev and the EU; and in the lifting of the Donetsk sanctions – not to be confused with the Crimea sanctions, which are less burdensome. The EU would like to see the situation in and around Ukraine stabilise. This would open the way for the restoration of relations with Russia and the lifting of most sanctions except those imposed over Crimea.

Taken together, all this creates a certain potential for a phased settlement of the conflict, given sufficient readiness by all sides to compromise and make concessions for the sake of peace, stability and cooperation. Moscow should make resolving the crisis in eastern Ukraine a foreign-policy priority. This would entail a willingness to accept a phased return to Kiev of sovereignty over specific territories of the Donetsk and Luhansk regions of Ukraine that are currently under the control of the DPR and LPR. Moscow should also agree that, after the Minsk agreements are fulfilled, control over the Russian–Ukrainian border in that region will be handed back to Kiev; and that elections will be held in that region according to Ukrainian law and under the auspices of international observers. Russia should take part in the restoration of the region's shattered economy and infrastructure, and stop its media campaign aimed at discrediting and defaming Ukraine. Finally, it should withdraw all military personnel and mercenaries, if any are present in the region.

Kiev should carry out its part of the Minsk agreements in full, including its provisions on pardons and amnesty; the exchange of all prisoners and hostages; the restoration of social transfers and economic ties; the unblocking of lines of contact; constitutional reform guaranteeing the decentralisation (or federation) of and special status for individual eastern Ukrainian regions; and the holding of elections there by agreement of all parties and under international control. Ukraine must take Russia's concerns about its strategic security seriously and be prepared to enshrine appropriate guarantees in legally binding agreements (bilateral and multilateral).

To implement these mutual measures, it will be necessary to restore direct and regular contacts between senior Russian and Ukrainian leaders, and to allow DPR and LPR representatives to participate if necessary. The hope is that this will be facilitated by Ukraine's presidential election. Certainly, the broad political mandate Zelensky has received from the citizens of Ukraine creates opportunities to move forward. The current leadership of the DPR and LPR, as well as the populations of those territories, should agree to the prospect of returning to the legal and political jurisdiction of Ukraine, and to full participation in the political and economic life of the country. Of course, this will be subject to their receiving all of the necessary guarantees associated with constitutional reform, broad decentralisation (federalisation), autonomy, guarantees of their rights and freedoms, pardons and amnesty, unrestricted cross-border ties with Russia, implementation of a programme for restoring the region's economy and infrastructure, the return of refugees and political representation in Ukrainian power structures.

The EU should contribute wherever possible to the implementation of the Minsk agreements (including within the framework of the 'Normandy format' bringing together France, Germany, Russia and Ukraine), acknowledge its own share of responsibility for the crisis, and participate in the restoration of the Ukrainian economy and the reconstruction of affected regions. Once the settlement process is under way and steps have been taken to normalise relations, the EU should lift the sanctions it imposed on Russia. The EU should also participate in the development and adoption of international legal security guarantees with respect to all its eastern neighbours, and particularly with regard to Ukraine and Russia.

The US must renounce all actions that could aggravate the confrontation between Russia and Ukraine, and take all steps within its power to achieve a final settlement of the conflict in eastern Ukraine. The US, Russia, the EU and Ukraine should develop and adopt measures and legal agreements providing additional security guarantees for all the countries of the region, including Ukraine and Russia. The implementation of these measures will require goodwill and considerable time, effort and resources from all of the parties, but the benefit gained from reaching a settlement and restoring positive relations would far outweigh the difficulties encountered along the way. Such a prospect more than warrants a firm commitment from all the parties.

Eastern Partnership countries
The countries of the EU Eastern Partnership programme, which are part of the EU neighbourhood policy covering Ukraine, Moldova, Belarus, Armenia, Georgia and Azerbaijan, have become an arena of competition between Russia and the EU, but it would be unwise to exaggerate the intensity of this competition or to cast it as a potential conflict. Rather, it is worth looking for opportunities for Russia and the EU to cooperate in the region.

Each of these six countries is unique and occupies a special place in the context of Russia–EU relations. Ukraine has already been discussed. Armenia and Belarus, through their membership of the Eurasian Economic Union (EAEU) and the Collective Security Treaty Organisation (CSTO), are participants in a process of Eurasian integration and security cooperation that is largely oriented towards Russia – although they are also expanding their mutually beneficial cooperation with the EU. Georgia, especially after the war in 2008, is focused entirely on the EU and the West, although the worst phase of its conflict with Russia is now past. Moldova is generally oriented towards the EU, but skilfully manages to strike a balance between the EU and Russia, diligently avoiding anything that would strain relations with either party. Drawing on a wealth of natural and financial resources, Azerbaijan conducts an independent and multipronged foreign policy, although Turkey remains its closest foreign-policy partner.

The EU's Eastern Partnership is a rather modest programme with limited resources, and the EU itself is preoccupied with its more pressing internal problems. By contrast, the region is a top priority for Russia, as noted in the country's Foreign Policy Concept.[16] This asymmetry between Russia's active presence and influence in the Eastern Partnership area and the EU's more limited involvement is likely to persist. Nevertheless, the development of Eurasian integration and a Eurasian system of security are, in principle, compatible with the building up of mutually beneficial cooperation between the EU and the members of the Commonwealth of Independent States (CIS), the EAEU and the CSTO. Armenia, for example, is a member of all three organisations and wishes to maintain a strong military and political alliance with Russia, yet is simultaneously interested in developing the broadest possible economic ties with the EU.[17] As part of its foreign-policy strategy, Armenia signed a Comprehensive and Enhanced Partnership Agreement with the EU – a new generation of agreement – in Brussels on 24 November 2017. The Armenian parliament quickly ratified the agreement and it conditionally entered into force on 1 June 2018. The agreement is intended to promote the development of political, industrial and trade relations between Armenia and the EU. Since 2014, the EU has allocated €120 million in financial assistance to Armenia and provided €412m in investment.[18] The two parties now share a simplified visa arrangement, and the EU has become Armenia's primary export market and its second-largest source of imports after Russia. Armenia benefits from the EU's Generalised Scheme of Preferences (GSP+) for trade, and 95% of its exports to the EU are not subject to export taxes. Moscow generally has no problem with this state of affairs: Maria Zakharova, a spokesperson for the Russian Foreign Ministry, said in 2017 that 'We promote our relations with countries, including Armenia, on a mutually beneficial basis and with full understanding that each country has its own foreign policy interests, goals and tasks. We respect that.'[19]

The Armenian model demonstrates that it is possible for a country to seek the closest possible relations with both the EAEU and the EU while not just avoiding conflicts, but also building mutually beneficial cooperation. It is telling that the EU and Kazakhstan signed a similar agreement in December 2015. Such a measured approach among all the parties in the post-Soviet space, and particularly in the area covered by the EU's Eastern Partnership programme, should make it possible to avoid rivalry and conflict. Of course, the EU should recognise and accommodate Russia's extensive interests in the region, including by agreeing to develop a trilateral negotiations format (that is, one that allows Russia in acute cases to participate in EU negotiations with Eastern Partnership countries). For its part, Russia should raise no objections to a deepening of cooperation between the EU and the countries covered by its Eastern Partnership programme, so long as such cooperation does not undermine Russia's security, trade or economic interests, or the development of the Russia-oriented Eurasian groupings.[20] The EU Eastern Partnership members should soberly assess their own national interests and maximise the benefits of building relationships with both Moscow and Brussels.

The EU should accommodate Russia's interests

Despite the strong economic links between the EU and the EAEU – the EU is the largest trade partner of the EAEU, with more than 50% of EAEU exports going to the EU and 41% of its total imports coming from the EU[21] – the relationship between the two organisations remains underdeveloped. EAEU bodies officially proposed establishing contacts with EU institutions in 2015, but such contacts have yet to be put in place. The EU, in addition to remaining highly sceptical of Eurasian integration and treating it as a rival process, projects its negative attitude towards Russia onto the whole grouping. Nevertheless, the possibility of establishing EU–EAEU relations is commanding growing interest.[22] It might be possible to deepen trust and spur trade and investment by establishing official contacts between the EU and EAEU, carrying out a broad exchange of information, and implementing joint programmes in such wide-ranging fields as the digitisation of customs procedures, the development of transport corridors, the safe use of strategic infrastructure facilities, the harmonisation of standards and procedures, and much more.[23] A more developed EU–EAEU relationship would create a neutral venue for dialogue and, potentially, harmonisation of Russian and EU positions, helping to reduce the Russia–EU rivalry in the post-Soviet space.

Building resilience

The EU has forcefully accused Russia of attempting to undermine its political stability, supporting radical anti-European forces in elections, waging cyber attacks against civilian and military facilities, using chemical weapons against EU citizens (the Skripal case) and using energy dependency to undermine the EU's strength and security, among other complaints. The Russian leadership has categorically denied all of these accusations as groundless, to no avail. After the attempt on Skripal's life, Brussels evicted a large number of Russian diplomats serving in a variety of EU countries.[24] The EU is also preparing to take action against so-called 'fake news' that it sees as destabilising to the domestic policies of EU countries, especially in the run-up to the European parliamentary elections in May 2019. Additionally, the EU plans to develop specific measures for countering cyber attacks and foreign hackers.[25] It has continued in its efforts to reduce its energy dependence on Russia, imposing increasingly stringent demands on Russian energy suppliers and displaying a generally negative attitude towards the Nord Stream 2.[26] Russia has no choice but to contend with the EU's concerns and complaints because they represent a significant obstacle to the restoration of institutional dialogue and a general improvement in relations. In addition, real damage could be done to projects of major economic importance to Russia, primarily in the field of energy, where Moscow risks losing significant market share.

Moscow must also stop the unbridled campaign by state-controlled media to discredit the EU and the West. Otherwise, it will prove impossible to restore mutual trust and create an atmosphere of cooperation. Russia and the EU should both abandon their mutually accusatory rhetoric, stop branding each other as enemies and end all discussion of the possibility of a military clash. Both sides should also drastically curtail all forms of dangerous and subversive activities by their intelligence services. These only poison relations and hinder every attempt at constructive dialogue. The same applies to all attempts to interfere in elections, spread fake news or support radical political forces. From now on, both sides should proceed from a shared understanding of the importance of supporting the internal stability of both the EU and Russia. This will require that both parties adopt strategies aimed not at undermining and weakening each other, but showing respect and cooperating in the interests of successful mutual development.

In particular, this will require opening a dialogue on ground rules and developing international standards in the sensitive and dangerous field of cyber security. Experts recommend adopting such principles as non-interference in political processes, establishing a common definition of a cyber attack, pledging not to attack states' critical infrastructure, internet resources or military facilities – especially its missile and nuclear facilities – and joining forces to stop hackers unaffiliated with specific states.[27] Doing so will require that a discussion of cyber security be either established or resumed in all the relevant forums, including the UN and the Organisation for Security and Cooperation in Europe (OSCE), between Russia and the EU, and between Russia and individual EU countries.

Selective engagement and exchanges

Both Russia and the EU recognise the need to preserve and develop selective engagement. Indeed, this is the only point on which both Moscow and Brussels agree unconditionally. Of course, selective engagement falls far short of the strategic partnership they strove for in the past, but it is still better than nothing. The broader and more concrete the cooperation, the stronger the mutual trust that will result, and the sooner practical prerequisites will be created for the resumption of a normal, multifaceted partnership. Official declarations are not enough: what is needed are practical steps and tools.

Selective engagement could be based on the list of issues that both sides have already agreed are important. Mogherini suggests that the parties reach settlements on Syria, Libya, the Persian Gulf, the Middle East peace process and the Ukrainian crisis; preserve the nuclear agreement with Iran; deal with the situations in the Western Balkans and the Korean Peninsula;

and foster cooperation among citizens and civil society.[28] Ederer also points to cross-border cooperation, cooperation in the Baltic region, developing trade and investment, student exchanges, the rising number of multiple-entry visas that the EU has granted Russian citizens and continued progress towards a simplified visa regime, and forming an energy partnership.[29] However, after the events in Ukraine in 2014 and the levelling of sanctions and counter-sanctions, the cooperation that had existed in many areas was frozen or significantly scaled back.

Even in the midst of what an EU–Russia Expert Network on Foreign Policy report describes as 'de-institutionalization and estrangement', members of the network are making systematic and valuable efforts to identify possible areas for selective engagement.[30] On the whole, the authors of the report are sceptical about the prospects for improving relations between Russia and the EU in the near future, noting that 'sustainable improvement of the relationship and greater convergence currently seem to be a vague aspiration rather than a realistic long-term goal.'[31] In their opinion, both sides are now 'unable and unwilling to change the status quo'.[32] The authors nevertheless propose a number of new areas of cooperation.

Within the framework of the common neighbourhood, the authors propose supporting confidence-building measures in eastern Ukraine, primarily aimed at achieving a sustainable ceasefire and creating conditions for the implementation of the Minsk agreements; initiating senior-level talks between the EU, the EAEU and signatory countries to the Deep and Comprehensive Free Trade Areas (Georgia, Moldova and Ukraine); and initiating senior-level talks between the EU, the EAEU, China and the Central Asian states to discuss China's Belt and Road Initiative and to establish permanent ties. Russia could cooperate with the EU in multilateral forums to preserve the nuclear deal with Iran, continue the search for joint positions and actions in Syria, and identify and add substance to the less politicised areas of cooperation such as climate change and environmental issues, the global commons (within the UN) and the development of economic relations (within the OSCE). The report recommends that Russia and the EU develop bilateral relations by studying possibilities for economic cooperation in areas not targeted by mutual sanctions. These include providing support for small and medium-sized businesses in Russia and avoiding the imposition of new economic barriers. It calls for creating conditions for more active and multifaceted civil cooperation (in education, science, culture and cross-border mobility, between representatives of civil society and between regions). It is necessary to improve citizens' ease of mobility as much as possible, even when that would require unilateral measures to facilitate the visa process. Finally, at a time when Russian and EU institutions have frozen all contact, it would make sense to initiate an expert dialogue on contentious issues to improve each side's understanding of the other's motives and arguments, and to create better conditions for restoring trust.

To advance this kind of selective engagement, the leaders of Russia, the EU and the individual EU countries must adopt, at the very least, a more positive attitude towards the efforts of agencies and non-state actors (business and civil society) to develop well-rounded cooperation. Indeed, they should set the example. The establishment of substantial and regular dialogue among the Russian and EU foreign ministries would send an important political signal on the renewal of cooperation, demonstrating that such cooperation is 'normal' and even desirable for all participants. As Andrei Zagorsky rightly notes, dialogue and cooperation at lower levels continues intermittently and deserves support, but cannot produce results without the restoration of dialogue at the highest level and without EU and Russian politicians formulating a common vision for the future format and goals of their relations.[33]

Both sides officially recognise the need to intensify cooperation between their respective civil societies. As noted, the EU considers support for civil society, and particularly youth, as one of the five priorities of its current Russia policy. Likewise, in its Foreign Policy Concept of 2016, Russia, with a few caveats (such as taking the national, cultural and other characteristics of each state into account), also declares its commitment to democratic values, including ensuring human rights and freedoms. Russia additionally recognises the need to involve institutions of civil society in solving international problems, to develop international cultural and humanitarian cooperation, and to increase interaction with international and non-governmental human-rights organisations.[34] At the same time, the EU has repeatedly levelled complaints against Russia for violating its stated principles. In 2018 alone, the EU published 17 official statements about the violation of human rights and the restriction of fundamental freedoms in Russia. These include statements condemning the imprisonment of the Ukrainian filmmaker Oleg Sentsov, the arrests of human-rights activists such as Oyub Titiev and Yuri Dmitriev, the persecution of Memorial Centre human-rights activists, the mass detentions of peaceful demonstrators, the Russian ban on the Jehovah's Witnesses organisation, the violation of human rights in Crimea and Sevastopol, the growing list of 'undesirable' (and hence banned) non-governmental organisations and the murder of Boris Nemtsov.[35] The EU generally views Russia as a country that systematically violates human rights and freedoms, including the freedom of the press and the right to assemble and demonstrate. It has criticised Russia's treatment of NGOs deemed 'foreign agents' and 'undesirable organisations', the country's restrictions on the holding of rallies and demonstrations, its broad interpretation of extremism and more. These policies, in addition to Moscow's generally negative attitude towards Russian NGOs receiving funding from abroad, greatly hamper the ability of Russian and EU civil-society actors to cooperate. More generally, the overall atmosphere of confrontation with the West cannot help but negatively influence interaction in the fields of science, higher education, culture and more.

Nevertheless, both parties must make every possible effort to develop such contacts. The EU should consider the Russian Foreign Ministry's proposal to resume the Russia–EU dialogue on human rights with a view to restoring their joint work on protecting human rights and freedoms (although the Russian proposal links such efforts with a resumption of work in other areas as well).[36] Efforts must be made to reduce, as much as possible, the negative atmosphere now surrounding possible contacts in the academic, scientific, educational, youth, environmental and other spheres. Moreover, there should be no interference in the joint work that various non-profit organisations perform in both Russia and the EU. This would help foster trust and create a general societal atmosphere that is conducive to the restoration of cooperation.

On the usefulness of old formats and agreements

In conclusion, it is worth mentioning the usefulness of old formats of cooperation and previous treaties and agreements. As Zagorsky rightly notes, there is still no viable alternative to the cooperation mechanisms established by the 1994 Partnership Cooperation Agreement between Russia and the EU,[37] and one is unlikely to appear in the near future. After the Ukrainian crisis in 2014, the EU halted the work of all official institutions and mechanisms stipulated by the agreement, as well as those established later. Some criticise the agreement as hopelessly outdated, and the previous mechanisms for cooperation as inadequate and ineffective. In fact, they provide the necessary and as yet only possible and legitimate framework for restoring dialogue at the political and technical levels. They also retain the potential to become more effective.[38] It would be in both sides' interest to hold high-level Russia–EU summits twice yearly, to have meetings between the Russian government and European Commission once every two years, and to establish a Partnership Cooperation Agreement Permanent Council at the relevant ministerial level, as well as a Parliamentary Cooperation Committee and numerous industry-specific dialogues and working groups.

A high-level political dialogue within the framework of Russia–EU summits could be useful for resolving current crises. Such a dialogue could, for example, serve as a platform for discussing joint efforts for settling the Ukrainian and Syrian crises. Renewing such summits would not mean that the EU recognises Russia's actions in Ukraine as legitimate. On the contrary, it would enable the EU to exercise greater influence and enhance its position in European and international politics. For Russia, the resumption of dialogue at the highest political level would create additional incentives to intensify efforts to resolve the crisis in eastern Ukraine, to achieve a phased lifting of sanctions and to restore normal, comprehensive cooperation with the EU. As argued above, the parties could demonstrate a willingness to compromise and hold a high-level constructive discussion on their main point of contention – the crisis in eastern Ukraine – while maintaining all of their positions of principle. Such a discussion could formulate general rules for non-confrontational interaction in those regions, additional guarantees for each side's internal stability and conditions for expanding civil contacts.

Reaching basic agreements on the thorniest issues would pave the way for reinvigorating cooperation in trade, the economy, finance, technology, security and others areas.

It would be best to start with a one-off, high-level Russia–EU summit, preceded by efforts by Russia and the other 'Normandy format' participants to achieve at least a modicum of progress towards settling the crisis in eastern Ukraine – as demonstrated by a complete ceasefire and the resumption of economic and social contacts there. Such progress would create the necessary atmosphere for holding a summit. (A direct dialogue between the Russian leadership and the new authorities in Kiev should also be established.) The summit could produce a political declaration – prepared and coordinated in advance – that contains the parties' common positions on the main issues of concern as well as steps for further joint action. The declaration could contain two main parts, with the first focusing on key political and security issues (the Ukrainian crisis, Syria, Iran, countries of the neighbourhood), and the second on renewing and expanding the dialogue and practical cooperation in specific areas that are important for both Russia and the EU. The parties should also take steps to narrow the gap between them in these areas, agreeing to resume dialogue at the ministerial and other relevant levels on human rights, energy, counter-terrorism, security, migration, finance, the economy, the harmonisation of regulation and technical standards, and the establishment of official EU–EAEU relations.[39] As a starting point, it would be enough to resume ministerial cooperation in five to seven areas. Moreover, at this stage, the parties could describe their efforts as temporary, without returning to the full-fledged format of a Permanent Partnership Cooperation Agreement Council.

Mogherini and Lavrov have already agreed that more regular Russia–EU meetings at the foreign-ministerial level should take place.[40] These meetings should be held at least three times per year, have full-fledged agendas, and produce practical decisions and recommendations for the Russian and EU political leaderships. For the actual implementation of top-level political decisions, working contacts should be resumed between the European Commission and the Russian government, with the signing of mandatory protocols for listing and implementing decisions.

It will not be possible to arrange for the lifting of all sanctions and counter-sanctions before the crisis in eastern Ukraine is resolved, but the resumption of formal dialogue at various levels, including the highest (albeit on a temporary and limited basis), would help to restore trust, accelerate efforts for settling crises and facilitate cooperation in broad areas not covered by sanctions, thereby creating the conditions for the sanctions' removal. Of course, this type of temporary and limited form of cooperation is less desirable than permanent, comprehensive and solidly institutionalised cooperation, but it would be better than the current state of affairs.

In such a deep crisis in relations as this, it is vital that the parties respect existing treaties, agreements and working papers such as 'road maps' so as to maintain continuity in relations and to not lose the little that the parties had managed to achieve in previous years. The issue of legitimacy is also important: relying on existing legal and political documents will make it easier to cope with the considerable forces in both the EU and Russia that advocate a complete severing of relations.

This is particularly true of Russia's membership in the Council of Europe. Russia's Foreign Policy Concept rightly characterises it as an 'independent universal European organization with a mandate to provide for a single legal and humanitarian space on the continent through its unique convention mechanisms'.[41] Russia has declared its commitment to work with the Council of Europe, as well as with the conventions adopted within its framework. The council is especially important for normalising Russia–EU relations, and as a forum for expressing common values and cooperating in the humanitarian sphere. Thus, recent statements by Russian officials about the possibility of Moscow withdrawing from the council are unacceptable.[42]

Russia and the EU need a strategic partnership. They share a broad foundation of common interests and projects, as well as significant experience working as partners. Even in the current climate, they should recognise those common interests and approaches, and reach compromises on the problems they face. Civil-society and economic interests are pushing the parties to normalise relations, and politicians should lose no time in doing so.

Notes

1 Yury Borko, 'Otnosheniya v treugol
'nike Rossiya – ES – SSHA' [Russia–
EU–US Relations], presentation at the
Russian Academy of Sciences Institute
of Europe, Moscow, 15 November
2018, http://www.instituteofeurope.
ru/nauchnaya-zhizn/novosti/
item/15112018.

2 'Markus Ederer: EU and Russia Are
and Will Remain Very Important
Energy Partners', Interfax, 9
November 2019, http://www.interfax.
com/interview.asp?id=869164.

3 See, for example, 'Three Years of
Sanctions: Losses and Gains', a
review of the effects of sanctions and
counter-sanctions on the EU and
Russia prepared by TASS experts
in 2017, available at https://tass.ru/
politika/4103932.

4 For example, the Russian president
met with core members of the German
Eastern Business Association on 1
November 2018, as reported on the
president's official website at http://
en.kremlin.ru/events/president/
news/59005.

5 These visits were reported on the official website of the Russian president
at http://en.kremlin.ru/.

6 See, for example, 'Foreign Minister
Sergey Lavrov's Remarks and Replies
to Media Questions During a Joint
News Conference Following Talks
with Minister of Foreign Affairs and
International Cooperation of Italy
Enzo Moavero Milanesi, Moscow,
October 8, 2018', http://www.mid.ru/
en/press_service/minister_speeches/-/
asset_publisher/7OvQR5KJWVmR/
content/id/3369071.

7 Lavrov's visits with foreign officials
were reported on the official website
of the Russian president at http://
en.kremlin.ru/.

8 See M. Entin and E. Entina, 'New
Agenda for Russia–EU Relations',
Russian International Affairs Council
Policy Brief, no. 4, May 2016; Ivan
Timofeev, Andrey Kortunov and
Sergey Utkin, 'Theses on Russia's
Foreign Policy and Global Positioning
(2017–2024)', Russian International
Affairs Council, 30 June 2017; and
Timofey Bordachev et al., 'The
European Union's Uncertain Future:
What Should Russia Do?', Valdai
Discussion Club Report, May 2017.

9 The US and several other countries
also imposed sanctions.

10 'The EU's Russia Policy: Five
Guiding Principles', European
Parliament Briefing, February
2018, available at http://www.
europarl.europa.eu/thinktank/en/
document.html?reference=EPRS_
BRI(2018)614698.

11 See Russian Foreign Minister
Sergey Lavrov's interview with
the Belarusian television network
RTR Belarus, 2 December 2017,
available at http://www.mid.ru/
en/vistupleniya_ministra/-/asset_
publisher/MCZ7HQuMdqBY/content/
id/2975550.

12 See, for example, 'Sovet pri Prezidente
Rossijskoj Federatsii po razvitiyu
grazhdanskogo obshestva I pravam
cheloveka' [Presidential Council
for Civil Society Development and
Human Rights], 15 May 2017, http://
president-sovet.ru/presscenter/news/

read/3916/.

13 See 'Meeting of the Valdai International Discussion Club', 18 October 2018, http://en.kremlin.ru/events/president/news/58848.

14 Alexey Arbatov et al., 'Mir Donbasu: Konflikt na yugo-vostoke Ukrainy: kak prodvinut'sya vpered' [Peace to Donbas: The Conflict in the Southeast of Ukraine: How to Move Forward], *Rossijskaya Gazeta*, 15 January 2018, https://rg.ru/2018/01/15/kak-prodvinutsia-v-uregulirovanii-konflikta-na-iugo-vostoke-ukrainy.html.

15 'Address by President of the Russian Federation', Moscow, 18 March 2014, http://en.kremlin.ru/events/president/news/20603.

16 'Foreign Policy Concept of the Russian Federation (Approved by President of the Russian Federation Vladimir Putin on November 30, 2016)', http://www.mid.ru/en/foreign_policy/official_documents/-/asset_publisher/CptICkB6BZ29/content/id/2542248.

17 The new Armenian leadership headed by Nikol Pashinyan has confirmed the continuity of this policy. See Richard Giragosian, 'Armenia's New Political Reality', *EaP Think Bridge*, no. 7, 2018, pp. 4–6, http://prismua.org/wp-content/uploads/2019/01/ETB_7_2018_en.pdf.

18 EU External Action, 'Fact Sheet on EU–Armenia Relations', https://eeas.europa.eu/headquarters/headQuarters-homepage/4080/node/4080_en.

19 'Briefing by Foreign Ministry Spokesperson Maria Zakharova, Moscow, November 23, 2017', Ministry of Foreign Affairs of the Russian Federation, http://www.mid.

ru/en/foreign_policy/news/-/asset_publisher/cKNonkJE02Bw/content/id/2964626.

20 See Bordachev et al., 'The European Union's Uncertain Future'.

21 Alexander Murychev, 'RSPP za razvitie economicheskogo partnerstva mezhdu Rossiej I stranami ES' [RUIE for the development of an economic partnership], 5 December 2017, http://xn--01aabe.xn--p1ai/viewpoint/view/970.

22 See, for example, N. Kondratieva, 'EU–EAEU Relations: Features of the Present Stage', *Sovremennaya Evropa*, vol. 82, no. 3, May 2018, pp. 60–70, DOI 10.15211/soveurope320186070.

23 See *ibid.*

24 'The Skripal Case', BBC, 27 March 2018, https://www.bbc.com/russian/news-43545689.

25 Olga Mishchenko, 'The EU Is Preparing to Take Action Against Russian Cyber Attacks', DW, 15 October 2018, https://www.dw.com/ru/%D0%B5%D1%81-%D0%B3%D0%BE%D1%82%D0%BE%D0%B2%D0%B8%D1%82%D1%81%D1%8F-%D0%BF%D1%80%D0%B8%D0%BD%D1%8F%D1%82%D1%8C-%D0%BC%D0%B5%D1%80%D1%8B-%D0%BF%D1%80%D0%BE%D1%82%D0%B8%D0%B2-%D0%BA%D0%B8%D0%B1%D0%B5%D1%80%D0%B0%D1%82%D0%B0%D0%BA-%D1%80%D0%BE%D1%81%D1%81%D0%B8%D0%B8/a-45888474.

26 Nikolay Kaveshnikov, 'The European Union as a Game Changer of the Rules of the Energy Game', Expert Online, 18 December 2017, http://expert.ru/2017/12/18/evrosoyuz-kak-game-changer-pravil-energeticheskoj-igryi/.

27 See, for example, Maria Smekalova, 'Cybersecurity and Intrigue in the Sandbox', Russian Council on International Affairs, 1 August 2018, http://russiancouncil.ru/analytics-and-comments/columns/cybercolumn/kiberbezopasnost-i-intrigi-v-pesochnitse/.

28 See 'Remarks by HR/VP Mogherini at the Joint Press Conference with Foreign Minister of the Russian Federation Sergey Lavrov', EU External Action, 24 April 2017, https://eeas.europa.eu/headquarters/headquarters-homepage/24982/remarks-hrvp-mogherini-joint-press-conference-foreign-minister-russian-federation-sergey_en.

29 'Markus Ederer: EU and Russia Are and Will Remain Very Important Energy Partners', Interfax, 9 November 2018, http://www.interfax.com/interview.asp?id=869164.

30 Sabine Fischer and Ivan Timofeev, 'Selective Engagement Between the EU and Russia', EUREN Interim Report, October 2018, p. 3, https://eeas.europa.eu/sites/eeas/files/eu-russia_network_interim_report_eng.pdf.

31 *Ibid.*, p. 8.

32 *Ibid.*, p. 2.

33 Andrei Zagorsky, *Russia–EU Relations at a Crossroads: Common and Divergent Interests* (Moscow: NPMP RIAC, 2016), p. 20.

34 'Foreign Policy Concept of the Russian Federation'.

35 See, for example, Delegation of the European Union to Russia, 'Statement by the Spokesperson on the Sentencing of Oyub Titiev, Director of the Memorial Human Rights Centre, Russian Federation',

18 March 2019, https://eeas.europa.eu/delegations/russia/59819/statement-spokesperson-sentencing-oyub-titiev-director-memorial-human-rights-centre-russian_en; Delegation of the European Union to Russia, 'Statement by the Spokesperson on the Sentencing of Dennis Christensen in Russia', 6 February 2019, https://eeas.europa.eu/delegations/russia/57728/statement-spokesperson-sentencing-dennis-christensen-russia_en; and EU External Action, 'Statement by the Spokesperson on the Continued Illegal Detention of Oleg Sentsov', 7 October 2018, https://eeas.europa.eu/headquarters/headquarters-homepage/51706/statement-spokesperson-continued-illegal-detention-oleg-sentsov_en.

36 'Foreign Minister Sergey Lavrov's Remarks and Answers to Media Questions at a Joint News Conference Following Talks with High Representative of the EU for Foreign Affairs and Security Policy Federica Mogherini, Moscow, 24 April 2017', http://www.mid.ru/press_service/minister_speeches/-/asset_publisher/7OvQR5KJWVmR/content/id/2736003.

37 Zagorsky, *Russia–EU Relations at a Crossroads*, p. 20.

38 See Mark Entin and Catherine Entina, 'Novaya povestka otnoshenij mezhdu Rossiej I ES' [The European Union squares its shoulders], Russian Council of International Affairs, May 2016, https://russiancouncil.ru/upload/PolicybriefRU-EU-rus.pdf.

39 *Ibid.*

40 See EU External Action, 'Remarks by High Representative/Vice-

President Federica Mogherini Following a Meeting with Foreign Minister of the Russian Federation, Sergey Lavrov', 11 July 2017, https://eeas.europa.eu/headquarters/headquarters-homepage/29710/node/29710_en.

41 'Foreign Policy Concept of the Russian Federation'.

42 See, for example, the statement by Federation Council Chairwoman Valentina Matviyenko: 'Valentina Matviyenko: The Federation Council is Firmly Committed to Promoting Constructive, Equitable and Mutually Beneficial Cooperation with All Its Partners', Federation Council of the Federal Assembly of the Russian Federation, 10 December 2018, http://council.gov.ru/en/events/news/99408/.

Rethinking Turkey's 'Rapprochements': Trouble with Germany and Beyond

Lisel Hintz

In September 2018, Turkish President Recep Tayyip Erdogan's first state visit to Germany in four years was greeted with a warm reception replete with full military honours. The cordial welcome marked a sharp contrast with previous bilateral tensions that had threatened to devolve into crisis. The diplomatic groundwork that made this visit possible, for example, included the much-anticipated release of German citizens from Turkish prisons amid accusations that Turkey was engaging in a form of 'hostage diplomacy' with a NATO ally.[1] With Berlin literally rolling out the red carpet for the Turkish leader, there was speculation that despite mutual displays of animosity, the two might achieve the rapprochement advocated by both countries' foreign ministries.[2]

Erdogan's visit to Germany was not the first time that Turkey had attempted to ameliorate a soured relationship. Indeed, Turkey's ties with many countries – including those with Israel, the Netherlands, Russia and the United States – defy neat classification. In the Israeli case, for example, a downgrade in diplomacy that had resulted from an Israeli attack on a Turkish aid flotilla attempting to break a Gaza blockade was officially repaired in 2016, only for relations to break down again in summer 2018 over the killing of Palestinians protesting the US embassy's move to Jerusalem.

For Germany and Turkey, a diplomatic crisis had erupted a year before Erdogan's visit that had threatened not just the countries' bilateral ties,

Lisel Hintz is an Assistant Professor of International Relations and European Studies at Johns Hopkins University's School of Advanced International Studies. Her first book, *Identity Politics Inside Out: National Identity Contestation and Foreign Policy in Turkey*, was recently released by Oxford University Press.

Survival | vol. 61 no. 3 | June–July 2019 | pp. 165–186   DOI 10.1080/00396338.2019.1614787

but Turkey's already rocky relationship with the European Union and with Europe more generally.[3] Tensions over refusals to allow members of Erdogan's Justice and Development Party (AKP) to campaign among Turkish citizens residing in Germany and the Netherlands in the run-up to a crucial referendum became severe when the Turkish president characterised both countries' actions as 'fascism'. In a bid to punish German Chancellor Angela Merkel and Dutch Prime Minister Mark Rutte as they contested their own elections – elections that may partly explain why these leaders pushed back on AKP campaigning in the first place – Erdogan urged voters of Turkish origin not to cast their ballots for 'Turkey's enemies'.[4] Erdogan doubled down on his anti-German rhetoric in a March 2017 speech in which he accused Merkel's government of denying freedom of thought. 'I thought Nazism was over in Germany,' he said, 'but it still continues.'[5]

Merkel moved to end Turkey's EU bid

While these insults did not lead to an official downgrading of diplomatic relations with Germany as they did with the Netherlands,[6] any potential for the rift to be quickly repaired dissipated several months later when Turkey placed German human-rights activist Peter Steudtner, Turkey's Amnesty International director İdil Eser and four others in pretrial detention on suspicion of aiding a terrorist organisation. By that time, eight other Germans, including *Die Welt* journalist Deniz Yücel, were already in jail on similar charges. Germany responded to Steudtner's arrest with a somewhat vague but ominous-sounding policy of 'reorientation' toward Turkey that encompassed warnings by then-foreign minister Sigmar Gabriel about travel to and investment in Turkey, as well as discussion of financial sanctions.[7] In September 2017, Merkel moved to end Turkey's EU bid, a step that Gabriel had discouraged for fear of providing Erdogan with more anti-European ammunition.[8] The rift only deepened when Gabriel declared a hold on arms exports to Turkey, citing domestic concerns about the use of German-manufactured *Leopard* tanks by the Turkish Armed Forces in Syria.[9] Given that Germany is Turkey's second-largest arms supplier after the United States, the decision did not go unnoticed. Arms sales did not resume until after Yücel was released in February 2018.

Rumours that Gabriel had brokered Yücel's release during a meeting with his Turkish counterpart, Mevlüt Çavuşoğlu, in Germany – multiple German opinion pieces questioned whether a 'dirty deal' was made[10] – were denied by the German minister, who insisted there was 'no deal, no quid pro quo'.[11] Yet the limits to rapprochement were palpable, notwithstanding the cordiality of Erdogan's visit. This is not to suggest that immutable cultural or civilisational fault lines such as those suggested by Samuel Huntington set those limits.[12] Identities and the interests they prescribe can change over time. Indeed, as German analyst Heinz Kramer has noted, West Germany served as a 'mentor for Turkey in Europe' during the Cold War.[13] Much more recently, during what Turkey scholars Ziya Öniş and Şuhnaz Yılmaz have termed Turkey's 'golden age' of Europeanisation, Germany's governing coalition comprising the Social Democratic Party (SPD) and the Green Party actively supported Turkey's full membership in the EU.[14]

It wasn't until Merkel's Christian Democratic Union unseated the SPD–Green coalition in 2005 that a German–Turkish partnership based on common values and interests started to seem unattainable. Merkel has always maintained that 'privileged membership' is the closest Turkey should come to joining the EU.[15] Although careful to deny allegations that she believes the Union is a 'Christian club', Merkel suggested in 2006 that EU values such as human and civil rights 'derive in large part from the teachings of Christianity'.[16] Many Turks responded to these and similar comments by suggesting that the EU discriminated against Turkey because it is a Muslim-majority country. Among the evidence for this claim is the fact that Catholic-majority Croatia joined the EU ten years after applying, while Turkey, which signed the Ankara Agreement in 1966 and applied for EU membership in 1987, has yet to join the Union. One AKP figure likened the relationship between Turkey and the EU to a marriage of bad faith.[17]

Leaving aside Turkey's failure to fulfil most of the EU's accession criteria, and the fact that Turkey is much larger than Croatia, Erdogan's understanding of Turkishness – what I have termed 'Ottoman Islamism'[18] – prescribes a foreign policy that places Turkey's focus largely outside of Europe. Although the AKP emphasised EU membership as a key foreign-policy pillar in its first years in power, Erdogan has since sought to assert Turkey's role as

Sunni Muslim leader in former Ottoman territories in the Balkans and the Middle East by dismantling Western-oriented and secularist institutional obstacles such as the military and the judiciary.

Given that Turkey and Germany appear to lack common values, a vision for a meaningful partnership or any long-term security interests,[19] it may be that the term 'rapprochement' unhelpfully sets expectations for a cordial Turkish–German relationship too high. Although both sides have political and economic reasons to improve relations, obstacles to achieving the necessary level of trust still exist, including Turkey's problematic influence over Turks in Germany. Moreover, Turkey's diplomacy with other countries, notably Russia and Israel, appears to signal an overall transactional trend in the country's foreign policy. For example, Erdogan's June 2016 letter to Moscow expressing regret over the downing of a Russian SU-24 jet that crossed into Turkish airspace in November 2015 came directly after targeted sanctions did serious damage to Turkey's food-export, banking and tourism sectors.[20] Likewise, Turkey's normalisation of relations with Israel, initiated at a moment of isolation made worse by Russia's cold shoulder,[21] produced valuable gains in trade, particularly in terms of potential energy collaboration and tourism,[22] but was short-lived. Turkey's current domestic political balance and the rise of nationalism will further complicate the country's relationship-building efforts.

Political and economic interests

The immediate motivations behind the September 2018 thaw in German–Turkish relations seem clear. The welcome on the German side likely reflected concern about Turkey's continued willingness to host Syrians fleeing the civil war in light of what appeared at the time to be an impending major assault by the Syrian regime on Idlib. Merkel had spearheaded the EU's negotiations with Ankara to curb refugee flows, culminating in a March 2016 agreement incentivising Turkey to host refugees within its borders. As the EU country that had accepted the largest number of Syrians, Germany was facing increasing domestic challenges from populists running on anti-immigrant and anti-Islam platforms. As similar pressures mounted in Turkey, where public opinion was souring on the presence of nearly four million refugees,[23] Merkel likely wanted reassurances for her domestic constituency that Erdogan would not renege on the agreement. Her concerns were not unfounded; Erdogan repeatedly intimated to Turkish audiences and to EU Commission President Jean-Claude Juncker that refugees would be loaded on buses and sent to Europe if Turkey's demands were not met, saying at one point, 'we don't have "sucker" written on our forehead'.[24]

In the end, a potential refugee surge was avoided, largely due to Turkey's brokering of a deal with Russia to create safe zones around Idlib. Yet the question of whether the Turkish–German relationship was merely experiencing a lull in hostilities remained. On the positive side, Germany participated (along with France) in an Istanbul summit that lent European legitimacy to the 'Astana track' spearheaded by Turkey and Russia for ending the Syrian civil war. Notably, Germany endorsed a statement rejecting 'separatist' agendas in Syria, a nod to Turkey's concerns about a potential Kurdish bid for autonomy.[25] On the negative side, Germany, along with the US, continued to support the Kurdish Democratic Union Party (PYD) in the fight against the Islamic State (ISIS). Turkey considers the PYD a terrorist organisation, along with its military wing, the People's Protection Units (YPG). German authorities have allowed the display of PYD and YPG flags and symbols in some states, but banned those of Turkey's Kurdistan Workers' Party (PKK).[26]

From Turkey's perspective, the seemingly warm welcome extended by Germany to Erdogan conferred the international legitimacy he needs to stabilise the Turkish lira and boost much-needed foreign investment. By September 2018, the lira's freefall against the US dollar had abated somewhat, but no substantive changes had been made to correct the deep structural problems in the Turkish economy.[27] Over-spending, over-borrowing and overly tight regulation of Turkey's Central Bank had exacerbated the country's economic problems, leading to speculation that Turkey was headed toward a crisis akin to the one it experienced in 2001.[28]

Ironically, the AKP came to power in 2002 largely because of that crisis, and the political and economic instability that precipitated it, with voters refusing to return any of the incumbent parties to parliament. The party's preferred moniker, the AK Party, includes the word *ak*, meaning 'white' or 'pure', to convey the party's distance from the corruption voters perceived as intrinsic to the pre-2001 period. A massive corruption scandal exposed in December 2013 by the party's allies-turned-enemies in the Gülen movement threatened to shake the impressive growth the AKP had presided over, but the economy remained relatively stable until 2018, when the practices facilitating that impressive growth increasingly proved unsustainable. US President Donald Trump's aggressive and eerily ill-timed tweet doubling tariffs on Turkish steel and aluminium imports just as Turkish Treasury and Finance Minister Berat Albayrak, Erdogan's son-in-law, was unveiling his plan to stabilise the economy made the burgeoning currency crisis worse, but cannot be blamed for the looming debt crisis.[29]

Given the severity of the situation, the three-day visit to Germany was aimed not only at increasing global investor confidence in general, but at cultivating support from Turkey's sixth-largest investor in particular. German foreign direct investment comprises approximately 6.3% of Turkey's total, and is concentrated in the country's large energy, manufacturing and insurance sectors. Although Berlin's limiting in 2017 of government credit guarantees for German firms investing in Turkey was largely symbolic, stricter limits could do real damage to the Turkish economy.[30]

Moreover, having rhetorically painted himself into a corner by expressing deep antipathy toward the International Monetary Fund, Erdogan needs to cultivate alternative sources of financial support.[31] The US is not an option, particularly since the US Congress took measures to oppose any credit offers to Turkey from international lending institutions in response to Turkey's refusal to release jailed American pastor Andrew Brunson.[32] Erdogan has secured a $3.6 billion loan from China and $15bn in investment from Qatar,[33] but additional financial support from the German government would certainly help avert a full economic meltdown.

Finally, Erdogan's visit was intended to help strengthen his support among Germans of Turkish origin. Numbering around three million, this population reflects many of the divides at play in Turkey's societal and political struggles back home – Kurdish–Turkish, Alevi–Sunni, religious–secular – if in somewhat different proportions. The mostly rural Turks who migrated to Germany as part of the Gastarbeiter agreement signed in 1961

tended to be more conservative and less educated than supporters of secu-
larist governments back home. This demographic factor, along with German
Turks' relatively low levels of integration into German society, mean that
Erdogan and the AKP receive proportionately higher levels of support
among Turks in Germany than they receive in Turkey. This population is
also responsible for nearly $1bn in annual remittances to family members in
Turkey, according to the German Central Bank.[34] In a bid to secure German
Turks' continued financial and electoral support, Erdogan spent part of his
visit to Germany in Cologne, inaugurating the country's largest mosque.
Thousands of fans attended the opening to express their approval, shouting:
'Who is the greatest? Turkey!'[35]

The long arm of Turkey's influence in Germany

AKP supporters in Germany are an important electoral asset for Erdogan,
and the tactics the party engages in outside of Turkey pose an obstacle to
establishing trust between the two countries. German security authorities
are concerned by evidence that Turkish groups falling somewhere between
civil-society organisations and paramilitary groups have spilled over into
Germany.[36] The group getting the most attention is Osmanen Germania
('Germania Ottomans'), a thuggish, self-defined 'boxing club' that has been
compared to a biker gang.[37] The group comprises 16 clubs, and its members
have been charged with attempted murder, extortion, drug trafficking,
deprivation of liberty and forced prostitution.[38] The group's extreme-right,
anti-Kurdish views pit it against a Kurdish diaspora in Germany that has
become the largest in the world as Kurds have fled ISIS violence in northern Syria.[39] Security analysts believe the boxing club to be closely linked to
the AKP, the Turkish National Intelligence Organization (Milli İstihbarat
Teşkilatı) and the AKP's lobbying group in Europe, the Union of European
Turkish Democrats (UETD). Wiretaps and surveillance suggest that Metin
Külünk, an AKP member of parliament and 'close confidant' of Erdogan,
provided money directly to the club for purchasing weapons to be used
against Kurds.[40] A police investigation found that Külünk advised group
members to harass Kurds, as well as Erdogan critics, living in Germany.
German intelligence also indicates that Külünk organised a demonstration

against a German bill recognising the Armenian genocide, after which he spoke with Erdogan, telling him he would 'await orders'.[41] Külünk also reportedly told a former UETD member to encourage Osmanen Germania to attack TV comedian Jan Böhmermann as punishment for a vulgar poem insulting Erdogan that he read during a March 2016 broadcast.[42] The German Interior Ministry banned Osmanen Germania two months before Erdogan's visit to Germany in 2018, but concerns about its violent activities remain.[43]

Critics are also concerned about the political activities of formal institutions such as the Islamische Gemeinschaft Millî Görüş (National Outlook Islamic Community), an ideological affiliate of the AKP, and the Turkish–Islamic Union for Religious Affairs (DITIB). With more than 900 mosques under its jurisdiction, DITIB is the largest Islamic umbrella organisation in Germany. It is an extension of Turkey's own Directorate of Religious Affairs (Diyanet İşleri Başkanlığı), and the imams it employs are sent from and funded by Turkey. The organisation is suspected of involvement in intelligence gathering on Gülen supporters. Meanwhile, there have been reports that Turkish consulates have encouraged teachers and parents to report any instruction in German schools that is critical of Erdogan.[44] These reports, as well as fears of rising extremism, have prompted Berlin to try to sever ties between German Muslims and Turkey. A top civil servant in the German Interior Ministry summed up Berlin's approach to reducing foreign influence by saying, 'The Turkish government has to accept that the days when they had total control over German mosques run by DITIB are over.'[45] While some Turks in Germany support the initiative to create 'homegrown imams', it is likely that Turkey will try to push back by raising the issue with intergovernmental Islamic organisations.[46]

The devolution of previous 'rapprochements'

The optimism surrounding discussions of Turkey's warming relations with Germany and other European countries, particularly in the wake of its dramatic fallout with the US in 2018–19, has been guarded. The persistence of challenges, and the diplomatic difficulties they can provoke when either side finds it politically profitable to stir the pot, underscore the utility of soberly evaluating the relationship's potential. Prospects for the complete normalisation of relations between Turkey and Germany will remain limited as long as Erdogan and the AKP continue to seek concessions in exchange for the release of prisoners; to stoke anti-Western, anti-Kurdish and other forms of nationalist sentiment at home and abroad in order to garner political support; and to constrict pluralism and dissent in the name of national security. For now, relations cannot usefully be classified as warmed or normalised; this is wary and opportunistic transactionalism, not cordial rapprochement.

This distinction is more than just semantics. The implications of acknowledging the actual nature of the countries' re-engagements following diplomatic crises are important for shaping expectations and interpreting subsequent interactions. Two themes germane to this point are reflected in the cases, mentioned above, of Turkey's so-called rapprochements with Russia and Israel. Firstly, Erdogan accepted no blame for the incidents that triggered the diplomatic crises in the dialogue that accompanied the simultaneous normalisations with Russia and Israel. This refusal to accept at least partial responsibility, which would require grappling with why he approved of the provocative action that was taken and how he could have acted differently, suggests that no meaningful change has taken place that could prevent future tensions.

In the Russian case, Areg Galstyan noted in the *National Interest* that by expressing condolences rather than offering an apology for the downing of the Russian jet, Erdogan's letter 'shrewdly' avoided concessions that 'would have made Ankara look weak'.[47] Less than a month after the letter was sent, a July 2016 coup attempt provided Erdogan's AKP with the opportunity to deflect blame for the crisis onto its ally-turned-rival, the Gülen movement. Just a few days after the failed putsch, two officers with alleged links to the Gülen movement were detained in connection with the downing of the jet, and Ankara mayor Melih Gökçek declared the incident as part of a plot to disrupt Turkey–Russia relations.[48] Russian President Vladimir Putin himself offered credence to this explanation,[49] while a think tank close to the Kremlin echoed rumours circulating in Turkey by blaming the downing of the jet on the involvement of 'US troops deployed at Incirlik' air base.[50]

In a similar way, Erdogan quickly absolved himself and his government of responsibility for the crisis in relations with Israel. In this case, he shifted blame for the arguably provocative decision to send the *Mavi Marmara* to break Israel's blockade of Gaza to the non-governmental organisation that planned and carried out the mission. Although the flotilla was under the auspices of the Humanitarian Relief Foundation (İHH), it is widely accepted that such a prominent move could not have taken place without Erdogan's approval. Indeed, at the time of the incident, the Turkish president defended the flotilla's actions, condemning Israel's attack that killed ten Turkish workers in return for resounding praise from Arab audiences for standing up to Israel.[51] Nevertheless, several days after the normalisation of ties with Israel, Erdogan eschewed any personal involvement in the decision and criticised the İHH, saying, 'We were already providing aid. While doing so, would we [send a flotilla] just for the sake of public display?'[52] When relations with Israel were eventually normalised, there was no effort to deal with the issue that had caused the discord in the first place.

Erdogan criticised Russia's actions in Crimea

Turkey's post-2016 relationship with Russia has been the subject of much inquiry, particularly from conservative analysts wondering whether the West has 'lost Turkey'.[53] Leaving aside criticism that such perspectives deny Turkey agency, this view also presumes an either–or alignment that Turkey does not seem to be pursuing.[54] Although Turkey has sought Russian approval for its military actions against Kurdish forces in Syria and refused to heed US calls to back down from a deal to purchase a Russian S-400 missile-defence system, Ankara had not yet closed the door on a possible US *Patriot* missile-system purchase instead by the time this issue went to press. Strong evidence also indicates that Turkey provided aid to Salafi jihadist forces such as Jabhat al-Nusra (now Hayat Tahrir al-Sham) in support of their goal to overthrow Syrian President Bashar al-Assad, another Erdogan ally-turned-enemy who is still Russia's closest Middle East partner.[55] Erdogan has also publicly criticised Russia's actions in Crimea even after the June 2016 letter that was meant to restore amicable ties, repeatedly criticising Russia's 'illegal annexation'[56] of the peninsula and stating in

November 2018 that 'we do not and will not recognise' Russia's sovereignty over the territory.[57] He has also commented critically on Russian influence in Donbas. Not surprisingly, Russian officials have responded harshly to Turkey's stance.[58]

Turkey's relationship with Russia has been described as a complex balancing act,[59] one perhaps best characterised as 'asymmetrical interdependence'[60] rather than any sort of partnership. While this may also be true of Turkey's contemporary relationship with Germany, the key difference is that Turkey has never counted Russia as a partner or ally. Quite the opposite – Turkey's membership of NATO was motivated by fears of Russian aggression and memories of numerous Ottoman defeats by the Russian Empire.[61]

Israel, on the other hand, is a better point of comparison. While perhaps there was never a 'golden age' of relations, Turkey was the first Muslim-majority state to recognise Israeli statehood in 1949. The two countries maintained close economic, diplomatic and security ties for more than 50 years despite the odd hiccup, such as Israel's worries over Turkey's fidelity upon its signing of the Baghdad Pact in 1955 and the temporary downgrading of relations in the wake of the Suez crisis in 1956. Since the AKP came to power, however, and particularly since it won a second term, several episodes have signalled a more contentious relationship, including Erdogan's criticism of Israeli president Shimon Peres at the 2009 World Economic Forum at Davos;[62] and the embarrassing 'chairgate' incident in which the Israeli Foreign Ministry summoned Turkish ambassador Ahmet Oğuz Çelikkol to discuss Israel's concerns about the negative portrayal of Israeli soldiers in the popular Turkish drama series *Kurtlar Vadisi* (*Valley of the Wolves*), only to offer him a lower chair at a table on which was displayed an Israeli flag but not a Turkish one, in what was a breach of diplomatic protocol.[63]

Even after US president Barack Obama encouraged Israeli Prime Minister Benjamin Netanyahu to apologise for the flotilla incident in March 2013, an apology that contributed to the restoration of full diplomatic ties between Israel and Turkey, posters appeared around Turkey depicting a recalcitrant Netanyahu and a victorious Erdogan separated by a flotilla and carrying the slogan 'Israel apologised to Turkey. We are grateful that you

[Erdogan] made our country experience this pride.' In reporting on normalisation negotiations, pro-government media outlets emphasised the
concessions Israel would be forced to make now that it had been brought
'to its knees',[64] including the payment of financial reparations and the granting of permission for Turkey to provide humanitarian aid to Gaza, while
omitting that Turkey's main demand, that the blockade be lifted, went
unfulfilled.[65] Journalists debated whether Turkey's negotiated settlement
should be deemed a 'victory' (*zafer*) or a 'thrashing' (*hezimet*).[66] Far from
an amicable reconciliation with optimistic prospects, the new relationship
between Turkey and Israel was portrayed as a Turkish triumph over a con-
trite enemy. Also telling was the increasingly open anti-Semitism in Turkish
public discourse, including insults and references to Adolf Hitler by top
AKP figures. Even after the rapprochement, Turkish Jews continued to emi-
grate, citing a discriminatory environment in general and threats via social
media specifically.[67]

Relations between Turkey and Israel took another bad turn in May 2018,
when Turkey recalled its ambassador to Israel over the killing of dozens of
Palestinian protesters in Gaza by Israeli forces. Erdogan chose particularly
forceful language in accusing Israel of being a 'terrorist state' and commit-
ting 'genocide'.[68] He also expelled Israel's ambassador to Turkey, allowing
Turkish TV crews to film him being subjected to a lengthy frisking by
airport security – a procedure from which ambassadors are usually exempt
by virtue of their diplomatic status.[69]

It is worth noting that the latest flare-up with Israel took place a month
before Turkey's June 2018 presidential and parliamentary elections, arguably the most important of Erdogan's career. In order to preside over the
consolidated presidential system he had worked so tirelessly to install,
Erdogan needed a victory that seemed uncertain in May 2018. His main
challenger for the presidency, Muharrem İnce, was moving up in the polls,
galvanising a somewhat dispirited and markedly fragmented opposition
that was excited to finally say 'enough!' ('*tamam!*') to the man who had led
their country, with an increasingly firm grip, for 15 years.[70] The economic
growth and public spending that had underpinned support for the AKP
had become unsustainable; inflation and unemployment were up; investor

confidence and the lira were down; and Erdogan's unorthodox views about interest rates were doing little to help.[71] Even after taking steps to secure his victory, such as moving the elections forward to avoid the effects of a worsening economy and declaring victory before ballot counting was finished, Erdogan only cleared the 50% threshold needed to avoid a run-off by about 2%.[72] In the aftermath of the election, the opposition made accusations of fraud, and there were suspicions that the Supreme Electoral Council had been hollowed out.[73]

The increasingly tough stance and harsh rhetoric Erdogan directed at Israel in the run-up to the 2018 presidential election was reminiscent of the Nazi references and accusations of harbouring terrorists aimed at Germany prior to the 2017 referendum on Erdogan's presidential system. Whether to court the votes of Turkish nationals frustrated with their host government in Germany, or those of Turks back home who were inclined to reward a leader for standing up to a country that some view as a European

Picking fights with Germany is a regular tactic

bully, picking diplomatic and rhetorical fights with Germany – as well as other countries – is a tactic Erdogan regularly deploys. This practice poses obvious problems for any meaningful and lasting rapprochement between Turkey and the countries that Erdogan attacks.

Following local elections in March 2019, Turkey is poised to enjoy a much-needed four-year respite from what has seemed like a continuous cycle of elections accompanied by the stoking of nationalist fervour, seemingly without regard for the foreign-policy consequences.[74] There is no guarantee, however, that the practice of exploiting rifts with Western countries will lose its political value even now that polls have closed. Although the power of the executive presidency is formidable, Erdogan and the AKP still feel obliged to court the favour of the AKP's junior coalition partner, the ultra-right Nationalist Movement Party (Milliyetçi Hareket Partisi or MHP). Indeed, with the AKP seemingly weakened in the March elections, at least in terms of popular support if not its ability to produce favourable outcomes for itself, the need to sustain MHP support may lead to an even more aggressive, virulently anti-Western foreign policy. What has been described as the junior party's 'hypernationalism' has been on display in its calls for ending EU accession talks,[75] as well as in its supporters' advocacy of violence, such as that attributed to members of Osmanen Germania, to keep Kurds out of politics. The MHP's increased influence and relevance thus cast doubt on hopes that the post-election period might create space for detente between Turkey and its neighbours. Erdogan's 'erratic, unstable, and personality-driven' temperament, to quote Turkey analyst Dan Arbell, could also produce more tensions irrespective of party influence.[76] Erdogan's references to Nazism in speeches criticising Merkel are but one example of his tendency to use inflammatory rhetoric even outside of election periods in Turkey.[77] This volatility, combined with the political incentives to stoke nationalism for domestic purposes, make any talk of rapprochement between Turkey and Germany seem premature at best, and naive at worst.

Notes

1 See Eric Edelman and Aykan Erdemir, 'Turkey's President Is Holding Americans Hostage. Why Aren't We Doing Anything About It?', *Washington Post*, 15 April 2018, https://www.washingtonpost.com/news/democracy-post/wp/2018/04/15/turkeys-president-is-holding-americans-hostage-why-arent-we-doing-anything-about-it/?utm_term=.93145598bda6.

2 See 'Germany Hints at Warming Relations with Germany', Al-Jazeera, 17 January 2018, https://www.aljazeera.com/news/2018/01/germany-hints-warming-relations-turkey-180117164059026.html; 'Are Relations between Turkey and Germany Getting Back to Normal?', *The Economist*, 27 September 2018, https://www.economist.com/the-economist-explains/2018/09/27/are-relations-between-turkey-and-germany-getting-back-to-normal; and 'Erdogan Comes Seeking Rapprochement with Wary Berlin', Reuters, 26 September 2018.

3 See, for example, Patrick Kingsley and Alissa J. Rubin, 'Turkey's Relations with Europe Sink amid Quarrel with Netherlands', *New York Times*, 12 March 2017, https://www.nytimes.com/2017/03/12/world/europe/netherlands-recep-tayyip-erdogan-turkey.html.

4 See 'Erdoğan Tells Voters in Germany Not to Vote for "Turkey's Enemies" Merkel, Schulz, Greens', *Hürriyet Daily News*, 18 August 2017, http://www.hurriyetdailynews.com/erdogan-tells-turks-in-germany-not-to-vote-for-turkeys-enemies-merkel-schulz-greens-116905; and 'Erdogan to Turks: Don't Vote for "Fascists" in Dutch Election', *Middle East Monitor*, 15 March 2017,

https://www.middleeastmonitor.
com/20170315-erdogan-to-turks-dont-
vote-for-fascists-in-dutch-election/.

5 Recep Tayyip Erdogan, speaking at a party rally in Istanbul on 5
March 2017, available on YouTube
at https://www.youtube.com/
watch?v=A2Rgd5SEc8M.

6 Government of the Netherlands,
'Statement of the Ministry of Foreign
Affairs of the Netherlands on the
Bilateral Relations with Turkey',
5 February 2018, https://www.
government.nl/latest/news/2018/02/05/
statement-of-the-ministry-of-foreign-
affairs-of-the-netherlands-on-the-
bilateral-relations-with-turkey.

7 'Turkey Rift: German Politicians
Demand Economic Pressure',
Deutsche Welle, 28 August 2017,
https://www.dw.com/en/turkey-rift-
german-politicans-demand-economic-
pressure/a-40262485.

8 Gabriela Baczynska and John
Irish, 'Merkel Call to Stop EU Bid
Draws Mixed Response', Reuters, 7
September 2017, https://www.reuters.
com/article/us-eu-turkey-finland/
merkel-call-to-stop-turkeys-
eu-bid-draws-mixed-response-
idUSKCN1BI1AE.

9 'German Arms Sales Hit Roadblock
as Turkey Continues Syria
Campaign', Defense News, 25 January
2018, https://www.defensenews.
com/global/europe/2018/01/25/
german-arms-sales-hit-roadblock-as-
turkey-continues-syria-campaign/.

10 See Damir Fras, 'Es wäre ein
schmutziger Deal', Frankfurter
Rundschau, 7 January 2018, https://
www.tagesschau.de/kommentar/
cavusoglu-145.html; Arnd Henze,

'Waffen gegen Freilassung: Einen
schmutzigen Deal darf es nicht
geben', Tagesschau, 6 January
2018, https://www.tagesschau.de/
kommentar/cavusoglu-145.html;
and 'Waffenexporte Genehmigt: Gab
es doch einen schmutzigen Deal?',
Tagesschau, 23 February 2018, https://
www.tagesschau.de/inland/yuecel-
ruestungsexporte-tuerkei-101.html.

11 'Gabriel zur Yücel-Freilassung: Kein
Deal, Kein Quid pro Quo', Tagesschau,
16 February 2018, https://www.
tagesschau.de/ausland/interview-
gabriel-109.html.

12 See Samuel Huntington, 'The Clash of
Civilizations?', Foreign Affairs, vol. 72,
no. 3, 1993.

13 Heinz Kramer, 'Türkei', in Siegmar
Schmidt, Gunther Hellmann and
Reinhard Wolff (eds), Handbuch zer
duetschen Aussenpolitik (Wiesbaden:
Verlag für Sozialwissenschaften,
2007), p. 483. Cited in Stephen Szabo,
Germany and Turkey: The Unavoidable
Partnership (Washington DC:
Brookings Institution, March 2018),
p. 2.

14 Ziya Öniş and Şuhnaz Yılmaz,
'Between Europeanization and Euro-
Asianism: Foreign Policy Activism in
Turkey During the AKP Era', Turkish
Studies, vol. 10, no. 1, 2009.

15 See 'Angela Merkel's "Privileged
Provocation" in Turkey', Spiegel
Online, 20 March 2010, http://www.
spiegel.de/international/europe/
the-world-from-berlin-angela-merkel-
s-privileged-provocation-in-tur-
key-a-686485.html.

16 'Germany's Angela Merkel
Keeps Turkey at Arm's Length',
Deutsche Welle, 22 June 2018,

https://www.dw.com/en/
germanys-angela-merkel-keeps-
turkey-at-arms-length/a-44340611.

17 Author's interview with ministerial-
    level AKP official, Ankara, August
    2013.

18 Lisel Hintz, *Identity Politics Inside
    Out: National Identity Contestation and
    Foreign Policy in Turkey* (New York:
    Oxford University Press, 2018).

19 The failure by Germany, Turkey,
    France and Russia to achieve any
    consensus during their much-touted
    but ultimately fruitless Istanbul
    summit is a strong indicator of this.
    See Aaron Stein and Faysal Itani, 'In
    Istanbul, Geopolitical Maneuvering
    But No Progress', SyriaSource,
    29 October 2018, https://www.
    atlanticcouncil.org/blogs/syriasource/
    in-istanbul-geopolitical-maneuvering-
    but-no-progress.

20 For example, after a ban on charter
    flights from Russia to Turkey, the
    number of Russian tourists visiting
    Turkey dropped to around 700,000
    in 2016 from 3.5 million the previ-
    ous year. See Iikka Korhonen, Heli
    Simola and Laura Solanko, 'Sanctions,
    Counter-sanctions and Russia: Effects
    on Economy, Trade and Finance',
    Bank of Finland Policy Brief, no. 4,
    2018, p. 18.

21 Metin Gurcan, 'What's Really
    Driving Turkish–Israeli
    Reconciliation', Al-Monitor, 1 July
    2016, https://www.al-monitor.
    com/pulse/originals/2016/06/
    turkey-israel-normalization-military-
    security-cooperation.html.

22 Shira Efron, *The Future of Israeli–
    Turkish Relations* (Santa Monica, CA:
    RAND Corporation, 2018), pp. 17–19.

23 '*Suriyeliler İstemiyoruz*', or 'We don't
    want Syrians', became a popular
    hashtag and slogan to express public
    discontent with the refugees' pres-
    ence, often deployed in response to
    reports of crimes supposedly commit-
    ted by Syrians. See 'Kriz ve Suriyeli
    Mülteciler', Evrensel.net, 5 October
    2018, https://www.evrensel.net/
    yazi/82385/kriz-ve-suriyeli-multeciler.

24 'Cumhurbaşkanı Erdoğan'dan
    BM'ye: Alnımızda Enayi Yazmıyor',
    NTV.com, 11 February 2016,
    https://www.ntv.com.tr/turkiye/
    cumhurbaskani-erdogandan-bmye-
    alnimizda-enayi-yazmiyor,kucK7cQA
    Wo69G4YOI5IWOA.

25 Stein and Itani, 'In Istanbul,
    Geopolitical Maneuvering But No
    Progress'.

26 Znar Shino, 'Germany Eases Up
    on PYD, YPG Bans', *Rudaw*, 11
    March 2018, http://www.rudaw.
    net/english/world/11032018.
    Government policy on this issue is
    shifting and inconsistent, however.
    See Nora Martin, 'Terrorism
    Policing: The YPG/YPJ, An Ally
    Abroad But a Danger at Home?',
    OpenDemocracy.net, 9 January 2019,
    https://www.opendemocracy.net/
    can-europe-make-it/nora-martin/
    terrorism-policing-ypgypj-ally-
    abroad-but-danger-at-home.

27 Constantine Courcoulas, 'Turkey's
    Lira Leads EM Recovery as Bonds
    Head for Record Gain', Bloomberg, 7
    September 2018.

28 Jim Edwards, 'UBS: Turkey Could Be
    Heading into a Balance of Payments
    Crisis', *Business Insider*, 14 August
    2018, https://www.businessinsider.
    com/turkey-lira-balance-of-payments-

crisis-2018-8.

29 Richard Partington, 'Turkey's Economic Crisis Deepens as Trump Doubles Tariffs', *Guardian*, 10 August 2018, https://www.the-guardian.com/world/2018/aug/10/turkeys-economic-crisis-deepens-as-trump-doubles-tariffs.

30 See Szabo, *Germany and Turkey: The Unavoidable Partnership*, p. 7.

31 See Colby Smith, 'Erdogan Can't Sidestep the IMF for Long', *Financial Times*, 16 August 2018, https://ftalphaville.ft.com/2018/08/16/1534410292000/Erdogan-can-t-sidestep-the-IMF-for-long/. Pro-government opinion columnists in Turkey have likened those suggesting that the country accept an IMF loan to coup plotters. See Cemil Ertem, 'When the IMF Dominated Turkey and the Current Facts', *Daily Sabah*, 20 March 2018, https://www.dailysabah.com/columns/cemil-ertem/2018/03/21/when-the-imf-dominated-turkey-and-the-current-facts.

32 Jennifer Epstein and Bill Faries, 'Turkey's Fragile Economy Faces New Risks in US Sanctions Threat', Bloomberg, 26 July 2018, https://www.bloomberg.com/news/articles/2018-07-26/pence-warns-turkey-u-s-to-impose-sanctions-if-pastor-not-freed.

33 Similar to the tit-for-tat approach apparent in Turkey–Germany relations, Qatar's aid to Turkey came after Ankara provided diplomatic, military and humanitarian aid to Doha during a crisis in its relationship with the Gulf Cooperation Council. Dominic Dudley, 'Qatar Repays Diplomatic and Military Debt to Turkey with Offer of $15B in Financial Support', *Forbes*, 16 August 2018, https://www.forbes.com/sites/dominicdudley/2018/08/16/qatar-repays-debt-turkey-15b-support/#44a075579f59.

34 Stefan Reccius, 'Migranten überwiesen 4,2 Milliarden Euro in Herkunftsländer', *Wirtschaftswoche*, 27 August 2017, https://www.wiwo.de/politik/deutschland/bundesbank-migranten-ueberwiesen-4-2-milliarden-euro-in-herkunftslaender/20234288.html.

35 'Erdogan Opens Huge Mosque in Germany Amid Rival Rallies', Al-Jazeera, 30 September 2018, https://www.aljazeera.com/news/2018/09/erdogan-opens-huge-mosque-germany-rival-rallies-180930074443295.html.

36 For a discussion of groups such as SADAT and Ottoman Hearths (Osmanlı Ocakları), see Howard Eissenstat, 'Uneasy Rests the Crown: Erdoğan and "Revolutionary Security" in Turkey', Project on Middle East Democracy Snapshot, December 2017, pp. 5–7, https://pomed.org/pomed-snapshot-uneasy-rests-the-crown-erdogan-and-revolutionary-security-in-turkey/.

37 Matern Boselager, 'Working Out with a Notorious German Biker Gang', Vice.com, 4 March 2016, https://www.vice.com/en_us/article/4w5ya9/meeting-germanys-newest-gang-the-osmanen-germania-876.

38 'German Interior Ministry Bans Biker Gang Osmanen Germania BC', Deutsche Welle, 10 July 2018, https://www.dw.com/en/german-interior-

ministry-bans-biker-gang-osmanen-germania-bc/a-44595773.

39 'Zahl der Kurden in Deutschland sprunghaft angestiegen', press briefing 52/0809-2015, Kurdische Gemeinde Deutchland, https://kurdische-gemeinde.de/zahl-der-kurden-in-deutschland-sprunghaft-angestiegen/.

40 'Turkish AKP Politician Linked to Osmanen Germania Boxing Gang in Germany', Deutsche Welle, 14 December 2017, https://www.dw.com/en/turkish-akp-politician-linked-to-osmanen-germania-boxing-gang-in-germany/a-41789389.

41 Jörg Diehl and Ansgar Siemens, 'Die Geheimsconnection zwischen den "Osmanen Germania" und Erdogan', Spiegel Online, 24 March 2018, http://www.spiegel.de/spiegel/osmanen-germania-und-ihre-conncetion-zu-recep-tayyip-erdogan-a-1199613.html.

42 'Turkish AKP Politician Linked to Osmanen Germania Boxing Gang in Germany'.

43 'German Interior Ministry Bans Biker Gang Osmanen Germania BC'.

44 Chase Winter, 'Did Turkey Order Spying in German Classrooms?', Deutsche Welle, 23 February 2017, https://www.dw.com/en/did-turkey-order-spying-in-german-classrooms/a-37693332.

45 Markus Kerber, cited in Tobias Buck, 'Berlin Moves to Cut Ties Between German Muslims and Turkey', Financial Times, 24 March 2019, https://www.ft.com/content/626ca230-4a2e-11e9-bbc9-6917dce3dc62.

46 See Menekşe Tokyay, '"Homegrown Islam" Project Could Lead to New Ankara–Berlin Tensions', Arab News, 26 March 2019, http://www.arabnews.com/node/1473046/middle-east.

47 Areg Galstyan, 'Turkey's "Apology" to Russia: More Than Meets the Eye', National Interest, 8 July 2016, https://nationalinterest.org/feature/turkeys-apology-russia-more-meets-the-eye-16909.

48 'Turkish Pilots Who Downed Russian Jet Detained', Al-Jazeera, 19 July 2016, https://www.aljazeera.com/news/2016/07/turkish-pilots-downed-russian-jet-detained-160719132950496.html.

49 'Ex-Turkish PM: I Was Told Pilot Who Shot Down Russian Jet Was Not Linked to Gülen Network', Hürriyet Daily News, 12 January 2017, http://www.hurriyetdailynews.com/ex-turkish-pm-i-was-told-pilot-who-shot-down-russian-jet-was-not-linked-to-gulen-network-108436.

50 Cansu Çamlıbel, 'Russian Strategist Claims US Soldiers at İncirlik "Involved in Jet Crisis"', Hürriyet Daily News, 7 November 2016, http://www.hurriyetdailynews.com/russian-strategist-claims-us-soldiers-at-incirlik-involved-in-jet-crisis--105835.

51 Marc Champion and Joshua Mitnick, 'Turkish Leader Proposes Gaza Visit, Setting up Possible Clash with Israel', Wall Street Journal, 20 July 2011, https://www.wsj.com/articles/SB10001424052702304567604576456263741978224.

52 'Erdoğan'dan Mavi Marmara Çıkışı: Günün Başkanına mi Sordunuz', Hürriyet Gazetesi, 29 June 2016, http://www.hurriyet.com.tr/gundem/erdogandan-mavi-marmara-cikisi-gunun-basbakanina-mi-sordunuz-40123952.

53   Patrick Buchanan, 'Is Turkey Lost to the West?', *American Conservative*, 14 March 2017, https://www.theamericanconservative.com/buchanan/is-turkey-lost-to-the-west/.

54   See, for example, Nicholas Danforth, 'Instead of Turning East, Turkey Is Going It Alone', *War on the Rocks*, 13 February 2018, https://warontherocks.com/2018/02/turkey/.

55   See 'MİT Tırları Soruşturması: Neler Olmuştu?', BBCTürkçe.com, 27 November 2015, https://www.bbc.com/turkce/haberler/2015/11/151127_mit_tirlari_neler_olmustu.

56   'Cumhurbaşkanı Erdoğan: Kırım'ın Yasa Dışı İlhakını Tanımadık Tanımayacağız', *Akşam Gazetesi*, 9 October 2017, https://www.aksam.com.tr/siyaset/cumhurbaskani-erdogan-ukraynada-konusuyor/haber-667769.

57   'Erdoğan: Kırım'ın Yasa Dışı İlhakını Tanımayacağımızı Tekraren Vurguladık', *Yeni Asya Gazetesi*, 3 November 2018, http://www.yeniasya.com.tr/gundem/erdogan-kirim-in-yasa-disi-ilhakini-tanimayacagimizi-tekraren-vurguladik_477328.

58   For a round-up of responses, see Yekaterina Chulkovskaya, 'Erdogan's Antics Keep Russia on Its Toes', Al-Monitor, 13 October 2017, https://www.al-monitor.com/pulse/originals/2017/10/turkey-russia-erdogan-antics-crimea-exports.html.

59   Semih Idiz, 'Turkey's Complex Balancing Act between Russia and Ukraine', Al-Monitor, 5 December 2018, https://www.al-monitor.com/pulse/originals/2018/12/turkey-russia-ankaras-complex-balancing-act.html.

60   Ziya Öniş and Şuhnaz Yılmaz, 'Turkey and Russia in a Shifting Global Order: Cooperation, Conflict, and Asymmetric Independence in a Turbulent Region', *Third World Quarterly*, vol. 37, no. 1, 2016.

61   See, for example, Suat Kınıklıoğlu and Valeriy Morkva, 'An Anatomy of Turkish–Russian Relations', *Journal of Southeast European and Black Sea Studies*, vol. 7, no. 4, 2007.

62   After insisting he had not been given enough time to speak on a panel, Erdogan interrupted moderator David Ignatius asking for 'one minute'. He then criticised Peres for Israel's killing of Palestinians in Gaza, saying 'you know well how to kill' and adding that Turkey was done with Davos before walking off the stage. See 'Recep Erdogan Storms out of Davos after Clash with Israeli President over Gaza', *Guardian*, 30 January 2009, https://www.the-guardian.com/world/2009/jan/30/turkish-prime-minister-gaza-davos.

63   Diplomatic protocol requires that both flags be present; the higher position in which Ayalon was seated added to the controversy, as did his comment in Hebrew to the cameraman: 'Pay attention that he is sitting in a lower chair … that there is only an Israeli flag on the table and that we are not smiling.' See Barak Ravid, 'Peres: Humiliation of Turkish Envoy Does Not Reflect Israel's Diplomacy', *Haaretz*, 13 January 2010, https://www.haaretz.com/1.5085307.

64   Ibrahim Karagül, 'İsrail'e Özür Diletmek…', *Yeni Şafak*, 23 March 2013, https://www.yenisafak.com/yazarlar/ibrahimkaragul/israile-ozur-diletmek-36898.

65 Barak Ravid, 'Israel Pays $20 Million in Reparations Agreed on in Reconciliation Deal', *Haaretz*, 20 September 2016, https://www.haaretz.com/israel-news/.premium-israel-pays-turkey-20-million-in-reparations-1.5444873.

66 Yasın Altıntaş and Berrin Naz Önsiper, 'Türkiye–İsrail Anlaşması: Zafer mi Heziyet Mi?', *Tesnim Haber Ajansı*, 22 August 2016, https://www.tasnimnews.com/tr/news/2016/08/22/1164807/t%C3%BCrkiye-israil-anla%C5%9Fmas%C4%B1-zafer-mi-hezimet-mi.

67 Sibel Ekin, 'More Turkish Jews Seek New Life in Israel', Ahval News, 3 March 2018, https://ahvalnews.com/turkey/more-turkish-jews-seek-new-life-israel.

68 'Cumhurbaşkanı Erdoğan: İsrail bir Terör Devletidir', Haberturk.com, 15 May 2018, https://www.haberturk.com/son-dakika-cumhurbaskani-erdogan-aciklama-yapiyor-1965642.

69 Israel quickly responded in kind, summoning the Turkish chargé d'affaires in Tel Aviv for his own dressing down. See 'İsrail, Türkiye Maslahatgüzarını Dışişleri Bakanlığı'na Çağırdı', NTV.com, 16 May 2018, https://www.ntv.com.tr/dunya/israil-turkiye-maslahatguzarini-disisleri-bakanligina-cagirdi,fdqgh5o9voWdFe53V8k4Yw.

70 Lisel Hintz, 'How a Hashtag and Memes Are Uniting Turkey's Opposition', *Washington Post*, Monkey Cage blog, 11 May 2018, https://www.washingtonpost.com/news/monkey-cage/wp/2018/05/11/how-a-hashtag-and-memes-are-uniting-turkeys-opposition/?utm_term=.cd44b2c327fo.

71 Alanna Petroff, 'Turkey's Currency Crash Puts Economy at Heart of Election', CNNBusiness.com, 21 June 2018, https://money.cnn.com/2018/06/21/news/economy/turkey-election-currency/index.html.

72 Laura Pitel, Funja Guler and Ayla Jean Yackley, 'Erdogan Claims Victory in Turkey Elections', *Financial Times*, 25 June 2018, https://www.ft.com/content/9ab2404e-7786-11e8-bc55-50daf11b720d.

73 Steven Cook, 'Turkey's Elections: Partially Free, Fair, and Fake', Council on Foreign Relations blog post, 25 June 2018, https://www.cfr.org/blog/turkeys-elections-partially-free-fair-and-fake.

74 This break from elections is conditional upon a potential re-run of the Istanbul mayoral election; results show that AKP candidate Binali Yıldırım lost to challenger Ekrem İmamoğlu, but as this issue went to press the result was being disputed by pro-AKP media as having been undermined by an 'election coup'. See Selçuk Türkyılmaz, 'The People's Will, the Election Coup, and the "Matter of Survival" in Turkey', *Yeni Şafak Gazetesi*, 4 April 2019, https://www.yenisafak.com/en/columns/selcukturkyilmaz/the-peoples-will-the-election-coup-and-the-matter-of-survival-in-turkey-2047000.

75 See, for example, Sinan Ülgen, 'Get Ready for a More Aggressive Turkey', *Foreign Policy*, 2 July 2018, https://foreignpolicy.com/2018/07/02/turkeys-foreign-policy-is-about-to-

take-a-turn-to-the-right/.

76 Dan Arbell, 'Pragmatism Pays Off
for Erdogan – How Long Can He
Keep It Up?', International Institute
for Strategic Studies blog post,
8 November 2018, https://www.
iiss.org/blogs/analysis/2018/11/
pragmatism-pays-off-erdogan.

77 'Erdogan Compares Merkel's
Comments on Turkey's EU Bid to
"Nazism"', *Times of Israel*, 6 September
2017, https://www.timesofisrael.com/
erdogan-compares-merkels-com-
ments-on-turkeys-eu-bid-to-nazism/.

China's Curious Nonchalance Towards the Indo-Pacific

Feng Zhang

'Nonchalant' is a word seldom used to describe Chinese foreign-policy attitudes. 'Prickly', 'assertive', 'truculent' or 'triumphalist' have been deployed far more often.[1] Yet a sort of nonchalance has characterised Beijing's attitude towards a major new regional strategic initiative that is widely considered anti-China in focus. This is the Indo-Pacific construct, embodied by the national strategies of Australia, Japan and the United States. Multilaterally, the initiative is represented by the Quadrilateral Security Dialogue (known informally as the 'Quad') among these countries and India, which was resurrected in 2017 after a ten-year hiatus. Washington's own Indo-Pacific strategy has drawn on years of discussions with Japan, Australia and India. President Donald Trump first mentioned the concept of 'a free and open Indo-Pacific' at the Asia-Pacific Economic Cooperation (APEC) summit in Vietnam in November 2017.[2] His administration's first National Security Strategy, released one month later, embraced it with gusto.[3]

The Chinese have refused to be impressed. In March 2018, Foreign Minister Wang Yi compared the Indo-Pacific idea to 'the sea foam in the Pacific or Indian Ocean', which 'may get some attention but soon will dissipate'.[4] Chinese scholars, while seeing it as a confrontational strategy, are sceptical about its effectiveness. Jin Canrong, an influential scholar from Renmin University in Beijing, described it as a 'bubble' that will disappear

Feng Zhang is Senior Lecturer in the Department of International Relations at the Australian National University's Coral Bell School of Asia Pacific Affairs, and Adjunct Professor at the National Institute for South China Sea Studies in China. He is the author of *Chinese Hegemony: Grand Strategy and International Institutions in East Asian History* (Stanford University Press, 2015).

Survival | vol. 61 no. 3 | June–July 2019 | pp. 187–212   DOI 10.1080/00396338.2019.1614791

as soon as the sun shines.[5] The *Global Times* has run a number of editorials prophesying that it will come to a whimpering end, just like Barack Obama's Asia 'rebalance' (or 'pivot') strategy.[6]

Nor has Beijing opted for focused confrontation against the Indo-Pacific, in contrast to its earlier assertiveness towards the rebalance. Even as tension rose at the November 2018 APEC summit in Papua New Guinea, President Xi Jinping contented himself with criticising American unilateralism and defending his Belt and Road Initiative (BRI), without unleashing any targeted counteroffensive.[7] Why?

It is tempting to explain China's nonchalance with reference to the country's dismissal of US strategic competence under Trump, who is not known for strategic foresight or coherence. But the causes run deeper. I suggest four reasons for Chinese forbearance during the first two years of the Trump administration: Beijing has learned the lesson of its overreaction to the rebalance; it believes itself in possession of new strategic leverage to fend off emerging challenges; it is in command of greater financial resources for regional economic initiatives and is open to third-party collaboration in the BRI; and it feels that it has adequate strategic space to navigate the treacherous waters of the Indo-Pacific.

The Trump administration's Indo-Pacific strategy, from its pronouncement in the December 2017 National Security Strategy to Vice President Mike Pence's articulation of its policy details in November 2018,[8] has been gradually clarified and solidified. One might reasonably have expected a corresponding evolution of Chinese attitudes towards it. Accordingly, in addition to drawing on public sources, I undertook two field trips to Beijing, in June and December 2018, during which I interviewed the same two leading government advisers to gauge changes in Chinese reactions. Surprisingly, although Beijing had begun to take the Indo-Pacific more seriously by December 2018 than it did in June 2018, the overall assessment remained the same: it was no big deal.[9]

Learning from mistakes

China's nonchalance towards the Indo-Pacific derives, to a significant extent, from its determination that it had overreacted to the Obama administration's rebalance. Experiential learning – defined as 'a change of beliefs (or the degree of confidence in one's beliefs) or the development of new beliefs, skills, or procedures as a result of the observation and interpretation of experience'[10] – can be an important cause of foreign-policy change. Decision-makers often engage in two kinds of learning: causal and diagnostic. Causal learning produces changing beliefs about the relationship of cause and effect, the consequences of actions and the optimal strategies under various conditions. Diagnostic learning, by contrast, generates changes in beliefs about how the overall situation, or the preferences, intentions or relative capabilities of others, should be defined.[11]

Chinese strategic experts, and the officials they influence, have engaged in both kinds of learning when considering their response to America's Indo-Pacific strategy. The Obama administration's rebalance strategy, announced in late 2011, has served as a useful reference point.[12] Beijing's initial assessment of the rebalance strategy was grave, seeing it as an almost entirely anti-China offensive.[13] This predilection was in part whipped up by nationalist denunciations of the rebalance as America's latest plot to contain China.

There were, to be sure, analysts such as Yuan Peng, a senior member of the prestigious China Institutes of Contemporary International Relations and an influential policy adviser, who appreciated the composite logic of the Obama strategy. Yuan took the view that the rebalance, which connected US diplomatic history with the contemporary realities of US statecraft, was not unreasonable from an American standpoint. Nevertheless, he maintained that it had comprehensively challenged China's interests in the security, diplomatic, economic and strategic domains.[14] Acknowledging the rebalance strategy's complex origins is one thing; letting it off the hook is something else.

Beijing gradually came to the judgement that a central motive of the strategy was hedging against and competing with China.[15] It may not have been an exclusively anti-China venture, but keeping China down was one of its chief purposes. This assessment was more emollient than the earlier 'containment' interpretation, but still alarmist. Thus, Fu Ying, a vice foreign minister in charge of Asia policy (2009–13), later noted that the 'intentions of the U.S. military alliances in the Asia-Pacific remain a particular source of concern for China', especially after the rebalance.[16]

The judgement that US Asia strategy was chiefly, if not entirely, directed at China produced paradoxical policy consequences. President Xi wanted to maintain a stable relationship with the United States, and so in February 2012, during a trip to the US when he was still vice-president, he suggested building a new type of cooperative relationship between the two countries.[17] The proposal developed into an attempt to build what China called 'a new model of major-country relationship', culminating in the Sunnylands summit between Obama and Xi in June 2013.[18] In striving for a new model of bilateral relations, Beijing averted its gaze from the rebalance.

Xi wanted a stable relationship

On the regional front, by contrast, China sought to confront the rebalance strategy with its own countermeasures. That meant, above all, a hardening of its positions in Asian maritime territorial disputes, especially in the South China Sea. Chinese analysts and officials accused Washington of fanning the flames of disputes between China and its neighbours, especially Vietnam, the Philippines and Japan.[19] These countries were perceived as relying on the US rebalance to make demands on China's sovereignty and maritime rights, and of proffering themselves as America's minions. China believed that it needed to respond with sufficient resolve to protect its own interests and resist these countries' provocations.[20] Failure to do so would not only inflate their ambitions at China's cost, but also embolden the US to further strengthen its own strategy. The upshot, then, was Beijing's determination to fight back – and a general assertiveness in its regional policy.

Yet this regional assertiveness stood in the way of building a new cooperative relationship with America. The way in which Beijing channelled its competitive instincts regionally, especially in asserting its sovereignty and maritime interests in the East and South China seas, made US policymakers more wary of Chinese intentions. They detected a contradiction between China's pursuit of a better relationship with the US and its behaviour in the region. Senior officials within the Obama administration initially responded positively, if not enthusiastically, to China's 'new model' diplomacy,[21] but by 2013 they had quietly rejected it. Beijing's decision to establish an air-defence identification zone in the East China Sea in November 2013, coupled with its island-building since late 2013, encouraged the perception that Chinese diplomacy was insincere, and even deceptive. Thus, China's regional assertiveness damaged its bilateral relationship with the US, an outcome that China had not foreseen.

Chinese analysts and policymakers have learned several important lessons from this. Firstly, they have re-evaluated the nature of the rebalance strategy and its potency,[22] concluding that the initial sense of the rebalance as an anti-China plot was exaggerated, and that the later, more moderate view that its chief aim was constraining China was more reasonable. To hardliners, the difference between 'containing' and 'constraining' China is trivial, but to policymakers who wish to preserve a stable Sino-US relationship, the difference is significant: seeing US strategy as 'containment' would entail a Chinese response of unbridled competition and confrontation, whereas a US strategy of 'constraining' China would leave room for cooperation. This more nuanced assessment of the rebalance reflected diagnostic learning concerning the accuracy of earlier judgements about the nature of the rebalance.

The causal learning experienced by Chinese officials was even more important. Influential Chinese experts saw a glaring contradiction between Xi's US strategy and his Asia strategy.[23] Xi was prepared to conciliate the US in a bilateral context while directing his offensive efforts towards the region. But he had shown little awareness of the need to reconcile the tension between bilateral compromise and regional assertiveness. The consequence of this contradiction was a worsening of China's relationship with the US, as well as with several of its Asian neighbours.

Chinese experts point to a further adverse effect of exaggerating the gravity of American strategy. Melodramatic fear mongering by the febrile nationalist press and social-media outlets unleashed additional pressure on the government to be tough, disrupting rational decision-making. Excited analysts played word games with the terms 'pivot' and 'rebalance', imputing all sorts of perfidious intentions to Washington. Such fervour and agitation reduced the space for calm analysis and shrewd judgement.[24]

Thus, confronted by the Indo-Pacific strategy in the first year of the Trump administration, influential experts counselled caution. They argued that in its earlier response to the rebalance, China had exaggerated its magnitude and potency, produced an internal contradiction in response and allowed domestic nationalist pressure to constrain policy. They recommended in internal policy meetings that these mistakes not be repeated, and that the government adopt a cool, wait-and-see attitude. Beijing listened, instructing research institutes and the media to desist from histrionic speculation and nationalist agitation.[25]

Expert learning is not the only cause of Chinese sobriety towards the Indo-Pacific. As a rule, learning is neither a necessary nor a sufficient condition for policy change. States alter their foreign policies for a host of reasons, and not all learning is translated into changes in policy.[26] But my interviews with elite advisers in Beijing suggest that it was an important conduit through which strategic caution was injected into the decision-making system. This was mainly accomplished through policy consultation between influential experts and officials. The writings of leading scholars – such as Shi Yinhong, a distinguished international-relations expert at Renmin University in Beijing – also played a key role. Shi has been cautioning against strategic overstretch since 2015.[27] This view is not only influential among scholars, but is also widely known within the government. Writers of this calibre are able to generate a discursive policy environment in which views at odds with the prevailing orthodoxy take on a life of their own. Either through the power of their argument, or by influencing elite experts who advise the government, they may shape policy. Thus, elite Chinese experts constitute an 'epistemic community' capable of driving learning-based foreign-policy change,[28] in this case imparting a measure of tranquillity to China's stance towards the Indo-Pacific construct.

New strategic leverage

In addition to the indirect effects of Chinese learning, there is a more straightforward reason for Chinese sangfroid: after a series of struggles with the rebalance, Beijing believes it has acquired new strategic leverage and is therefore in a better position to deal with the Indo-Pacific. Indeed,

Beijing today fears America's Asia strategy less than at any time during the Obama administration.

China's reaction to the rebalance was alarmist because the country felt threatened on multiple fronts. In the security domain, US redeployments intended to bring the proportion of US naval assets in the Pacific up to 60% (from 50%),[29] and a series of military plans targeting China, challenged its near-sea defence system. Brisk bilateral and multilateral military exercises around China's periphery aggravated its regional security environment. Significant deployments of new military assets in the region, including in Australia, Guam, Japan, the Philippines, Singapore and South Korea, cast a long shadow over the Sino-US military relationship. In the diplomatic domain, the rebalance strengthened America's existing alliance system and fostered a new networked approach to regional partnerships, increasing pressure on China. Beijing grumbled in particular about the rebalance's alleged exacerbation of maritime territorial disputes. Meanwhile, in the economic realm, the push for a Trans-Pacific Partnership (TPP) was seen to have disrupted the tempo of East Asian economic integration and challenged China's regional economic strategy.[30]

China's regional pushback strategy enacted during Xi's first term (2013–18) allowed it to emerge in a stronger position in Asia, at least in the short term. In October 2013, Xi hosted China's first conference on diplomacy towards countries on its periphery. Attended by representatives from the Communist Party, local and central government, the military, state-owned enterprises and the diplomatic corps, this conference marked a milestone in China's Asian regional strategy. Yan Xuetong, an esteemed international-relations scholar at Tsinghua University in Beijing, saw in the conference a strategic shift from 'keeping a low profile' to 'striving for achievement'.[31]

This 'striving for achievement' manifested itself in a two-pronged regional approach: a Chinese 'pivot' towards the Eurasian continent in the economic sphere, and a new resolve to protect its interests in maritime Asia in the security sphere. Not reducible to a simple Sino-US competition, this approach was not a direct response to the rebalance, though the rebalance played a role in establishing a foreboding geopolitical context for Chinese policymaking.

The Eurasian pivot, initially suggested by Peking University scholar Wang Jisi in an influential article,[32] became Xi's much-hyped BRI. With great fanfare, Beijing transfigured Xi's two 2013 speeches on the BRI into China's 'project of the century' aimed at building a rich and powerful China. Initially, however, the BRI had been part of China's answer to the TPP, the economic pillar of the rebalance. Kurt M. Campbell, assistant secretary of state for East Asian and Pacific affairs during Obama's first term in office and a key advocate of the rebalance, had described the TPP as the policy's 'true sine qua non';[33] while Ashton Carter, Obama's last secretary of defense, had declared that passing the TPP was as important to him as acquiring another aircraft carrier.[34] Yet Obama ran out of time to have the TPP ratified by Congress, and Trump, who ran for president on an anti-Obama and anti-multilateralism platform, withdrew US participation altogether. China had reason to be jubilant about this outcome, since the successor to the TPP, the Comprehensive and Progressive Agreement for Trans-Pacific Partnership (CPATPP),[35] is far less of a threat without the US. And while the BRI has met with resistance, it has not experienced a setback as grievous as Washington's abandonment of the TPP.[36]

In the security domain, Beijing stiffened its resolve in its maritime territorial disputes, wresting control of Scarborough Shoal in a bloodless confrontation with the Philippines in 2012, hauling an oil rig to waters seen by Vietnam as within its exclusive economic zone, and carrying out land reclamation and island-building in the Spratly Islands from late 2013, which by June 2015 had allowed it to claim more than 2,900 acres of land. Since then, it has installed military as well as civilian facilities that can accommodate fighter jets, missiles and communications equipment.[37]

American attitudes towards Chinese island fortification have shifted from a dismissive cockiness to growing anxiety. In a 2015 report on the US–China military balance, RAND analysts asserted that the islands 'are unlikely to be a significant factor in high-intensity military operations against U.S. forces beyond the first hours of a conflict'.[38] Three years later, in April 2018, Admiral Philip Davidson, nominated as commander of the Indo-Pacific Command, observed in his testimony to Congress that 'China is now capable of controlling the South China Sea in all scenarios short of war with the United States'.[39] These two observations are not wholly con-tradictory, since they both point to the vulnerability of the islands during a Sino-US hot war. Yet Davidson's remarks belie an intensifying unease about China's consolidation of its control over a large portion of the South China Sea during peacetime. The perception that the US has lost the initiative and that China is prevailing is widespread in Washington and regional capi-tals.[40] American analysts are now grappling with the challenge of devising new strategies for countering Chinese advances.[41]

Beijing has also made notable progress on the diplomatic front. Under the rebalance, the US enhanced its diplomatic and strategic relations with key Asian countries, including both its traditional allies and new security partners. In Northeast Asia, the April 2015 upgrade of the Guidelines for US–Japan Defense Cooperation represented the latest in a series of enhancements since the 1997 revision of the guidelines.[42] In Southeast Asia, the

China is no longer in siege mode

Obama administration opened new ties with Myanmar, elevated relations with Vietnam, forged a new partnership with Indonesia, strengthened an already solid relationship with Singapore and boosted the traditional alli-ance with the Philippines with a new defence-cooperation agreement. The relationship with the Association of Southeast Asian Nations (ASEAN) also received an upgrade. Washington acceded to the ASEAN Treaty of Amity and Cooperation in Southeast Asia, joined the East Asia Summit and hosted, for the first time, a US–ASEAN summit on American soil in February 2016.[43] These developments rang alarm bells in Beijing.

Less than two years into the Trump administration, however, China is no longer in siege mode. Its relationship with Japan has thawed, in part because both countries oppose Trump's trade offensive.[44] Prime Minister Shinzo Abe visited Beijing in October 2018, the first official visit to China by a Japanese leader since 2011. Abe announced that the relationship had shifted 'from competition to cooperation' and characterised the two coun-tries as 'partners'.[45] These pronouncements should be taken, of course, with a pinch of salt – balancing against China is still Japan's underlying security strategy, and the two countries' territorial dispute over the Senkaku/Diaoyu islands remains intractable. Nevertheless, the relationship has experienced an undeniable improvement. Japan's pledge to work with China on the latter's BRI projects, a major outcome of Abe's visit, is a noteworthy signal of Tokyo's new pragmatism.[46]

China also achieved a striking strategic reversal with ASEAN and its member states. Blandishing both economic largesse and the prospect of a new diplomatic code of conduct, Beijing has managed to reduce tension with ASEAN over the South China Sea since July 2016.[47] The 2015 upgrade of the ASEAN–China Free Trade Agreement and the rolling out of the BRI in Southeast Asia represent the economic pillar of this strategy, while diplomatic consultations on a code of conduct have all but depleted ASEAN's capacity for raising hackles over the disputes.

Bilaterally, China's relationships with Southeast Asian states saw a general, albeit uneven, improvement. Regional states are, to varying degrees, getting along with China. These include the traditional bandwagoners of Cambodia and Laos, the careful hedgers of Indonesia and Singapore, and the former challengers of the Philippines and Vietnam. Of these, the crown jewel of Chinese achievement is the Philippines. Since June 2016, in a remarkable volte-face from the approach of Benigno Aquino III, President Rodrigo Duterte has comported himself as if Manila were an ally of China rather than the US, perhaps swayed by Chinese promises of a whopping $24 billion economic package for shelving disputes.[48] To be sure, China's relationship with Vietnam remains tense, especially after Chinese pressure forced Hanoi to suspend oil drilling in disputed areas.[49] And Beijing also suffered a setback in Malaysia after the electoral defeat of the Sinophile Najib Razak at the hands of his former mentor Mahathir Mohamad in May 2018.[50] Overall, however, China has come close to atoning for its assertiveness in Southeast Asia with a cocktail of economic inducements, security deterrence and diplomatic cajoling. No serious region-wide backlash is in sight.

Although calling this a 'win' for China might be a stretch, Beijing certainly does not think it is losing. The TPP is no more, and the CPATPP, while still acting as a regional economic constraint, is not an American-led threat as the TPP had been. In the South China Sea, it is the US, not China, that has been wrongfooted. And Beijing's diplomatic, economic and security position in Southeast Asia, and especially vis-à-vis ASEAN, has been enhanced. There is no danger of the region slinking into the American fold, as once was possible during the height of the rebalance. Of course, the cost of China's enhanced regional position is rising tension and a badly deteriorating relationship with the US. That is a cost China has to accept.

Resource advantages and openness to BRI collaboration

A third reason why China has remained calm about America's growing investment in its Indo-Pacific strategy is that it considers itself better resourced to implement its own regional initiative, the BRI. Chinese elites are confident that the US is not in a position to dole out a new 'Marshall Plan' to regional countries in economic competition with China.[51] Beijing is even prepared to welcome the infrastructure initiatives of Quad members if they can complement – or even work with – the BRI to deliver greater prosperity and stability for the region.

To be sure, the Trump administration has been ramping up resources devoted to its own Indo-Pacific strategy. In July 2018, Secretary of State Michael Pompeo announced $113 million to support initiatives in the realms of digital economy, energy and infrastructure. Mindful of the puniness of the funds, he characterised them as 'just a down payment on a new era in U.S. economic commitment to peace and prosperity in the Indo-Pacific region'.[52] In the field of infrastructure, where much of the competition with China takes place, Pompeo announced the creation of a new inter-agency body called the Infrastructure Transaction and Assistance Network, as well as a new Indo-Pacific Transaction Advisory Fund. He also highlighted the BUILD (Better Utilization of Investments Leading to Development) Act, which would more than double the US government's development-finance capacity to $60bn.[53] One week later, while attending the ASEAN Foreign Ministers' Meeting, Pompeo offered $300m to support the security component of the Indo-Pacific strategy, with an emphasis on strengthening maritime security.[54]

Vice President Pence gave further weight to the strategy at the November 2018 APEC summit. In the economic arena, he pledged $400m for an Indo-Pacific Transparency Initiative. In infrastructure development, he announced a partnership with Japan to invest $10bn in the region's energy infrastructure and, with Japan and Australia, to bring electricity to 70% of Papua New Guinea by 2030. In July 2018, America, Australia and Japan cemented a trilateral partnership for infrastructure investment in the Indo-Pacific,[55] through which Pence promised 'a vast array of private development projects'. In the field of security, he announced America's intention to develop the Lombrum Naval Base on Manus Island with Papua New Guinea and Australia.[56]

Many have interpreted this slew of measures as a significant pushback against China.[57] Yet, while these measures may have niggled at Beijing, they have not yet caused significant alarm, for two reasons. The first is the equation of resource commitments. American investments, granting the 'down payment' caveat, are paltry compared with China's, totalling about $60.8bn including the BUILD Act's $60bn. Compare that with China's intended investments in the BRI alone, estimates of which range from $1 trillion to $8trn.[58] The China–Pakistan Economic Corridor, a signature project, is valued at between $46bn and $62bn. Yang Jiechi, China's top-ranking foreign-policy official, claimed in July 2018 that China had already invested $70bn during the BRI's first five years.[59]

This resource advantage is by no means the only, or even the most important, reason behind China's equanimity in the face of growing international resistance to the BRI. It may not be a reliable advantage anyway, given that China's state coffers are not bottomless. A more important reason is the consensus among Chinese elites that other countries' infrastructure initiatives should not necessarily be perceived as 'competition' against the BRI. A positive-sum perspective emphasising mutual benefit is seen as more appropriate than a counterproductive, zero-sum mindset. Following this logic, Beijing is prepared to welcome the infrastructure policies of the Quad countries if they can further the economic and social development of regional countries. Indeed, China has already begun to accept the collaboration of some regional countries, notably Singapore and Japan.[60] After all, the BRI is supposed to be based on the principles of 'discussion, collaboration, and sharing' (*gongshang, gongjian, gongxiang*),[61] and anything that contributes to a more prosperous and stable region is seen as in China's interest.[62]

An adequate strategic space

Finally, in the security domain, although the Trump administration has pushed back hard in the South China Sea and the South Pacific, China believes it still possesses an adequate strategic space in which to manoeuvre.[63] The Quad is not a monolithic anti-China bloc, and China believes that India, and to a lesser extent Japan and Australia, can be weaned off a Sinophobic agenda. Asia's multilayered institutional architecture affords additional strategic space. ASEAN, for instance, is averse to choosing sides between America and China.

The Indo-Pacific strategy, especially the Quad mechanism, faces three challenges: coordination among the four Quad powers, their relationship with ASEAN and institutional constraints within the regional order. The problem of coordination is pervasive in multilateral undertakings – it was, for example, a principal cause of the inability of the Six-Party Talks to resolve the North Korean nuclear-weapons crisis from 2003 to 2008[64] – and there is no reason to believe that the Quad will be able to overcome it easily. Coordination in 'low politics' areas, such as counter-terrorism and humanitarian assistance, is relatively straightforward. But when it comes to the task of constraining China, universally believed to be the Quad's chief purpose, cracks are likely to emerge.

Indeed, signs of disunity have already been in evidence since the initial Quad meeting convened at the urging of Japan in May 2007. In less than a year, the Australian government under Kevin Rudd had dropped out for fear of offending China.[65] Ten years later, in November 2017, again at the prompting of Japan, the Quad was resurrected, this time with more feisty support from Australia and America. But India, held back by its long-standing non-alignment tradition and the need to rub along with China over a skein of issues, stands in the way of an overtly anti-China agenda. And this despite a significant worsening of its relationship with China following the 73-day stand-off at Doklam in June–August 2017, during which Indian troops confronted a Chinese construction crew staffed by members of the People's Liberation Army that had come to the disputed area to build a road.[66]

The statements issued after the November 2017 meeting by each country are a clear illustration of the coordination problem.[67] That each Quad member chose to issue a separate statement rather than agree to a joint statement is noteworthy in itself. The statements also display subtle but important differences in India's vision of the Indo-Pacific compared to those of the America–Australia–Japan troika. While the troika endorsed a vision of an Indo-Pacific that is 'free and open', India's statement used the term 'inclusive' and emphasised 'the long-term interests of all countries in the region and of the world at large'. Absent from the Indian statement was any mention of freedom of navigation, respect for international law or maritime security, all issues at the heart of the disputes in the South China Sea and all highlighted by the troika. Common democratic values and principles are cited as the foundation of the Quad by the troika, while India highlights its 'Act East' policy as the cornerstone of its engagement in the Indo-Pacific. Indeed, India, unlike the US and Australia, avoided any mention of a 'quad-rilateral' at all. Judging from these differences, the Quad looks like an uneasy 3+1 rather than a monolithic quartet.

Unsettled by the Doklam stand-off, Beijing and New Delhi tried to patch up their quarrels through an informal summit meeting between Xi and Prime Minister Narendra Modi in April 2018 in the Chinese city of Wuhan. The meeting was successful in that it appeared to prevent the countries' relationship, one that had been plunged into confusion due to Doklam and a series of other disputes, from becoming explicitly adversarial. The Xi–Modi summit, according to Beijing, redefined the two countries as 'neighbors, friends and partners'.[68] The Indian view, while less rosy, encompassed a pledge to strengthen the Closer Development Partnership and to strive for a 'peaceful, stable, and balanced relationship'.[69] In June 2018, Modi delivered the keynote address at the IISS Shangri-La Dialogue in Singapore, during which he mentioned the understanding with China achieved at the Wuhan summit. More gratifying to the Chinese, however, was his declaration that 'India does not see the Indo-Pacific region as a strategy or as a club of limited members, nor as a grouping that seeks to dominate. And by no means do we consider it as directed against any country.'[70] This dismissal of the Indo-Pacific as a geopolitical strategy stood in stark contrast to the way it was depicted by then-US defense secretary Jim Mattis in his speech the following day, which presented the Indo-Pacific as America's whole-of-government strategy.[71]

India has good reason to be wary of joining with America, Australia and Japan in forming a Sinophobic Quad. One constraint is India's tradition of non-alignment.[72] Moreover, India's land-border disputes with China have tended to drain resources from the Indo-Pacific maritime front,[73] and its interests lie mainly in the Indian Ocean, meaning that its engagement with the Pacific is likely to 'remain largely diplomatic, economic and rhetorical' in the short term, according to *Survival* contributors Rahul Roy-Chaudhury and Kate Sullivan de Estrada.[74] This is ironic considering that the America–Australia–Japan troika has embraced the Indo-Pacific above all to woo India, a rising power just like China but, unlike China, also an agreeable democracy committed to a rules-based order.[75] On the US side, the inclusion of India represents a weighty upgrade to the Obama administration's rebalance strategy. If India sidles away, both the strategy and the Quad will lose their clout.

India has good reason to be wary

Signs that the Quad has become 'softer' as the result of India's dilution of its anti-China agenda are already visible. Following the second Quad meeting in June 2018, none of the four countries used the term 'quadrilateral' in its statement, and all used the term 'inclusive' to modify the 'Indo-Pacific', a clear nod to the Indian vision. In addition, all four pledged to partner with other countries and institutions in the region.[76] This appeared primarily as an overture to ASEAN, but also as an effort to dispel any suspicion of its anti-China exclusivity. Yet even though this second meeting appears to have narrowed the gap between India's vision of the Indo-Pacific and those of the other three powers, a common strategy remains elusive. Modi's rejection of the Indo-Pacific as an Indian strategy presents a significant obstacle to a coherent and uniform Quad strategy. It is also worth noting that all four Quad meetings convened between 2007 and 2018 (May 2007, November 2017, June and November 2018) were at the sub-cabinet level. Beijing would not see any particular challenge in this.

Tactically, China needs only to hold India to neutralise the Quad. It may also have a crack at Japan and Australia.[77] As noted, relations with Japan have already begun to thaw. Official ties with Australia were 'frozen' after 2017 as China seethed about then-prime minister Malcolm Turnbull's allegations that it was conducting 'influence operations',[78] but since an apparently conciliatory Scott Morrison became prime minister in August 2018, Beijing has relented. In November 2018, Marise Payne became the first Australian foreign minister in almost three years to visit Beijing.[79] Japan's and Australia's commitment to the Quad is greater than India's, and their bilateral relationships with China have inherent limits. Nevertheless, China can use these relationships to drive a wedge in the Quad. Beijing is betting that India and Japan, as two major Asian countries, will recognise that their relations with China need to be based on beneficial cooperation, not vicious competition.[80]

Chinese elites are not oblivious to the security risks presented by America's Indo-Pacific strategy. They are alert to any US attempt to divide the region and undermine China's relations with its neighbours. But they are also relieved by what they see as the limits of the US strategy. If Washington pushes too hard, the Quad will break apart and the US will lose the support of many regional countries, especially those in Southeast Asia.[81] No regional country will intentionally seek a bad relationship with China, making any fallout from the Indo-Pacific strategy containable.

Another lever that China has at its disposal is its improving relationship with ASEAN. For America's Indo-Pacific strategy and the Quad to be effective, they must have some ASEAN support. Southeast Asia, which semi-encloses the South China Sea, lies at the critical intersection between the Indian and Pacific oceans, and is a major arena for great-power competition. ASEAN, the premier regional organisation, has been the region's central platform for multilateral order-building since the end of the Cold War.[82]

Yet ASEAN fears a potential blow to its centrality from the Indo-Pacific construct. If the Quad were to dominate regional strategic initiatives, that would undermine ASEAN's ability to frustrate the designs of major powers and, along with it, a key institutional principle of the post-Cold War regional order.[83] ASEAN has shaped this order through a series of multilateral institutions centred on itself, including ASEAN+1 dialogues with partner states, ASEAN+3 (China, Japan and South Korea), the ASEAN Regional Forum and the East Asia Summit. Describing the current period as 'very grave', Vivian

Balakrishnan, Singapore's foreign minister, when hosting the ASEAN Foreign Ministers' Meeting in August 2018, exhorted ASEAN to 'remain anchored to the core principles of ASEAN unity and centrality, maintain an open, inclusive and rules-based regional architecture, and double down on community-building efforts'.[84] The Indo-Pacific initiative must reckon with this ASEAN agenda.

A predominantly China-focused Indo-Pacific security strategy is unlikely to win ASEAN's support, since the grouping is loath to choose sides in this great-power competition and has consciously avoided doing so. Asked about the Quad ahead of the ASEAN–Australia summit in March 2018, Singapore's Prime Minister Lee Hsien Loong demurred, saying that 'We do not want to end up with rival blocs forming or countries having to take one side or the other.'[85] Likewise, Bilahari Kausikan, a veteran Singaporean diplomat, described the Quad countries' focus on China and the BRI as 'too narrow a basis to attract wider support'.[86] Chinese elites are confident that ASEAN will oppose policies that risk making the region more competitive than cooperative.[87] China's *Global Times*, noting that having to choose sides between China and the US is ASEAN's 'worst nightmare', gleefully declared in August 2018 that the Indo-Pacific strategy is unpopular in ASEAN.[88]

> ## ASEAN is loath to choose sides

Kausikan believes that the Indo-Pacific strategy cannot succeed without ASEAN's support.[89] To win that support, Quad members will have to commit to maintaining ASEAN's centrality and develop an economic strategy to meet the region's development needs. Indeed, since the 2018 Shangri-La Dialogue, all the Quad countries have pledged to support ASEAN's centrality and its related institutions in regional order-building.[90] They are wooing ASEAN in earnest. But Chinese elites see American reassurance about ASEAN's centrality as a charade.[91] ASEAN's centrality would blunt the Indo-Pacific offensive. Where then would be the sting for China?

As it is, the Quad can be seen as just another layer in an already complex regional institutional architecture comprising a host of bilateral, trilateral and other plurilateral configurations. These include the post-war hub-and-spokes system of bilateral alliances created by the US; the trilateral security dialogues among the US, Japan and Australia and the US, Japan and India; the multilateral groupings of ASEAN+1 and ASEAN+3; the ASEAN Regional Forum; the East Asia Summit; APEC; the Asian Infrastructure Investment Bank (AIIB); and Track Two security forums such as the Council for Security Cooperation in the Asia Pacific that exist alongside Track One security dialogues. As Victor Cha has noted, the Quad would incite Chinese insecurities if it were the only regional grouping available.[92] Yet Beijing is currently able to engage with all the Quad powers in the context of the East Asia Summit; with Japan in the context of ASEAN+3; with Australia and India in the context of the AIIB; and with its fellow members of the BRICS grouping (Brazil, Russia, India, China and South Africa). This capacity helps to reduce, if not eliminate, Chinese anxiety.[93]

China's regional and global diplomacy is today focused on forging strategic partnerships. Its signature partnership in the Indo-Pacific region is with ASEAN.[94] It has also cemented partnership relationships with both Australia and India, although not with America or Japan, still two of its most difficult bilateral relationships. Winning friends through such partnerships would doubtless also mitigate the brunt of the Indo-Pacific strategy.

*   *   *

China's nonchalance towards the Indo-Pacific strategic construct presents a striking contrast to its assertiveness during Xi's first term. Beijing drew lessons from its injudicious response to the Obama administration's rebalance, heeding the counsel of experts who advised caution. It also emerged in a strong strategic position following its struggles with the rebalance and with neighbours over disputed territories, particularly in the South China Sea. It is now well placed to address any challenge from the Indo-Pacific.

China does not see American-led regional infrastructure initiatives as a threat to its own BRI, given that its own projects are well resourced and that it is open to collaboration with other countries, including the US. Moreover, China believes it can exploit the coordination problem among the four Quad powers, focusing on India as the easiest target. It can cajole ASEAN to withhold support for the Indo-Pacific, thus depriving it of much potency in the vital region of Southeast Asia. And it can use Asia's complex, multilayered regional architecture to cushion any fallout. If Beijing has any concerns deriving from the series of concrete policies announced by the Trump administration in 2018, it appears to still regard these as eminently manageable.

Notes

1   See, for example, Barry Buzan, 'China in International Society: Is "Peaceful Rise" Possible?', *Chinese Journal of International Politics*, vol. 3, no. 1, 2010, p. 33; Alastair Iain Johnston, 'How New and Assertive Is China's New Assertiveness?', *International Security*, vol. 37, no. 4, 2013, pp. 7–48; and Orville Schell, 'China Strikes Back!', *New York Review of Books*, 23 October 2014, https://www.nybooks.com/articles/2014/10/23/china-strikes-back/.

2   'Remarks by President Trump at APEC CEO Summit', Da Nang, Vietnam, 10 November 2017, https://www.whitehouse.gov/briefings-statements/remarks-president-trump-apec-ceo-summit-da-nang-vietnam/.

3   White House, 'National Security Strategy of the United States of America', December 2017, pp. 45–7.

4   Ministry of Foreign Affairs of the People's Republic of China, 'Foreign Minister Wang Yi Meets the Press', 9 March 2018, http://www.fmprc.gov.cn/mfa_eng/wjb_663304/wjbz_663308/2461_663310/t1540928.shtml.

5   Dingding Chen, 'What China Thinks of the Indo-Pacific Strategy', *Diplomat*, 27 April 2018, https://thediplomat.com/2018/05/what-china-thinks-of-the-indo-pacific-strategy/.

6   See Liu Dian, 'Indo-Pacific Alliance Could End Prematurely', *Global Times*, 13 November 2017, http://www.globaltimes.cn/content/1074998.shtml; and Liang Fang, 'Indo-Pacific Strategy Will Likely Share the Same Fate as Rebalance to Asia-Pacific', *Global Times*, 3 December 2017, http://www.globaltimes.cn/content/1078470.shtml.

7   Xi Jinping, 'Tongzhou gongji chuang-zao meihao weilai' [Helping each other and creating a fine future], Port Moresby, 17 November 2018, https://www.fmprc.gov.cn/web/zyxw/t1614036.shtml.

8   'Remarks by Vice President Pence at the 2018 APEC CEO Summit', Port Moresby, 16 November 2018, https://www.whitehouse.gov/briefings-statements/remarks-vice-president-pence-2018-apec-ceo-summit-port-moresby-papua-new-guinea/.

9   Author interview with scholar A based at government think tank A, Beijing, June and December 2018; author interview with scholar B based at government think tank B, Beijing, June and December 2018.

10   Jack S. Levy, 'Learning and Foreign Policy: Sweeping a Conceptual Minefield', *International Organization*,

vol. 48, no. 2, 1994, p. 283.

11 *Ibid.*, p. 285.

12 See Kurt M. Campbell, *The Pivot: The Future of American Statecraft in Asia* (New York: Twelve, 2016).

13 Author interview with scholar A, Beijing, June 2018.

14 Yuan Peng, 'Xunqiu zhongmei yatai liangxing hudong' [In search of positive US–China interactions in the Asia-Pacific region], *Guoji anquan yanjiu* [Journal of International Security Studies], no. 1, 2013, p. 60.

15 Ruan Zongze, 'Meiguo "yatai zaip-ingheng" zhanlüe qianjing lunxi' [An analysis of the prospects of the US 'Asian rebalance strategy'], *Shijie jingji yu zhengzhi* [World Economy and Politics], no. 4, 2014, p. 10. Ruan, a leading American foreign-policy expert, is the deputy dean of the China Institute of International Studies in Beijing, a think tank supervised by the Ministry of Foreign Affairs.

16 Fu Ying, 'How China Sees Russia', *Foreign Affairs*, vol. 95, no. 1, 2016, p. 104.

17 'Remarks by Vice President Biden and Chinese Vice President Xi at the State Department Luncheon', 14 February 2012, https://obamawhitehouse.archives.gov/the-press-office/2012/02/14/remarks-vice-president-biden-and-chinese-vice-president-xi-state-departm.

18 'Remarks by President Obama and President Xi Jinping of the People's Republic of China After Bilateral Meeting', Sunnylands Retreat, Rancho Mirage, 8 June 2013, https://obamawhitehouse.archives.gov/the-press-office/2013/06/08/remarks-president-obama-and-president-xi-jinping-peoples-republic-china-.

19 See Wu Xinbo and Michael Green, 'Regional Security Roles and Challenges', in Nina Hachigian (ed.), *Debating China: The US–China Relationship in Ten Conversations* (Oxford: Oxford University Press, 2014), pp. 201–5; and Fu, 'How China Sees Russia', p. 104.

20 See Lin Hongyu and Zhang Shuai, 'Chaoyue kunjing: 2010 nian yilai zhongmei anquan boyi jiqi yingxiang' [Beyond dilemma: the security game between China and America since 2010], *Guoji anquan yanjiu* [Journal of International Security Studies], vol. 33, no. 2, 2015, p. 66.

21 See, for example, 'Remarks by Tom Donilon, National Security Advisor to the President: "The United States and the Asia-Pacific in 2013"', The Asia Society, New York, 11 March 2013, https://obamawhitehouse.archives.gov/the-press-office/2013/03/11/remarks-tom-donilon-national-security-advisor-president-united-states-an.

22 Author interview with scholar A, Beijing, June 2018.

23 *Ibid.*

24 *Ibid.*

25 Interviews with scholar A, Beijing, June 2018; with scholar B, Beijing, December 2018; and with scholar C based at a major university, Beijing, June 2018.

26 Levy, 'Learning and Foreign Policy', pp. 289–90.

27 Shi Yinhong, 'Guanyu zhongguo duiwai zhanlüe youhua he zhanlüe shenshen wenti de sikao' [Reflections on China's strategy in foreign rela-tions: issues of improvement and prudence], *Taipingyang xuebao* [Pacific Journal], vol. 23, no. 6, 2015, pp. 1–5.

28 Levy, 'Learning and Foreign Policy', p. 293.

29 See 'Remarks by Secretary Panetta at the Shangri-La Dialogue in Singapore', 2 June 2012, http://archive. defense.gov/transcripts/transcript. aspx?transcriptid=5049.

30 Yuan, 'Xunqiu zhongmei yatai liangxing hudong', p. 58.

31 Yan Xuetong, 'From Keeping a Low Profile to Striving for Achievement', *Chinese Journal of International Politics*, vol. 7, no. 2, 2014, pp. 153–84.

32 Wang Jisi, '"Xijin", zhongguo diyuan zhanlüe de zaipingheng' ['Pivot towards the West', the rebalance of China's geopolitical strategy], *Huanqiu shibbao* [Global Times], 17 October 2012, http://opinion.huanqiu.com/ opinion_world/2012-10/3193760.html.

33 Campbell, *The Pivot*, p. 266.

34 See Jamil Anderlini, 'A Shaky Trade Pact that Signals American Decline', *Financial Times*, 5 October 2016.

35 Ernesto Londoño and Motoko Rich, 'US Allies Sign Sweeping Trade Deal in Challenge to Trump', *New York Times*, 8 March 2018, https://www. nytimes.com/2018/03/08/world/asia/ us-trump-tpp-signed.html.

36 'China Has a Vastly Ambitious Plan to Connect the World', *The Economist*, 26 July 2018, https://www. economist.com/briefing/2018/07/26/ china-has-a-vastly-ambitious-plan-to- connect-the-world.

37 Asia Maritime Transparency Initiative, 'An Accounting of China's Deployments to the Spratly Islands', 9 May 2018, https://amti.csis.org/ accounting-chinas-deployments- spratly-islands/.

38 Eric Heginbotham et al., *The US–China Military Scorecard: Forces, Geography, and the Evolving Balance of Power, 1996–2017* (Santa Monica, CA: RAND Corporation, 2015), p. 89.

39 United States Senate Committee on Armed Forces, 'Advance Policy Questions for Admiral Philip Davidson, USN Expected Nominee for Commander, US Pacific Command', 17 April 2018, p. 18, https://www. armed-services.senate.gov/imo/media/ doc/Davidson_APQs_04-17-18.pdf.

40 See Hugh White, 'Without America: Australia in the New Asia', *Quarterly Essay*, no. 68, 2017, p. 12; and Lynn Kuok, 'China Is Winning in the South China Sea', *Wall Street Journal*, 17 July 2018, https://www.wsj.com/articles/ china-is-winning-in-the-south-china- sea-1531868329.

41 See Michael J. Green et al., 'Countering Coercion in Maritime Asia: The Theory and Practice of Gray Zone Deterrence' (Washington DC: Center for Strategic and International Studies, 2017); and Ross Babbage, 'Countering China's Adventurism in the South China Sea: Strategy Options for the Trump Administration' (Washington DC: Center for Strategic and Budgetary Assessments, 15 December 2016).

42 See Michael Auslin, 'Japan's New Realism: Abe Gets Tough', *Foreign Affairs*, vol. 95, no. 2, 2016, p. 133.

43 Patrick M. Cronin, 'Sustaining the Rebalance in Southeast Asia: Challenges and Opportunities Facing the Next Administration' (Washington DC: Center for a New American Security, 2016), p. 5.

44 Willy Wo-lap Lam, 'The Many Sides of Tentative Sino-Japanese

Rapprochement', *China Brief*, vol. 18, no. 9, May 2018, pp. 4–6.

45 Steven Lee Myers and Motoko Rich, 'Shinzo Abe Says Japan Is China's "Partner," and No Longer Its Aid Donor', *New York Times*, 26 October 2018, https://www.nytimes.com/2018/10/26/world/asia/shinzo-abe-china-japan.html.

46 Shiro Armstrong, 'Japan Joins to Shape China's Belt and Road', East Asia Forum, 28 October 2018, http://www.eastasiaforum.org/2018/10/28/japan-joins-to-shape-chinas-belt-and-road/.

47 See Feng Zhang, 'Assessing China's Response to the South China Sea Arbitration Ruling', *Australian Journal of International Affairs*, vol. 71, no. 4, 2017, pp. 440–59.

48 Richard Javad Heydarian, 'Duterte Confuses, Risks Making China Bolder in South China Sea', *Straits Times*, 24 October 2016, http://www.straitstimes.com/opinion/duterte-confuses-risks-making-china-bolder-in-south-china-sea.

49 See Bonnie S. Glaser and Gregory Poling, 'Vanishing Borders in the South China Sea', *Foreign Affairs*, 5 June 2018, https://www.foreignaffairs.com/articles/china/2018-06-05/vanishing-borders-south-china-sea.

50 Richard C. Paddock, 'Malaysia Opposition, Led by 92-year-old, Wins Upset Victory', *New York Times*, 9 May 2018, https://www.nytimes.com/2018/05/09/world/asia/malaysia-election-najib-mahathir.html.

51 Author interview with scholar B, Beijing, December 2018.

52 'Remarks on "America's Indo-Pacific Economic Vision"', 30 July 2018, https://www.state.gov/secretary/remarks/2018/07/284722.htm.

53 *Ibid.*

54 'Press Availability at the 51st ASEAN Foreign Ministers' Meeting and Related Meetings', Singapore, 4 August 2018, https://www.state.gov/secretary/remarks/2018/08/284924.htm.

55 Julie Bishop, 'Australia, US and Japan Announce Trilateral Partnership for Infrastructure Investment in the Indo-Pacific', media release, 31 July 2018, https://foreignminister.gov.au/releases/Pages/2018/jb_mr_180731.aspx.

56 'Remarks by Vice President Pence at the 2018 APEC CEO Summit'.

57 See, for example, Rory Medcalf, '2018 APEC Summit Possible Turning Point for China's Powerplay in the Pacific', *Australian Financial Review*, 18 November 2018, https://www.afr.com/news/economy/2018-apec-summit-possible-turning-point-for-chinas-powerplay-in-the-pacific-20181118-h180y2.

58 'China Has a Vastly Ambitious Plan to Connect the World'.

59 Yang Jiechi, 'Working Together to Build a World of Lasting Peace and Universal Security and a Community with a Shared Future for Mankind', Beijing, 14 July 2018, http://www.fmprc.gov.cn/mfa_eng/zxxx_662805/t1577242.shtml.

60 For Singapore, see Tan Dawn Wei, 'China, Singapore Agree to Deepen Ties in Various Areas', *Straits Times*, 15 November 2018, https://www.straitstimes.com/singapore/china-singapore-agree-to-deepen-ties-in-various-areas. For Japan, see Armstrong, 'Japan Joins to Shape China's Belt and Road'.

61 The National Development and
    Reform Commission, Ministry of
    Foreign Affairs, and Ministry of
    Commerce of the People's Republic
    of China, with State Council
    Authorization, 'Tuidong gongjian
    sichou zhilu jingjidai he 21 shiji
    haishang sichou zhilu de yuanjing
    yu xingdong' [Vision and actions on
    jointly building Silk Road Economic
    Belt and Twenty-first-century
    Maritime Silk Road], 1 April 2015,
    http://www.fmprc.gov.cn/ce/cevn/
    chn/sghkt/t1251121.htm.

62 Author interview with scholars A and
    B, Beijing, December 2018.

63 Author interview with scholar A,
    Beijing, December 2018.

64 Stephan Haggard and Marcus Noland,
    *Hard Target: Sanctions, Inducements, and
    the Case of North Korea* (Stanford, CA:
    Stanford University Press, 2017).

65 Tanvi Madan, 'The Rise, Fall, and
    Rebirth of the "Quad"', *War on the
    Rocks*, 16 November 2017, https://
    warontherocks.com/2017/11/
    rise-fall-rebirth-quad/.

66 'China and India Are Trying to Get
    Along Better', *The Economist*, 26 April
    2018, https://www.economist.com/
    asia/2018/04/26/china-and-india-are-
    trying-to-get-along-better.

67 Heather Nauert, 'Australia–India–
    Japan–US Consultations on the
    Indo-Pacific', US Department of State,
    12 November 2017, https://www.
    state.gov/r/pa/prs/ps/2017/11/275464.
    htm; Ministry of Foreign Affairs of
    Japan, 'Australia–India–Japan–US
    Consultations on the Indo-Pacific',
    press release, 12 November 2017,
    https://www.mofa.go.jp/press/release/
    press4e_001789.html; Department of

    Foreign Affairs and Trade of Australia,
    'Australia–India–Japan–United States
    Consultations on the Indo-Pacific',
    media release, 12 November 2017,
    https://dfat.gov.au/news/media/Pages/
    aus-india-japan-us-consultations-
    on-the-indo-pacific.aspx; Ministry
    of External Affairs of India, 'India–
    Australia–Japan–US Consultations
    on Indo-Pacific (November 12,
    2017)', press release, http://mea.gov.
    in/press-releases.htm?dtl/29110/
    IndiaAustraliaJapanUS_
    Consultations_on_IndoPacific_
    November_12_2017.

68 Ministry of Foreign Affairs of the
    People's Republic of China, 'Leaders
    of China and India Reach Broad
    Consensus in Informal Meeting', 28
    April 2018, http://www.fmprc.gov.cn/
    mfa_eng/zxxx_662805/t1556558.shtml.

69 Ministry of External Affairs of India,
    'India–China Informal Summit at
    Wuhan', press release, 28 April 2018,
    http://www.mea.gov.in/press-releases.
    htm?dtl/29853/IndiaChina+Informal+S
    ummit+at+Wuhan.

70 Narendra Modi, 'Keynote Address',
    17th Asia Security Summit: The IISS
    Shangri-La Dialogue, Singapore, 1
    June 2018, https://www.iiss.org/-/
    media/images/dialogues/sld/sld-2018/
    documents/narendra-modi-sld18.ashx
    ?la=en&hash=66F993469C4220817C49
    26310711FEE4A2C9E017.

71 James Mattis, 'US Leadership and the
    Challenges of Indo-Pacific Security',
    First Plenary Session, 17th Asia
    Security Summit: The IISS Shangri-La
    Dialogue, Singapore, 2 June 2018,
    'Remarks by Secretary Mattis', https://
    www.iiss.org/-/media/images/
    dialogues/sld/sld-2018/documents/

james-mattis-sld18.ashx?la=en&hash=
020D1562882D7460CDA17BC67B0037
BFE1DDE748.

72 See Harsh V. Pant and Abhijnan Rej,
'Is India Ready for the Indo-Pacific?',
Washington Quarterly, vol. 41, no. 2,
2018, pp. 47–61, especially p. 52.

73 *Ibid.*

74 Rahul Roy-Chaudhury and Kate
Sullivan de Estrada, 'India, the Indo-
Pacific and the Quad', *Survival*, vol. 60,
no. 3, June–July 2018, p. 181.

75 *Ibid.*, p. 182.

76 US Department of State, 'US–
Australia–India–Japan Consultations',
media note, 7 June 2018, https://www.
state.gov/r/pa/prs/ps/2018/06/283013.
htm; Department of Foreign
Affairs and Trade of Australia,
'Australia–India–Japan–United States
Consultations', media release, 7 June
2018, https://dfat.gov.au/news/media/
Pages/australia-india-japan-united-
states-consultations.aspx; Ministry
of External Affairs of India, 'India–
Australia–Japan–US Consultations',
press release, 7 June 2018, https://
www.mea.gov.in/press-releases.
htm?dtl/29961/IndiaAustraliaJapanU
S+Consultations; Ministry of Foreign
Affairs of Japan, 'Japan–Australia–
India–US consultations', press release,
7 June 2018, https://www.mofa.go.jp/
press/release/press4e_002062.html.

77 Author interview with scholar B,
Beijing, December 2018.

78 See Geoff Raby, 'China Relations Can
Only Be Unfrozen with Julie Bishop's
Sacking', *Australian Financial Review*,
14 May 2018, https://www.afr.com/
opinion/columnists/china-relations-
can-only-be-unfrozen-with-julie-
bishops-sacking-20180514-h100w9.

79 Jamie Smyth, 'Beijing and Canberra
Aim for Diplomatic Reset',
Financial Times, 6 November 2018,
https://www.ft.com/content/
e1fbe912-e169-11e8-a6e5-792428919cee.

80 Author interview with scholar B,
Beijing, December 2018.

81 *Ibid.*

82 Kishore Mahbubani and Jeffery Sng,
The ASEAN Miracle: A Catalyst for Peace
(Singapore: NUS Press, 2017).

83 Bilahari Kausikan, 'ASEAN Is
Imperfect but Its Incoherence
Sometimes Is Not a Bad Thing',
Mothership, 4 October 2017,
https://mothership.sg/2017/10/
bilahari-kausikan-asean-is-imperfect-
but-its-incoherence-sometimes-is-not-
a-bad-thing/.

84 Nur Asyiqin Mohamad Salleh, 'Asean
Must Find Right Balance to Weather
"Grave Period" in World History:
Vivian Balakrishnan', *Straits Times*, 2
August 2018, https://www.straitstimes.
com/politics/asean-must-find-right-
balance-to-weather-grave-period-in-
world-history-vivian-balakrishnan.

85 David Wroe, 'Asia Must Not Fragment
into "Rival Blocs" as Region Reshapes:
Singapore PM', *Sydney Morning
Herald*, 16 March 2018, https://
www.smh.com.au/politics/federal/
asia-must-not-fragment-into-rival-
blocs-as-region-reshapes-singapore-
pm-20180315-p4z4hq.html.

86 Bilahari Kausikan, 'ASEAN:
Agnostic on the Free and Open Indo-
Pacific', *Diplomat*, 27 April 2018,
https://thediplomat.com/2018/05/
asean-agnostic-on-the-free-and-
open-indo-pacific/.

87 Author interview with scholar B,
Beijing, December 2018.

88 'Indo-Pacific Strategy Unpopular
in ASEAN', *Global Times*, 3 August
2018, http://www.globaltimes.cn/
content/1113773.shtml.

89 Kausikan, 'ASEAN: Agnostic on the
Free and Open Indo-Pacific'.

90 See Mattis, 'US Leadership and the
Challenges of Indo-Pacific Security';
Modi, 'Keynote Address'; US
Department of State, 'US–Australia–
India–Japan Consultations', 2018;
Department of Foreign Affairs and
Trade of Australia, 'Australia–India–
Japan–United States Consultations',
2018; Ministry of External Affairs of
India, 'India–Australia–Japan–US con-
sultations', 2018; Ministry of Foreign
Affairs of Japan, 'Japan–Australia–
India–US Consultations', 2018.

91 Author interview with scholar B,
Beijing, December 2018.

92 Victor D. Cha, 'Complex Patchworks:
US Alliances as Part of Asia's Regional
Architecture', *Asia Policy*, no. 11,
January 2011, pp. 27–50; Victor D.
Cha, 'American Alliances and Asia's
Regional Architecture', in Saadia
M. Pekkanen, John Ravenhill and
Rosemary Foot (eds), *Oxford Handbook
of the International Relations of Asia*
(Oxford: Oxford University Press,
2014), pp. 737–57.

93 Cha, 'Complex Patchworks', pp. 47–8.

94 See Feng Zhang, 'China as a Global
Force', *Asia & the Pacific Policy Studies*,
vol. 3, no. 1, 2016, p. 118.

Review Essay

The Virtues of Arrogance

Jonathan Stevenson

**Our Man: Richard Holbrooke and the End of the
American Century**
George Packer. New York: Alfred A. Knopf, 2019. $30.00. 608 pp.

Richard Holbrooke was one of the most talented and dedicated American
diplomats of his generation. His signature achievement was forging peace
among the three recalcitrant sides in the vicious and near-genocidal war in
Bosnia-Herzegovina when few thought it possible. He was also a famously
self-regarding blowhard who sucked the oxygen out of every room he occupied, a heedless womaniser who cuckolded his best friend and never took
responsibility for it, an often despicable careerist and a climber who discounted an underling's physical heroism and left the other man looking like
a coward without ever correcting the record.

George Packer, whom Holbrooke's family afforded unique access to his
papers, sees him as a warts-and-all embodiment of the United States in the
American century: a paragon of the nobility that America found in overcoming the insularity of the 1930s, winning the Second World War and building
the liberal international order that allowed the West to prevail in the Cold
War; but also, to a far lesser degree, a living example of the overweening
exceptionalism that produced the morbidly protracted and senselessly
destructive Vietnam War, where Holbrooke cut his teeth as a young Foreign

Jonathan Stevenson is Managing Editor of *Survival* and IISS Senior Fellow for US Defence.

Survival | vol. 61 no. 3 | June–July 2019 | pp. 213–224   DOI 10.1080/00396338.2019.1614792

Service officer, and the invasion and occupation of Iraq, which arguably proved even more damaging from a strategic standpoint. Neither the quiet American nor the ugly one, Holbrooke was, like his country, exasperatingly and often brilliantly complicated.[1]

Packer is an extraordinary journalist and chronicler of American lives. He nailed the two key stories of post-9/11 America: domestically, the rupture of its domestic politics; overseas, Iraq. In *The Unwinding: An Inner History of the New America* (2013), he deciphered the alienation of the white working class and foresaw the fissiparation of the broad-based Democratic coalition, a phenomenon that would enable Donald Trump's election in 2016. In *The*

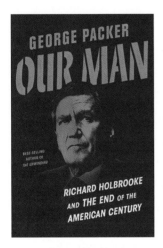

Assassins' Gate: America in Iraq (2005), he explained the folly of the United States' 2003 intervention in Iraq, which he had initially supported. But, even for such an astute observer and gifted writer, Holbrooke's singular flaws made the task of casting him in a credibly positive light a daunting one.

Packer marshals a delicate sufficiency of literary flourish, diverting to first- and second-person asides to assure the reader of his knowingness and his critical eye, the better to make a nuanced case for a man who was, at best, 'almost great' (p. 9). At the end of the prologue, writing after Trump had become president, the author prefaces what will be a long, granularly eloquent argument by noting that:

> What's called the American century was really just a little more than half a century, and that was the span of Holbrooke's life. It began with the Second World War and the creative burst that followed – the United Nations, the Atlantic alliance, containment, the free world – and it went through dizzying lows and highs, until it expired the day before yesterday. The thing that brings on doom to great powers, and great men – is it simple hubris, or decadence and squander, a kind of inattention, loss of faith, or just the passage of years? – at some point that thing set in, and so we are talking about an age gone by. It wasn't a golden age, there

was plenty of folly and wrong, but I already miss it. The best about us was inseparable from the worst. Our feeling that we could do anything gave us the Marshall Plan and Vietnam, the peace at Dayton and the endless Afghan war. Our confidence and energy, our reach and grasp, our excess and blindness – they were not so different from Holbrooke's. He was our man. That's the reason to tell you this story. That's why I can't get his voice out of my head. (p. 9)

It's an achingly melancholy note of candour that buoys both the narrative and the argument.

Vietnam, Vietnam, Vietnam – we've all been there

Like many of his generation, Holbrooke went into government enamoured of Dean Acheson, George Kennan and George Marshall, who had been present at the creation of the US-led world order, and impelled by John Kennedy's soaring inaugural address to lift it to greater heights. At 21, he was the youngest in his Foreign Service class, fresh out of Brown University, and would spend most of the next six years in the Mekong Delta. As Packer notes, against the current backdrop of a State Department sobered by a cascade of post-9/11 policy frustrations and hollowed out by Trump's malign bureaucratic neglect, it is hard to imagine a new recruit 'aglow with molten ambition' (p. 19), but that phrase described Holbrooke. He found kindred spirits in deadeye war reporters like David Halberstam and Neil Sheehan. Each would write a book on the delusions of Vietnam that still anchors the canon, and which Holbrooke would internalise as part of his own orthodoxy.[2]

America's failure in Vietnam did not subdue him; rather, it galvanised him to do better. In the classified study of the war that Robert McNamara, in his last year as secretary of defense, commissioned – it came to be called the 'Pentagon Papers' after Daniel Ellsberg leaked it – 'Holbrooke', unlike most of his peers, 'wrote with a point of view. He focused on the Sisyphean irony of an American effort to get the Vietnamese to save their own country with American ideas, on an American schedule' (p. 126). And, showing his penchant for the telling historical analogy, Holbrooke noted in a dissenting briefing memo for the president:

> Hanoi uses time the way the Russians used terrain before Napoleon's advance in Moscow, always retreating, losing every battle, but eventually creating conditions in which the enemy can no longer function. For Napoleon it was his long supply lines and the cold Russian winter; Hanoi hopes that for us it will be the mounting dissension, impatience, and frustration caused by a protracted war without fronts or other visible signs of success; a growing need to choose between guns and butter; and an increasing American repugnance at finding, for the first time, their own country cast as 'the heavy' with massive fire power brought to bear against a 'small Asian nation.' (p. 128)

Analytically, he pretty much cracked Vietnam right there, as clearly as Charles Joseph Minard had sussed out the disaster of Napoleon's Russian campaign in his renowned 1869 chart. Holbrooke also plumbed the experience reflectively, manifesting considerable empathy. His diaries, swathes of which Packer strategically inserts into his narrative, included this observation: 'We arrive here with no knowledge of the country or of the situation and immediately start giving advice, some of which we can really turn almost into orders because of the materials and money and transportation that we fully control. I think that no American would stand for such a deep and continuing interference in our affairs, even if it appeared that survival was at stake. Yet the Vietnamese accept it, and with rather good grace' (p. 61). Still, Holbrooke's tragic flaw, says Packer, was an incapacity for introspection, and that made it hard for him to apply his insights in other assignments. In retrospect, his recorded nuggets of wisdom can seem like bemused bloviations to himself, sterile and isolated and to be regarded sardonically in retrospect.

In the moment, he and his contemporaries in government faced this reality: 'They went in as true believers, and Vietnam upset every one of their assumptions about what it meant to serve the United States. How could there be a next Acheson or Kennan if America was going into decline? They were still insiders, and neither conviction nor ambition would let them walk away from their chosen profession. But Vietnam was just too big for them to move on' (p. 153). In that light, it may have been convenient that the

Nixon campaign had surreptitiously promised Saigon a more favourable US policy than a Democratic administration would have offered. For that sort of thing, Packer isn't alone in being unable to come up with a better word than 'treason' (p. 136). Holbrooke now had the opportunity to act on principle. Between Nixon's election and his inauguration, Holbrooke told Henry Kissinger that he couldn't work for Nixon and left the front lines of government for a year-long fellowship at Princeton University, followed by a stint as Peace Corps country director in Morocco.

Louche and footloose

Holbrooke's departure could also be read as a vain display that serviced his truth-to-power self-image and wider reputation. He himself had asked for the meeting with Kissinger, and while he may have considered Kissinger 'devious', Kissinger thought Holbrooke 'viperous' (pp. 164–5). In later hiatuses from government service, Holbrooke's extravagant lifestyle called for high paychecks at investment banks and the like. This first time, though, he became editor of *Foreign Policy*, a new magazine with an iconoclastically oblong shape, conceived as a snarky antidote to the rather staid *Foreign Affairs*, and then situated at the Carnegie Endowment for International Peace – 'a high perch to wait out Republican rule' (p. 155). This state of limbo, in Washington but not in government, seemed to liberate some of his ugliest proclivities. He became 'a star-fucker' given to, for instance, 'cajoling a bereaved widow to include him among her late husband's eulogists, then rearranging name cards so that he can chat up the right dinner guests after the service' (p. 152).

It was also during this relatively untethered period that Holbrooke informed his wife Litty that 'he loved someone else and found it ... one of the most powerful experiences of his life' (p. 144). Packer's deadpan presentation of the episode only amplifies Holbrooke's cluelessness – did he know anything about women? – and cruelty. To make matters worse, the woman in question turned out to be the wife of Anthony Lake, whom he had worked with cheek-by-jowl in Vietnam and who had theretofore been one of his closest friends. His romantic relationships in general – he married three times and strayed quite a bit – leaned towards the tempestuous. But despite inspiring some personal rancour in his professional community, and leaving Jimmy Carter cold in their first face-to-face meeting during the transition, Holbrooke demonstrated his capabilities and worked his connections well enough to be appointed assistant secretary of state for East Asian and Pacific Affairs at age 35.

He favoured secretary of state Cyrus Vance in the burgeoning confrontation between the courtly Vance and the abrasive Zbigniew Brzezinski, Carter's national security advisor. He managed to offend both. The dysfunction almost torpedoed the administration's effort to normalise relations with China, which Brzezinski steered while wilfully marginalising Holbrooke's attempt to orchestrate a rapprochement with Vietnam. Owing to his lack of bureaucratic clout, his opposition to the United States' passive support for the Khmer Rouge in Cambodia against Vietnam – notwithstanding Pol Pot's genocidal campaign – was overruled. Holbrooke had to 'swallow hard' (p. 196) in backing the Carter administration's decision to officially recognise the Khmer Rouge-led government in the UN General Assembly. Political expediency had suppressed the United States' humanitarian impulses. But 'human suffering didn't plunge him into psychological paralysis or philosophical despair. It drove him to furious action' (p. 201). As Southeast Asian refugees multiplied, Holbrooke pushed Congress to address the problem, and by 1982 the United States had admitted half a million such refugees, more than any other country. No doubt with Syria, Yemen and Trump's immigration policies in mind, Packer notes trenchantly: 'It shames us today' (p. 203).

Destiny fulfilled

The ignominious end of Carter's one-term presidency is well known – Packer felicitously if uncharitably writes him off as 'an accident of Watergate' (p. 208) – and it left Democrats out of power for 12 years. Holbrooke would not get another chance at glory until the mid-1990s. But the chance that arose in the Balkans was tailored to the particular virtues of his arrogance – the bluster, the bullying, the grandiosity, the sense of history and his place in it. To exploit the opportunity, however, he still needed to finesse his own reputation.

By the time Bill Clinton was elected president, Holbrooke was known in policy circles as an insufferably disruptive noodge as well as a supremely talented operator, so it was hard for him to find a place on Clinton's foreign-policy team. It didn't help that Lake, whose wife he had seduced, was Clinton's national security advisor, and that Warren Christopher, whose receding colourlessness was distinctly at odds with Holbrooke's look-at-me flamboyance, his secretary of state. Here, however, Holbrooke's irrepressible self-promotion came into play. On the pretext of fact-finding for the International Rescue Committee, of which he was a board member, Holbrooke spent the winter holidays in the Balkans.

As Packer puts it: 'Holbrooke was a diplomat in search of a job, and you know him well enough by now to understand why the job ranked not an inch lower on his scale of values than the war. Egotism and ideal-ism, incomprehensibly allied in their irreconcilable antagonism! To do something about Bosnia, he needed power' (p. 260). He sent a memo to Lake and Christopher describing the siege of Sarajevo and advocating that the US bomb Bosnian Serb targets, allow weapons to get through to the Bosnian Croats and Muslims despite the UN arms embargo, and pursue war criminals. The overarching message was that the Bosnian problem called for American leadership. Lake, a balanced and evidently forgiving man, was receptive, and Holbrooke's ideas dovetailed with Lake's own policy entrepreneurship on Bosnia. The administration's eventual policy was to lift the arms embargo and protect Muslim civil-ians with limited airstrikes.

The bone Christopher threw Holbrooke was an appointment as US ambassador to Germany, a position that enabled him to insinuate himself into Bosnia. 'Now', muses Packer – he churns out his fair share of *bons mots* – 'greatness is looking over his shoulder while spite mutters in his ear' (p. 289). In less than a year, Christopher elevated Holbrooke to assistant sec-retary of state for European and Canadian affairs. Energised by Bosnian Serb forces' massacre of more than 8,000 Muslim civilians, mainly men and boys, at Srebrenica in July 1995, 'lift and strike' would eventually bring the Serbs to the bargaining table. Meanwhile, Holbrooke provided a strategic framework for evolving US policy in *Foreign Affairs* that linked the existing impulse to expand NATO eastward to the imperative of NATO's efficacy in Bosnia.[3] While it is a mild exaggeration to cast the piece as 'the kind of strategic thinking that government rarely produces' (p. 307), it did wrap key American post-Cold War interests around humanitarian values in a compelling way.

Holbrooke continued to behave churlishly, being quoted in a *New York Times* article castigating Lake and others for their supposed lethargy and indecision. Lake's nod to Holbrooke as our man in Dayton was testament to his generosity of spirit as well as his hard-nosed pragmatism. As others have done, Packer makes a convincing argument that Holbrooke was the right, possibly the only, man for the job in Dayton – tireless, swaggering, theatrical, overbearing, manipulative and willing to ingratiate himself with Slobodan Milosevic, the amoral president of Serbia. Certainly the Dayton Agreement was the centrepiece of NATO's largely successful Balkan interventions.[4]

The author also relates a damning anecdote about Holbrooke's character. In August 1995, Holbrooke and General Wesley Clark, then the US military adviser to Holbrooke's diplomatic team, were racing to a meeting with Milosevic in Sarajevo on a treacherous mountain road, travelling in a Humvee trailed by a French armoured personnel carrier. Forced to brake suddenly, the carrier pitched over a steep embankment, rolled repeatedly over 300 metres, and caught fire, killing several French and American diplomatic and military personnel. Clark did run to the scene and helped coordinate the rescue operation, but it was Randall Banky, an American lieutenant colonel who had been riding in the Humvee, who scrambled down the embankment, braving mines and exploding ammunition, to aid survivors and identify the dead. The way Holbrooke related the story in an after-action phone conversation with Clinton, it was Clark – 'your fellow Arkansas Rhodes Scholar' (p. 347) – and not Banky who made the rescue effort. In his memoir of the Bosnia war, Holbrooke disposes of Banky, now a narrative inconvenience, with the line 'Colonel Banky had disappeared'.[5]

Despite a bitter confrontation with Banky at a book event in Minneapolis, Holbrooke never set the record straight. Packer clearly considers Holbrooke's dissembling repellent, as it was. He does offer an explanation, but it's no less damning. He suggests that from Holbrooke's point of view, without the 'origin myth' that he manufactured, whereby a fellow great man rather than a lowly lieutenant colonel set the tone of American involvement in Bosnia, Clinton might have felt 'a subtle deflation' and 'the American drive for peace' might have faltered. 'Holbrooke, who loved history, told the kind of story that history loves' (p. 348). Maybe so, but the idea that Holbrooke's lie might have somehow helped vouchsafe peace in Bosnia strains credulity, and the lie stands as fatuously gratuitous as well as unethical.

The denouement

Holbrooke was inevitably in the mix to replace Christopher as secretary of state, but just as inevitably he lost out to Madeleine Albright. Despite his undeniable talents, his grating demands for special treatment and attention made him a locker-room liability. In Strobe Talbott's words, he was 'high value, high maintenance' but also 'a royal pain in the ass' (p. 390). Still, his influence, girded by Dayton, endured. Albright's celebrated notion that the United States was 'the indispensable nation' was of a piece with Holbrooke's deeply held strategic view, which he had put into practice. 'He believed', writes Packer, 'that power brought responsibilities, and if we failed to face them the world's suffering would worsen, and eventually other people's problems would be ours, and if we didn't act no one else would. Not necessarily with force, but with the full weight of American influence' (p. 396). Packer explicitly declines to equate the Holbrooke doctrine, as it were, with American hubris, to connect Dayton to Iraq. 'I thought he represented what was best about us', the author says (p. 397).

Thus, in the last third or so of this remarkable book, the first person seems to arise more often, and Packer gets down more intently to special pleading for Holbrooke as an Almost Great Man of history: a saviour, a prophet, a truth-teller. As ambassador to the UN during the last couple of years of Clinton's presidency, Holbrooke 'saved the United Nations from the dissolution that would have come with the loss of American leadership' (p. 416) and 'understood ahead of his time that diplomacy would change in the twenty-first century – that it would have more to do with organizing individuals and groups outside of government … than with table talk between men in suits' (p. 417). After his eight years in the wilderness during the George W. Bush administration, the world had changed in other ways. Post-9/11, the Middle East became the US strategic centre of gravity. Holbrooke had managed to avoid the region during his career. As a secular Jew who downplayed his Jewishness, he didn't relish delicately navigating American Jewish organisations. But now the region, at least broadly construed, was impossible to escape for a diplomat keen on securing his place in history.

Holbrooke's kiss-up-piss-everywhere-else shtick didn't fool or impress Barack Obama or his lieutenants, but again Holbrooke's talents trumped his foibles – he was appointed US special envoy for Afghanistan and Pakistan. But Obama was still put off by Holbrooke's windy pedantry, his reflexive rhetorical leveraging of Vietnam and his blithe officiousness, and he was not the only one. In retaliation for his colleagues' eye-rolling, Holbrooke ignored them. 'No one was spared his inattention' (p. 479). He may have felt exclusive in his understanding that military victory in Afghanistan was practically impossible and that if the United States wanted lasting peace, Washington and the Afghan government had little choice but to talk with the Taliban. But the viability of the argument was not lost on Obama's other national-security principals or the wider policy community. They also considered the alternative of a less committed approach centred on counter-terrorism.[6]

After an attempt at an Iraq-like surge that Holbrooke only tacitly opposed, the administration ultimately chose a calibrated counter-terrorism approach. Written off as too grandiose and simply too much trouble, Holbrooke looked, bureaucratically, like a dead man walking at the end of 2009. Improbably, he survived – Hillary Clinton, then secretary of state, stayed in his corner – and his ideas for a diplomatic solution got some traction, as the National Security Council staff stood up a Conflict Resolution Cell. But nobody had Holbrooke in mind as the lead negotiator, and, in his standing compulsion both to make a difference and to distinguish himself, he overplayed a tenuous hand by fancifully suggesting that the administration open a diplomatic track between India and Pakistan on Afghanistan.[7]

*   *   *

The final chapter of *Our Man* is as riveting and poignant as the end of a Robert Stone novel. For several years, Holbrooke and his doctors had known of his heart condition, involving atrial fibrillation and then an aortic aneurysm, and its symptoms were getting worse. By late 2010, his belly was distended, his face red, his feet chronically swollen. But he delayed getting treatment, his egotism and patriotic vanity suppressing his instinct for self-preservation.

On 10 December, after a flattening audience with David Axelrod at the White House, Holbrooke proceeded to a meeting with Hillary Clinton at her office on the state of US diplomacy on Afghanistan. There he was stricken by an acute aortic dissection and taken to George Washington Hospital. In those frenetic moments, he expressed his love for his family and friends, admonished his aide, announced his official importance, flirted with the cardiologist and interrogated the surgeon. By Packer's reckoning, it was vintage Holbrooke; it was who he really was. After 20 hours of surgery, he died. It might have pleased him that on his last day on Earth, just a few blocks from the State Department, he commanded the rapt attention of a team of experts trying to prolong his life.

The attributes Packer sees in Holbrooke – 'crystal brilliance', 'inward occlusion', a 'blind spot growing bigger' (p. 524) – are also those of the United States itself. But Holbrooke would be dismayed at just how big the American blind spot has become, and by the solemn epitaph that Packer has pronounced for the American moment: 'All that accumulated experience – we Americans don't want it. We're almost embarrassed by it, except when we're burying it. So we forget our mistakes or recoil from them, we swing wildly between superhuman exertion and sullen withdrawal, always looking for answers in our own goodness and wisdom instead of where they lie, out in the world and in history. I'm amazed we came through our half century as well as we did. Now it's over' (p. 552). The author adds, elegiacally, 'now that Holbrooke is gone, and we're getting to know the alternatives, don't you, too, feel some regret?' (p. 554). You bet I do. Packer has made his case.

Notes

1 For a fine collection of essays on Holbrooke and a selection of his own writing, see Derek Chollet and Samantha Power (eds), *The Unquiet American: Richard Holbrooke in the World* (New York: PublicAffairs, 2011).

2 David Halberstam, *The Best and the Brightest* (New York: Random House, 1972); Neil Sheehan, *A Bright Shining Lie: John Paul Vann and America in Vietnam* (New York: Random House, 1988).

3 Richard Holbrooke, 'America, A European Power', *Foreign Affairs*, vol. 74, no. 2, March/April 1995, pp. 38–51.

4 See, for instance, Dana H. Allin, *NATO's Balkan Interventions*, IISS Adelphi Paper 347 (Oxford: Oxford University Press, 2002).

5 Richard Holbrooke, *To End a War* (New York: Random House, 1998), p. 11.

6 See, for example, Steven Simon and Jonathan Stevenson, 'Afghanistan: How Much Is Enough?', *Survival*, vol. 51, no. 5, October–November 2009, pp. 47–67.

7 On Holbrooke's travails in the Obama administration, see also Michael Hirsh, 'Richard Holbrooke's Decline and Fall, as Told in Clinton Emails', Politico, 1 July 2015, https://www.politico.com/story/2015/07/richard-holbrookes-hillary-clinton-emails-119649.

Book Reviews

Europe
Erik Jones

Romania Confronts Its Communist Past: Democracy, Memory, and Moral Justice
Vladimir Tismaneanu and Marius Stan. Cambridge: Cambridge
University Press, 2018. £75.00. 205 pp.

Romania went through an abysmal time under communism, particularly between the end of the Second World War and the start of the 1960s, and from the beginning of the 1970s to the popular revolution that overthrew the dictatorship of Nicolae and Elena Ceauşescu. It would be easy to pretend that this brutal half-century was the product of foreign manipulation of Romania's small political elite and its security service, the Securitate, but the reality is more complicated. The Romanian elite was small but still large enough to encompass a number of prominent individuals, many of whom retained their status long after the Ceauşescus were dead. Meanwhile, the Securitate had tentacles that reached across politics and society in the form of allies and informants. The architects and engineers of Romania's misery were thus Romanian, not foreign. Romanians have to live with that awkward fact. Remembering the past only makes things more awkward, not less.

Nevertheless, Vladimir Tismaneanu and his co-author, Marius Stan, believe that confronting Romania's communist past is essential to stabilise and legitimate the country's political future. Specifically, they believe Romanians should acknowledge that communism was every bit as terrible as fascism; that Romanian communism was always both Stalinist and nationalist – meaning that the dictatorship of the Ceauşescus was not all that different from the dictatorship created by their predecessor, Gheorghe Gheorghiu-Dej; and that only

Survival | vol. 61 no. 3 | June–July 2019 | pp. 225–232   DOI 10.1080/00396338.2019.1614793

a vibrant civil society can foster the culture of responsibility and reconciliation needed to ensure that Romanians do not repeat the mistakes of the past. This argument is openly political and programmatic. It is also morally charged. Tismaneanu and Stan are vocal in their attack on former Romanian president Ion Iliescu and his Social Democratic Party, for example. They also excoriate the right-wing nationalist Corneliu Vadim Tudor (now deceased). Both Iliescu and Tudor were prominent during the communist regime. More importantly, they both threatened to take Romania in the wrong direction. This is not to put Iliescu and Tudor on the same moral plane. Iliescu played a vitally important role in Romania's transition from communism; Tismaneanu's frustration is that he was not even more progressive. Tudor was an altogether different case.

The focal point of this argument is the final report Tismaneanu shepherded as chair of the Presidential Commission for the Analysis of the Communist Dictatorship in Romania. President Traian Băsescu created the commission in April 2006 and Tismaneanu's group presented its final report in December – to a rowdy and vituperative parliamentary reception. The 600-plus pages of the report laid bare a number of unpleasant truths about Romanian communism, and exposed politicians like Iliescu and Tudor by name. What followed was more than a decade of conflict and recrimination, mostly among intellectuals and politicians rather than the general public. Moreover, that debate was often more about choosing between contemporary political groups than any recon-ciliation with the past. The reason for *Romania Confronts Its Communist Past* is to give Tismaneanu (and Stan) the opportunity to set the record straight.

It is still unclear whether Romanians have actually confronted their past and, if so, whether that confrontation has made the future any less perilous in terms of the country's political development. Romanians now have better school textbooks and better access to official documents. They may also have a better understanding of the breadth of the country's collective complicity in a half-century of Stalinist nationalism. Whether they will use that insight to build a better country remains to be seen. The politics of memory is potent but not omnipotent.

**Time and Power: Visions of History in German Politics,
from the Thirty Years' War to the Third Reich**
Christopher Clark. Princeton, NJ: Princeton University Press,
2019. £24.00/$29.95. 293 pp.

Vladimir Tismaneanu's attempt to render judgement on Romania's communist regime (see previous review) is only one illustration of how the role of history in modern politics has taken on new meaning. Over the past ten years of review-ing books in these pages, I have sketched many others. Less common, however, are works that explore how the notion of history – rather than the precise interpretation of events – connects to political power. Christopher Clark's *Time and Power* is a welcome addition to that particular conversation. Using case studies drawn from Germany's past four centuries, Clark shows how political leaders try to shape 'the lived relationship between past and present' (p. 210) through the assumptions they make about what history means in broad terms.

Clark's argument is both intriguing and alarming. It is intriguing insofar as he highlights how the interpretation of history plays a role in the legitimation of political authority. It is alarming because he reveals the full extent to which the public can be manipulated by 'the warping of temporality by power' (p. 212).

The importance of history in politics derives from the complex relationship between prediction, purpose and progress. Prediction lies at the heart of strategic thinking. Time and again, Germany's political leaders have had to face uncertain choices. Time and again, they have sought to narrate those choices as a necessary feature of their authority. In this sense, history is a relentless machine for choosing between possible futures.

This decision-making can serve a number of purposes. One of these is progressive: policymakers strive to make the world a better place. Another is more existential: the goal of statecraft is to preserve what already exists. In some instances, German leaders emphasised the teleology of progress. In others, they focused narrowly on the contingency of the moment and the reason of state.

This contrast between teleology and contingency created space for a third, more terrifying alternative. Clark identifies this alternative in the 'ultra-essentialist and biologistic account of the genesis and evolution of German life in Europe' (pp. 195–6) promoted by the Nazi regime. This peculiar vision of history represented a 'triumph of prophecy' (p. 198) over contingency and prediction by anticipating 'an end that is already given' (p. 202). When the future is prophecy, politicians bear no responsibility for the decisions they make. Hence, the 'final solution' becomes just one of many overlapping 'end games' (p. 206).

Given the power of this kind of abuse of history – in which history serves not as a narrative, but as a way of connecting past, present and future – remembering the atrocities of the Nazi regime is insufficient to prevent them from recurring. Understanding how our sense of time and meaning is shaped by the people who make history is also necessary. This is true particularly in moments at which the notion of progress is contested, and when the stability of the political system is most at risk. Clark's case studies focus on revolutionary moments of the past, such as the Thirty Years' War, the revolutions of 1848 and the Treaty of Versailles – episodes that may seem remote, yet have powerful implications for the present.

The Responsive Union: National Elections and European Governance
Christina J. Schneider. Cambridge: Cambridge University Press, 2018. £75.00. 345 pp.

The European Union may be more democratic – or at least more responsive to democratic pressures – than some might think. The proof of this lies in the intergovernmental bargaining that takes place in the Council of Ministers (or, more accurately, the Council of the European Union). The national politicians who come together to make decisions are all elected – or at least, their coalitions are. Hence, they have an incentive to demonstrate that they are pursuing the interests of the voters they represent. In an ideal world, they would secure policies that work to the advantage of their electorates. At a minimum, they have an incentive to delay any policy decisions likely to go against their voters' interests until some quiet moment between elections. The signalling, bargaining and delaying tactics they employ together constitute a kind of 'democratic responsiveness'. This is perhaps not as elegant as having an all-powerful European Parliament, but it is still more democratic than the usual tropes about Brussels bureaucrats are prepared to acknowledge, and is probably as much democracy as the system can support given the central role of national politics in determining EU policy.

Christina Schneider uses an array of analytic strategies to demonstrate how this democratic responsiveness works within a European context. She deploys experimental techniques to show that voters are paying attention, and uses a series of statistical models and datasets to show the implications of her argument as they play out in multi-annual budget negotiations and in the more general legislative process. She also sets out case studies based in part on interviews with many of the participants to show how the budget negotiations evolved in the early 2000s under the shadow of Europe's historic enlargement, and how the Germans failed to slow down the bailout required at the start of the Greek sovereign-debt crisis. The conclusion she offers is that politicians can try to be responsive, but that does not mean that either they or their voters always get what they want. Democracy at the European level is as imperfect as everywhere else.

Schneider's argument is impressive in terms of both the simplicity of her message and the sophistication of her data collection and analysis. Her book is sure to become a touchstone in debates about Europe's 'democratic deficit'. Even so, her argument raises questions. To begin with, Schneider focuses her large-scale statistical analysis on national elections, but her case study on the Greek bailout hinges on the regional elections in North Rhine-Westphalia in Germany. That case study also included two very different German governments – a grand coalition that existed until national elections in September 2009 and a centre-right coalition that came after. These governments had opposite perspectives on Greek finances, but it was the Social Democratic finance minister in Germany who, facing the prospect of national elections, chose in February 2009 to signal his support for a backstop. Why did he do so, contrary to the expectations of Schneider's model? And how do we know *ex ante* which contests matter?

Another set of questions concerns the role of elections to the European Parliament. These are elections that involve all member states and in which we would expect European policy issues to be most salient. They are also elections that create a natural break in the legislative process, not just because they interrupt the parliament's operations but because they correspond to the appointment of a new European Commission. If Schneider's model is correct, these events should show particularly high levels of democratic responsiveness. The late Peter Mair (cited by Schneider) worried that they did not. It would be useful to know if he was right. Democracy in the Council of the European Union is important, but a responsive European Parliament is even more so.

Close to Home: Local Ties and Voting Radical Right in Europe
Jennifer Fitzgerald. Cambridge: Cambridge University Press, 2018. £75.00. 247 pp.

Debates about the future of European democracy tend to focus on the national level, but the local level may be more important. Support for radical groups varies significantly from one locality to the next. Such variation is hard to explain exclusively on the basis of macroeconomic or macro-political variables. The composition of support within localities varies as well, often in ways that cannot be explained using the stories we tell about whole parties. The 'losers-from-globalisation' thesis does not offer a compelling explanation for the attachment of left-leaning women to new radical-right parties, for example.

Jennifer Fitzgerald offers her own explanation for this localised variation in support. She argues that emotional attachment to one's local community is an important component in support for the new radical right. Indeed, such attachment is a strong predictor of support among left-leaning women for groups such as the National Rally in France or the Swiss People's Party. Moreover, we can see the influence of that emotional attachment on national electoral results whenever local issues come to the fore. In practice, this means that countries which run their national and local electoral contests closely together are likely to see more support for parties on the radical right in national elections, support that cannot be explained using the standard losers-from-globalisation story.

Fitzgerald's argument is subtle, and she qualifies it in at least three important ways. The first qualification is explicit: Fitzgerald makes it clear that emotional attachment to the local community is not the same as local involvement. On the contrary, the more people are actually involved in local affairs, the less likely they are to support new radical-right parties. In this sense, the 'local ties' that Fitzgerald emphasises are to 'imagined' local communities (borrowing from Benedict Anderson) rather than to real people or institutions. The other two qualifications are implicit. To begin with, holding one idea does not 'cause' someone to hold another. That is why the word 'predictor' is so important in the previous paragraph. Fitzgerald can show in her statistical models that some ideas tend to cluster together in certain demographic groups – such as left-leaning, emotional attachment and support for the new radical right among women – but not why these clusters are so common. Finally, these idea clusters do not capture large numbers of people. The standard stories for new radical-right support explain most of the variation across localities within countries, and from one country to the next. Nevertheless, Fitzgerald's argument unlocks important variation that the standard stories do not.

In the current electoral climate in Europe, even small unexplained variations in support can be decisive. Emmanuel Macron only led in the first round of the 2017 French presidential elections by a narrow margin; the differences across political parties in the Dutch parliament are even smaller. Moreover, the cluster of ideas that Fitzgerald identifies also includes a strong anti-EU sentiment. Here Fitzgerald's research set-up may even suggest a causal argument. She finds the cluster to be strongest 'in areas with either high levels of local autonomy or areas that recently lost such autonomy' (p. 162). This finding suggests that the source of the cluster may be a threat to local status, whether imagined or real. Such a threat can come from many sources, among which immigration is only one and perhaps not even the most important (p. 171). This is all the more encouragement for scholars researching democratic responsiveness in Europe (such as Christina Schneider, whose book is reviewed above) to think creatively about ways to take subnational levels of democratic politics into account.

Europe's Future: Decoupling and Reforming
Sergio Fabbrini. Cambridge: Cambridge University Press, 2019.
£16.99. 170 pp.

The paradox surrounding the European project is that popular attitudes toward Europe have deteriorated despite the fact that European institutions have succeeded in navigating an unprecedented crisis that has unfolded across multiple policy dimensions; and that Europe's heads of state and government have engaged in a flurry of initiatives that have pushed the project forward. Worse, the mainstream political parties that have traditionally supported the European project have ceded electoral ground to a raft of nationalist–populist alternatives. Relations between the member states have grown ever tenser and more contentious. Even without the spectacle of Britain's departure, there is a palpable sense of crisis. The question is whether and how proponents of 'Europe' can shore up its institutions and membership so that the project as a whole does not run aground.

Sergio Fabbrini believes he has found an answer. His solution is to distinguish between the EU's two main patterns of decision-making, one intergovernmental and the other supranational. In the current arrangement, the two patterns overlap, with supranational institutions managing most of the market-making structures during normal times and the intergovernmental institutions tackling more contentious matters, such as taxation and foreign policy, both in substantive terms and in times of crisis. The problem, Fabbrini argues, is that the recent crisis upset the EU's delicate constitutional balance. Yes, European heads of state and government created an impressive array of new institutions, but they also entrenched the practices associated with intergovernmental decision-making. This new emphasis on intergovernmentalism has overridden the EU's horizontal checks and balances and so made it easier for larger countries to dominate what are supposed to be deliberative forums through the exercise of power politics. It is small wonder, therefore, that many weaker member states have become disenchanted both with the process of decision-making and with the distribution of burdens as agreed through the policy process.

Fabbrini believes this situation can be rectified by decoupling the supranational and intergovernmental constitutional arrangements. Drawing upon the experience of federalism in the United States and Switzerland, he argues that the EU should split into a large and relatively loose common market governed by supranational institutions, and a smaller but more intense federal union that could divide sovereignty between the member states and 'Europe'. This federal union would not aspire to statehood in the Westphalian sense, and neither would it aim to replace national identities. Nevertheless, it would have authority over key policy domains that would require legitimation across the whole of its participants. In this way, Fabbrini concludes, those countries that strive only for the economic benefits of membership could be released from the obligations of political union, while those countries that share a view on Europe as a political objective could move toward an ever closer union.

Fabbrini's argument is both innovative and, in many respects, persuasive. The central problem is the relationship between Brexit and the internal market. The British objected not to monetary union or even migration policy so much as they objected to regulations from Brussels and freedom of movement. Fabbrini tries to resist the parallel by distinguishing between sovereign-tists in Britain and those on the continent (p. 60), by highlighting Britain's unique history of 'self-sufficiency' (p. 71), and by ascribing British scepticism of Europe to 'the idiosyncrasies of an island' (p. 130). He may be right. But experience with 'beyond-the-border' trade negotiations suggests that market integration is no longer a matter of 'low domestic political salience' (p. 24). Meanwhile, tensions in the Franco-German relationship suggest there may be fundamental disagreement over Europe's political goals. The 'decoupling' Fabbrini advocates is a creative solution, but it may not be enough to address the EU's underlying problems.

Africa
'Funmi Olonisakin

Go Tell the Crocodiles: Chasing Prosperity in Mozambique
Rowan Moore Gerety. New York: The New Press, 2018. $26.95.
343 pp.

The Mozambican Civil War, which killed more than one million people, was fought between FRELIMO, the ruling party, and RENAMO, an opposition insurgency, from 1977 to 1992. After it ended, the country became something of a 'donor darling' and supposedly enjoyed a period of sustained, impressive economic growth. In 2012, however, RENAMO once more turned to violence against the FRELIMO government, and in 2016 a debt crisis exposed the problematic nature of the country's economic expansion.

Rowan Moore Gerety's book reveals how any notion of increasing prosperity and genuine security among ordinary Mozambicans was a mirage. It does so through conversational case studies showcasing the day-to-day lives of an eclectic mixture of locals, including street hustlers (Chapter One), warlord politicians (Chapter Two), crocodile conservationists (Chapter Six) and a retired white mercenary (Chapter Seven), to name a few.

Early chapters are helpful in providing layman readers with a good understanding of the issues at the heart of Mozambicans' current plight. The introduction clarifies that it was always misguided to suggest that Mozambique was experiencing some kind of post-war economic miracle. Gerety cites the example of Mozal – a private aluminium-smelting project that accounts for one-third of Mozambique's exports and consumes nearly half of its electricity – which earns $21 for its foreign backers for every $1 it earns for the Mozambican government (p. 9).

Chapter Two provides an insightful portrait of Afonso Dhlakama, the leader of RENAMO until his death in May 2018. Gerety observes that 'Dhlakama the politician … never managed to match his exploits as a warlord' (p. 49), receiving a steadily declining share of the popular vote after the first post-war election in 1992. Having become frustrated with a FRELIMO-dominated legislature and government machinery, Dhlakama 'returned to the Bush' in October 2012. The book covers this new phase of violence until a 2016 Christmas truce between FRELIMO and RENAMO, and therefore does not discuss Dhlakama's subsequent death. But Gerety observes that, during his lifetime, 'the bulk of [Dhlakama's] political leverage [derived] from the threat, real or imagined, of a return to full-fledged armed conflict' (p. 49). The rest of the book's stories all take place in the midst of unresolved tensions between

Survival | vol. 61 no. 3 | June–July 2019 | pp. 233–239   DOI 10.1080/00396338.2019.1614794

the oppressive, corrupt FRELIMO government and the frustrated, potentially violent RENAMO opposition.

Many of these stories speak to broader themes prevalent in Mozambique and indeed across Africa, such as the role of the informal economy (Chapters One and Nine); refugee and human-trafficking issues (Chapter Three); land-acquisition disputes (Chapter Four); and citizens' justified mistrust of corrupt government officials, foreign businesses and non-governmental organisations (Chapter Five). In this way, *Go Tell the Crocodiles* avoids the trap of providing a journalistic, light-hearted adventure narrative featuring locals overcoming adversity while ignoring the serious structural issues that clearly persist. Instead, it portrays the colourful, problematic, sometimes tragi-comic lives of real Mozambicans with thoughtfulness and compassion, while weaving in a well-articulated history and contemporary analysis of Mozambique.

A drawback of the book is its dearth of female voices and stories, which Gerety apologetically acknowledges in the introduction (p. 20). The author also makes no direct effort to draw clear conclusions, or to answer his own questions, such as 'can you fix a refugee system that abets human trafficking?' and 'can you move beyond the spectre of violence when a warlord leads the political opposition?' (p. 20). But this adds to the charm of the book: there are, after all, no clear or easy answers to such ponderings, so readers are left to draw their own conclusions. The story he tells captures both modern Mozambique as well as Africa more generally: a sad, troubled place that seems at times impossibly complicated, but that is at the same time hopeful, resilient, entrepreneurial and ever-changing.

**Fighting for Peace in Somalia: A History and Analysis of
the African Union Mission (AMISOM), 2007–2017**
Paul D. Williams. Oxford: Oxford University Press, 2018. £70.00.
366 pp.

The African Union Mission in Somalia (AMISOM) began as a small, limited deployment of Ugandan-only peacekeepers in 2007. It evolved to become the longest-running, most deadly AU mission – and largest uniformed peace-keeping deployment – in the world by 2017. AMISOM's 'model' involved AU members providing troops, the EU paying them, the UN providing logistics, and key partners (especially the US and UK) supplying equipment, training and other security assistance to troop-contributing countries (p. 347). Costs for the mission quickly escalated, reaching a peak of $1 billion per annum (p. 2). The mission's fight against al-Shabaab shifted in scope, size and mandate considerably as it grappled with an intensely hostile Somali environment and a complex international political economy. Its progress and achievements have likewise fluctuated. The mission saw commendable successes against al-Shabaab, as well as considerable failures along the way, until the signing of the May 2017 London Security Pact which, after ten years, meant that AMISOM 'had a political pathway out of Somalia', at least on paper (p. 208).

Williams's detailed history of AMISOM is presented in two sections. The first provides a historical overview of the distinct phases of AMISOM operations. It discusses the mission's genesis, its entry into the chaos of battle, and its struggles through phases of stalemate, offensives, expansion and consolidation, culminating in the January 2014 'surge' which eventually led to the London Security Pact. The second section details the many issues and challenges that AMISOM faced during the course of these phases, including logistics, security-sector reform, civilian protection, strategic communications, stabilisation and questions of how to exit.

Williams makes it abundantly clear that AMISOM was never a peacekeeping mission: this was a war-fighting force operating in an intensely unstable civil-war environment (p. 47). He is unashamedly disparaging of Ethiopian prime minister Meles Zenawi's decision in 2006 to attack the Islamic Courts Union, which had at least brought a semblance of stability to Mogadishu, and to install the Transitional Federal Government (TFG) instead (p. 32). This meant that locals could not see AMISOM as a legitimate actor until after September 2012, when the despised, deeply corrupt TFG was replaced by a new federal government (p. 155). AMISOM's most controversial feature was the harm it caused to civilians, through instances of indiscriminate killings, theft and the selling of equipment, and abuse of local women (pp. 266–70). Whatever the myriad complexities and challenges the mission faced, however, Williams concludes that 'the most fundamental challenge was the aligning of AMISOM's military and political tasks, namely victory against Al-Shabab and installation of a credible central government authority' (p. 347).

This is an insightful, clinical analysis of AMISOM's first ten years of operations. The exceptional nature of the mission means that it is unlikely to be repeated, but Williams succeeds in his aim of providing important policy insights of potential use to whatever AU or UN peacekeeping missions are required in future. Williams states unequivocally that without AMISOM, al-Shabaab would have overrun Mogadishu in January 2009 after Ethiopia withdrew (p. 13). At the same time, he concludes that AMISOM's model 'should not and could not be reassembled as the basis for conducting sustained peace enforcement tasks' (p. 349). Despite the London Security Pact, it is not yet clear exactly when or even if the mission will leave Somalia, but Williams concludes that it will certainly evolve and adapt to whatever new era awaits the country, as it has done throughout its existence.

Fighting Corruption Is Dangerous: The Story Behind the Headlines
Ngozi Okonjo-Iweala. Cambridge, MA: The MIT Press, 2018.
$29.95. 173 pp.

Ngozi Okonjo-Iweala provides a vivid account of the dynamics at play in the fight against corruption in Africa's largest economy, Nigeria, from the point of view of a former public official who played an integral part in this fight. While corruption has remained a constant challenge for post-independence Nigeria since its early years, the author focuses particularly on her time as Nigeria's finance minister and coordinating minister of the economy between 2011 and 2015, when she served in then-president Goodluck Jonathan's administration.

Like most developing countries that struggle with endemic corruption, Nigeria has attempted to institute various reforms aimed at curtailing a problem that has earned it a negative international reputation. The reforms of various administrations have yielded some positive results, tightening loopholes and blocking leakages, but these reforms have also come at a heavy cost, especially to those who have been courageous enough to make bold decisions that challenged vested interests (p. 10). There is also much still to do, as the author acknowledges. Reform efforts frequently appear to be truncated by the beneficiaries of the status quo, both within the government and in the private sector (p. 28).

Okonjo-Iweala notes that corruption has been perpetuated in Nigeria in ways that are particular to that country. She identifies one of these as the worrisome closeness between oil marketers and those within the corridors of power (p. 35). The author also reveals how the passing of the national budget has become an issue of contention in Nigeria and is often delayed by interest-driven legislators in the National Assembly (p. 78). This anomaly has come to be referred to as 'budget padding'.

Another way in which corruption has been pursued at high levels is through opaque and hasty deals with businesses of dubious authenticity. Okonjo-Iweala also points to the challenges associated with the public service in Nigeria, which has over the years become a conduit for fraud and corruption. She particularly alerts readers to the issues of 'ghost workers' and 'ghost pensioners' – phenomena that have perennially drained state resources.

Searching for Boko Haram: A History of Violence in Central Africa
Scott MacEachern. Oxford: Oxford University Press, 2018.
£21.99. 233 pp.

Writing on Boko Haram has typically focused on its insurgency and its ideological and religious underpinnings. Scott MacEachern focuses elsewhere, on the territory from which Boko Haram emerged and the historical processes that produced the group, a perspective to which he brings more than three and a half decades of archaeological research. By examining 'the lands of Boko Haram' (p. 3), particularly the area between Lake Chad and the Mandara Mountains, as well as the people of this region and their history, the author successfully debunks the assumption that the territories occupied by Boko Haram are remote and inaccessible, and that Africa in general is populated mainly by unchanging 'traditional' societies within a static natural environment (p. 25).

MacEachern's compelling thesis is that we can understand much of the violence associated with Boko Haram as a manifestation of historical processes that have been shaping the southern Lake Chad Basin for centuries, even millennia. Asking why the group has used violence, and whether there have been continuities in the way violence has been used over time, is not just an intellectual exercise designed to explain away the violence. There are cultural logics at play that need to be explained. MacEachern looks at changes in the natural environment, as well as in the sociopolitical relationships among different groups of people, by using data extracted from archaeology, genetics and linguistics. Along the way, he makes a good case that there is much to be learned by investigating how human landscapes have developed in the region over time.

The area south of Lake Chad (encompassing present-day Chad, Cameroon, Niger and Nigeria) first appears in historical accounts only a thousand years ago, but MacEachern argues convincingly that the gap between recorded history and the prehistoric age can be unearthed through archaeology. Genetics and linguistics provide some evidence of the movement and interactions among Chadic-speaking peoples in the region – what happened to them when they encountered each other and how they adapted to changing climatic conditions. When archaeology connects with historical accounts, we learn even more (p. 41). MacEachern reveals that the forces that sustain Boko Haram, which remains largely a regional (rather than global) movement based in the Lake Chad Basin, have existed in the region for centuries. These include flows of materials, ideology and wealth (p. 189). The author draws parallels between the present day and the first millennium, when Kanem rulers were first exposed to Islam and the slave trade across the Sahara. He shows that technological transfers and the appearance of foreign weapons in the region are not new phenomena (pp. 188–9).

Transforming Sudan: Decolonization, Economic Development, and State Formation
Alden Young. Cambridge: Cambridge University Press, 2017.
£75.00. 180 pp.

A series of crises in Sudan, which in the 2000s saw the country being discussed in the company of countries such as Rwanda and Somalia, is often explained as the result of old, lingering ethnic and religious hatreds. But Alden Young offers a well-researched and compelling alternative explanation, arguing that an 'economizing logic' that became the 'policy making lens' in Sudan (p. 10) is to blame. This logic privileged economic growth and caused national sovereignty to be perceived in a way that 'continues to haunt the country until today' (p. 15).

Young's analysis focuses on the decolonisation era in Sudan. By examining policy decisions in the decades before and after Sudanese independence, the author reveals a consistent logic in the policy choices of British colonial officials and the Sudanese officials who replaced them. Sudanese leaders wrestled from the start with the question of whether and how to keep the country together as a single political and economic unit. Contradictory visions of southern Sudan, either as crucial to Sudan's future prosperity or as economically barren with only limited potential, invariably influenced political debates about whether to unify and develop the whole territory or to narrowly focus on Khartoum and neighbouring regions.

While much attention has been focused on the political drivers of post-colonial discontent, there is much to be learned from examining how those who adopted an economising logic – 'planning in numbers' – won the day over those who favoured 'planning in prose' and argued for listening to the voices of the excluded or marginalised provinces (p. 77). Viewing Sudan as a single economic unit, as the colonial (Anglo-Egyptian) department of finance did, meant that limited focus was given to the idea of regional development. Attention was focused instead on areas that seemed likely to bring prosperity to the state, with the potential of the southern provinces deemed less important.

The finance officials who held sway over the country delegitimised the development forecasts based on prose and were persuaded by the quantifiable. This logic serves to explain why, for example, the rising prices and ready markets for cotton during the 1940s led to increased production for export when, at the same time, chronic food shortages plagued Darfur and the southern provinces. While regional inequality had become a concern by the end of Sudan's first five-year development plan after the Second World War, the opportunity to place this concern at the core of the second development plan was missed, not least because of ambivalence among finance officials.

Young is clear that the Sudanese experience was not dissimilar to experiences elsewhere at the time, writing that 'the processes at work in the Sudan of the 1950s and 1960s were the same processes at work globally. After all, Sudanese financial bureaucrats were not particularly corrupt; their behaviour can be explained by their economizing logic of bureaucracy' (p. 149). Sudan started to become known as a 'failed state' by the 1980s, but the groundwork for the failure had been laid several decades earlier.

Latin America
Russell Crandall with Sarah Sears

The Line Becomes a River
Francisco Cantú. London: The Bodley Head, 2018. £14.99.
247 pp.

Francisco Cantú studied international relations as an undergraduate at Georgetown University in Washington DC and expected to pursue a career in public policy. Infused with the wanderlust so common to those coming of age, Cantú also wanted to work in the outdoors and experience real life outside the Washington Beltway. As a bilingual, third-generation Mexican American reared near the border, whose mother was a National Park ranger, he felt drawn to the US Border Patrol, a force bigger than either the FBI or the US Drug Enforcement Administration that employs roughly 18,000 Americans (about half of whom are Latinos). In his memoir, *The Line Becomes a River*, Cantú recalls explaining to his dubious mother that 'I'm tired of reading about the border in books', and adding that 'stepping into a system doesn't mean that the system becomes you' (pp. 22, 25). He joined the Border Patrol in 2008, at the tender age of 23. During his first year or so he was stationed at the border itself, after which he carried out relatively staid, desk-bound intelligence work in Arizona, New Mexico and Texas – the vast, arid and often inhospitable borderlands of which straddle the 3,000-kilometre-long US–Mexican frontier.

Cantú wrote this exquisitely crafted, distressing memoir of his time working for *la migra* – the term used by Hispanic migrants to refer to the Border Patrol – after leaving the agency in 2012. In it he expresses ambivalence about the agency's professionalism and humanity, writing of agents slicing the water containers that desperately parched migrants depend on for their lives, and of a higher-up assigning migrants to one of two categories: 'scumbags' and 'P.O.W.s' – 'plain 'ol wetbacks' (p. 101). In an especially harrowing and heartrending scene coming after Cantú's departure from the agency, an unauthorised Mexican migrant with whom Cantú had developed a friendship is deported. Virtually powerless to do anything other than help his friend pursue a conventional legal response, Cantú's despair is on full display. 'It's like I never quit', he tells his mother. 'It's like I'm still part of this thing that crushes' (p. 229).

The book's publication in 2018 set off a veritable storm of media coverage and controversy, much of it linked to the notion that, despite his own ancestry, Cantú is an apologist for an abusive, racist Border Patrol. At book signings, some protesters have shouted '*vendido*' (sell-out). Yet nothing in the book seems even remotely close to a justification of the US Border Patrol. Rather, the book is a courageous account by a young, idealistic Mexican American who loved his country enough to sign up for the Border Patrol. *The Line Becomes a River* also reveals a young writer with immense talent and potential. Let's hope that Cantú keeps researching and writing on his beloved borderlands as this, rather than being a frontier cop, is surely his true calling.

Homelands: Four Friends, Two Countries, and the Fate of the Great Mexican–American Migration
Alfredo Corchado. New York: Bloomsbury Publishing, 2018.
$27.00. 304 pp.

'Searching for answers on both sides of the border, my heart tore at its seams. The so-called tortilla curtain was now made of steel', writes journalist Alfredo Corchado in his memoir *Homelands*, an exploration of the modern Mexican-American experience (p. 204). Born in Durango, Mexico, Corchado moved to California in the mid-1960s during the tail end of the Bracero Program, a guest-worker programme that allowed millions of Mexican workers into the US on short-term labour contracts. His parents worked in agriculture in California before moving their family to El Paso, Texas, and opening a Mexican restaurant. Corchado interweaves reflections on his own bi-national life with those of three Mexican-American friends he met at a restaurant in Philadelphia: human-rights activist Primo Oceguera, restaurateur David Sura-Piñera and lawyer Kenneth Trujillo. The four friends' vastly different life trajectories and outcomes together form a deeply personal and complex story of the origins, present and future of the 36-million-strong Mexican diaspora in the United States, which Corchado describes as being poised 'on the cusp of the unknown' (p. 136). He writes of the emergence of 'two Mexicos, *él de aquí y él de allá*, north and south of the border' (p. 133), identifying both Mexicos as home.

Discussing the causes and consequences of the Mexican diasporic experience, Corchado deftly balances a historical overview of relevant government policies with personal reflections on the economic relationship between the US and Mexico. He provides a borderlander's perspective on NAFTA, recalling that 'part of me was excited about NAFTA, a treaty that justified our existence on the border' (p. 109). At the same time, however, Corchado condemns what he calls a 'marriage of convenience' between the US and Mexico, one 'based on trade, cold and loveless, moving blindly into the future' (p. 112). He demands accountability from both countries for mistreating the vulnerable working poor, noting that 'everywhere where a job required a hardworking human, a Mexican was there' (p. 274).

Over the past decade, more Mexicans have returned to their home country than have migrated to the United States. Nevertheless, Corchado asserts the centrality of Mexican Americans to the cultural and political fabric of both nations. He concludes with a call to action to his fellow Mexican Americans, encouraging them to engage with mainstream American culture. 'If I, if my family, didn't commit to being American – not just paying taxes but voting and becoming players in the system – we would always be in the fields', he writes (p. 94). No matter how messy – and often toxic – the relationship between Mexico and the United States can be, Corchado ultimately insists that the persistent flow of people between the two nations has forever altered the cultural dynamic on the continent. 'We may end up becoming *norteamericanos*', he says – 'people really of a continent' (p. 147).

Our Woman in Havana: A Diplomat's Chronicle of
America's Long Struggle with Castro's Cuba
Vicki Huddleston. New York: The Overlook Press, 2018. $29.95.
304 pp.

It was in the initial aftermath of the end of the Cold War that Vicki Huddleston first started working on Cuba as a US Foreign Service officer. (She would later work at the Pentagon, where I worked with her in 2009–10.) With the American embargo only tightening and annual Soviet subsidies of around $5 billion ending, it was an especially precarious time for Fidel Castro's regime. In her gripping memoir, *Our Woman in Havana*, Huddleston recounts her experiences as chief of the US Interests Section (effectively the ambassador) in Havana during the Bill Clinton and George W. Bush presidencies.

Huddleston pulls no punches in explaining to readers what is at stake as Washington and Havana come to grips with their past relationship and try to forge a new one. She has no patience for the 'myths and contradictions' that have emboldened Cuban-American communities to 'fight to regain the country they lost' (p. 12). As she tells it, otherwise reasonable observers have failed to grasp that Washington's 'Cuba policy is actually domestic policy, not foreign policy', driven by the Cuban-American lobby's desire for harsh, punitive measures against the Cuban regime. The author adds that this seemingly indomitable Cuban-American voting bloc has 'seduced Democrats and Republicans alike' (p. 12): hardcore conservatives like Ronald Reagan and George W. Bush played to the Cuban-American electorate, but so did John F. Kennedy and Bill Clinton. During the 2000 presidential election, the so-called *voto castigo* (punishment vote) went against Al Gore as payback for Clinton's (mis)handling of the Elián González repatriation case, giving the election to Bush.

Huddleston's rejoinder to the inertial Cuban-Americanisation of US Cuba policy is categorical:

> It is well past time that we stop making Cuba a glaring exception to the way we engage with countries around the world whose political systems we oppose. Cuba is the only country against which we maintain a comprehensive unilateral economic embargo and the only country in which we occupy part of its territory against its wishes. (pp. 12–13)

She takes a strongly anti-authoritarian stance, but argues against punitive measures: 'Economic embargoes hurt people more than they hurt governments', she writes, critiquing one of the foundational elements of the United States' policy toward Cuba going back 50 years. Without political and economic engagement, Huddleston is certain that Washington will needlessly alienate a 'potential strategic ally' while fomenting unnecessary division among its existing allies (p. 13).

The author was elated when Barack Obama created a diplomatic opening with Cuba in late 2014. She believes that conditions are even better today for a thaw in relations, now that Fidel Castro's brother Raúl has stepped down, meaning that, for the first time in almost 60 years, 'a Castro will no longer rule Cuba' (p. 13). The rub, of course, is Donald Trump's efforts to undo the historic bilateral agreements that were part of the Obama thaw. Ultimately, Huddleston finds hope in the new generations of Cubans who see their future in Havana, not Miami.

The Tango War: The Struggle for the Hearts, Minds and Riches of Latin America During World War II
Mary Jo McConahay. New York: St. Martin's Press, 2018. $29.99.
336 pp.

Picture a group of people casually eating apfelstrudel and discussing Nazi politics at a café on a street named Tiergartenstrasse. One could be forgiven for thinking that such a scene could only have unfolded in Germany or Austria in the 1930s and early 1940s, but as veteran journalist Mary Jo McConahay reminds us in her Second World War history *The Tango War*, this scene could also have occurred across southern Brazil, where upwards of one million Germans lived. Latin America was also home to populations of ethnic Japanese and Italians, whose homelands were to become US enemies in 1941. Although the prospect of a Nazi threat originating in the United States' geostrategic backyard terrified president Franklin Roosevelt's foreign-policy team, it is easy to underplay the perceived security threat today, simply because we know how the war turned out. In *The Tango War*, McConahay seeks to highlight the overlooked 'shadow war' that played out between the Allied and Axis powers for control over a region stretching from the Rio Grande to Tierra del Fuego (pp. xii–xiii). 'It is difficult to imagine how strong the Reich was before 1943, how grievous a threat to the Allies, how unsure anyone was about which way the conflict would go', she writes. 'In the run-up to the war and during the hostilities in Europe and the Pacific, the Latin American region was up for grabs' (p. xiii).

McConahay reveals just how central Latin America was to US strategy during the Second World War, noting that the Executive Branch's Joint Planning Committee held hundreds of national-security meetings in 1939 and 1940, all but six of which had Latin America as a key subject. 'The Axis and the Allies competed', she writes, 'for the hearts and minds of the continent's people, for their sea lanes and natural resources – from oil and rubber to wolfram and industrial diamonds – to feed their war machines. Their spies operated out of embassies, corporate offices, dockside bars. Each side closely shadowed the steps of the other, like dancers in a tango' (p. xii). Although difficult to imagine today, US officials considered Argentina pro-Nazi.

Through interviews and archival research, McConahay also sheds light on the largely secret movement of ethnic Italians, Germans and Japanese within and across national boundaries in Latin America. For example, a system known as 'Ratlines' relocated fascist war criminals from Europe to Latin America, and officials within the Roman Catholic Church used international church networks to facilitate the escape of Nazi war criminals such as concentration-camp physician Josef Mengele and Gestapo officer Klaus Barbie to South America. The US also pressured Latin American nations to kidnap and relocate thousands of Japanese, Italian and German residents as a national-security measure. Entire families were abducted in the middle of the night and whisked to the United States to serve as bargaining chips in a clandestine prisoner swap with Japan.

All in all, McConahay's *The Tango War* fills a long-overlooked gap in histories of the Second World War, framing it as a truly global conflict. By revealing the untold story of Latin America's role in the war, McConahay suggests that the geostrategic struggle over the continent in the 1940s had serious implications in the decades that followed. She draws 'connection[s] between the tyrannies' of European fascism and Latin American authoritarianism, building a historical bridge between the continent's involvement in the war and its subsequent dirty wars, with their attendant political violence and human-rights abuses (p. 274).

Vanishing Frontiers: The Forces Driving Mexico and the United States Together
Andrew Selee. New York: PublicAffairs, 2018. $28.00. 336 pp.

When Donald Trump announced his candidacy for the presidency in June 2015, he infamously said of illegal immigrants from Mexico: 'They're bringing drugs. They're bringing crime. They're rapists. And some, I assume are good people.' Trump's strategy, which vaulted him to an electoral victory on a platform of fear and resentment of immigrants (and domestic liberals), was to take the exception and make it the rule. His easy fix to the problems he had conjured was to build 'a big, beautiful wall' along the US–Mexico border, a solution that between one-quarter and one-third of Americans strongly supported.

In this timely and impassioned book, Andrew Selee attempts to take a sledgehammer to Trump's bombastic, simplistic and very successful political rhetoric on Mexico. The director of the respected Migration Policy Institute in Washington DC, Selee argues that despite Trump's inflammatory anti-Mexico rhetoric, the US and Mexico are more culturally and economically intertwined than ever before. He presents case studies demonstrating that bidirectional flows of people and capital are producing 'vanishing frontiers'.

Selee stresses that while media attention has fixated on the undeniable and incessant gangland horrors in Mexico, the country has also experienced an economic and social revolution over the past three decades. In a single generation, Mexicans' life expectancy jumped four years, bringing it within two years of Americans' own life expectancy. Median income has risen by one-third since the early 1990s, and education levels over the same period increased by over half. Today, a quarter of Mexican children will attend institutions of higher learning – triple the rate of previous decades. Indeed, Mexico is a middle-class country (40% of the population is defined as such). These changes explain why Mexicans are no longer entering the United States illegally as they once did, contrary to Trump's nativistic rants.

Selee reveals that borders are vanishing not just in the expected places such as the San Diego–Tijuana region, where a joint international airport operates on the Mexican side of the border and Republican politicians extol their unified economic zone, but also in places located far from Mexico, such as Hazleton, Pennsylvania, and Knoxville, Tennessee. In Rust Belt cities across the northeast, vanishing borders are apparent in the Mexican bakery giant that employs American workers and the *taquerías* that are adored by gringos.

Selee updates a well-known 1980s book on the bilateral relationship, *Distant Neighbors*, writing that today the relationship between the US and Mexico is more akin to that of 'intimate strangers, deeply connected to each other yet with few of the tools we need to understand our growing intimacy' (p. 25). While both nations' current presidents promote inward-looking, nationalistic goals, Selee suggests that the frontier between Mexico and the US will continue to vanish, if not because of neighbourly sentiments, then simply for the pragmatic reasons of economic efficiency and steady cultural fusion.

Moscow Rules

Nicholas Redman

I

In many regions of the world, Russia is at loggerheads with the United States and its closest allies. Russia and the West back different sides and have different approaches to the conflict in Syria. In Venezuela, Moscow recognises and supports Nicolás Maduro as president, while many Western and Latin American states now regard Juan Guaidó as the country's rightful leader. Russia has sided with heavy-handed African governments when Western states have sought to take action against them in the UN Security Council. A similar dynamic is observable with regard to human-rights violations in Myanmar.

It is tempting to apprehend Russia as being motivated mainly by a determination to protect its national and commercial interests and a desire to pay back the US for the support it has given to anti-Russian governments in Ukraine, Georgia and the Baltic states over the last two decades. In Venezuela, for instance, Russia's state oil champion, Rosneft, has commercial equities in the oil sector, and Russian entities have lent billions of dollars to Caracas, while also having supplied the country with arms for many years. Russia has delighted in backing the Chavista regime to the chagrin of Washington, and has periodically sent warplanes to the Caribbean to signal solidarity with an implacably anti-US state.

Nicholas Redman is IISS Director of Editorial and editor of *Strategic Survey* and the *Adelphi* books.

Survival | vol. 61 no. 3 | June–July 2019 | pp. 247–254   DOI 10.1080/00396338.2019.1614797

In Syria, Russia has defended a government that has long purchased Russian arms, hosted a Russian naval facility and permitted significant Russian investment into its energy sector. By backing President Bashar al-Assad, Moscow has also frustrated the efforts of Western states to change the regime and in the process gained the grudging admiration of other Middle Eastern states for turning the tide of the war. Syria has served as a platform for a renewed Russian engagement in the Gulf, the Levant and North Africa, marking its return as a regional powerbroker.

In parts of Africa too, Russia's pursuit of policies inimical to the West's is intended partly to gain friends and open new markets in response to Western sanctions. This has been especially apparent in the Central African Republic, where Russian mercenaries have deployed and Russia is trying to ease sanctions, including the arms embargo, against the government, which would yield business opportunities for Moscow. In the last two years, Russia has also stepped up its presence in the Horn of Africa, the African Great Lakes and parts of Southern Africa. Until Sudanese president Omar al-Bashir was overthrown on 11 April, Russia had protected his government from Western-led censure at the Security Council over his imposition of a harsh, nationwide state of emergency. Moscow has also aligned with some African states to shield the government of Burundi from criticism by France, the US and the UK in the Security Council over its record on human rights and internal security.

While some commentators see in Russia's pattern of anti-Western behaviour the geopolitical objective of countering Western efforts to marginalise it, they miss the attendant theoretical challenge to the Western conception of contemporary international relations. Russia is not only promoting its interests and seeking to frustrate the US; it is also systematically practising and promoting a classical view of international relations that upholds the primacy of states and the principle of non-interference in their domestic affairs. Such a framework dramatically curtails the scope for the international community to interfere in the affairs of a UN member state in instances of internal insecurity.

The original signatories of the Treaty of Westphalia have, to varying degrees, moved beyond the idea that governments are free to act as they wish within their own territory, so long as the consequences largely remain there. They care about stolen elections and repressed minorities. Russian President Vladimir Putin, by contrast, clings grimly to a Westphalian view of international relations, and he is not alone. In backing Maduro, Putin is not only looking after his country's loans to Venezuela and creating problems for the US in its backyard; he is also acting to bolster the principle of non-interference, regardless of any humanitarian or political crisis caused by a particular government. The United States' and other governments' recognition of Guaidó, the head of Venezuela's legislature, as interim president in early 2019 has brought the clash of outlooks to a head. The US has tightened sanctions on Venezuela to persuade the armed forces and the leadership of state oil monopoly PDVSA to abandon Maduro, and sought to deliver humanitarian aid without the consent of the Venezuelan authorities. Russia has castigated the US for threatening force against Venezuela, for seeking to block its military assistance and for using humanitarian aid as cover for destabilising the country. Moscow perceives US backing for the opposition as impeding national reconciliation by rendering the opposition irreconcilable.

II

The same logic of preventing external interference led Moscow to block any effort at the Security Council to coerce the Syrian government – even when it appeared that Assad was doomed, in which case a deal with the opposition would have served Moscow's commercial interests. Ever since the civil war started in 2011, Russia has refused to accept externally imposed preconditions on any political settlement – in particular, demands that Assad should step down – and held that Syrians alone should determine a political solution. Moscow's explicit political support gave Assad a huge advantage over his opponents by limiting external intervention on their behalf. At every turn, Russia contrasted the legality of its policies with the illegality of Western approaches: it supported the recognised Syrian government and deployed its military forces in the country with the consent of Damascus. Western states, by contrast, sought to weaken Assad and aid his opponents with airpower and special-operations forces. Putin purported to champion the UN Charter and cast Western states as under-mining it.

Russia's adherence to the principle of non-interference in the face of Western challenges was also apparent in January 2019 in a dispute over elections in the Democratic Republic of the Congo (DRC). President Joseph Kabila, desperate to retain power, had persistently delayed the scheduled election. Eventually the vote was held in late 2018 and tallies suggested that Kabila's candidate, Emmanuel Ramazani Shadary, had finished a distant third, with opposition candidate Martin Fayulu winning nearly 60% of the vote. Yet official results declared in January 2019 gave victory to Felix Tshisekedi, a political veteran, amid rumours that he had cut a deal with Kabila. Several Western states called for a recount and their African coun-terparts seemed torn as to how to proceed. Russia, however, accepted the result, and its foreign minister criticised France, the US and 'other former colonial powers' for meddling. Moscow again took the position that any interference in the domestic affairs of a sovereign state was unacceptable.

Except as to the former Soviet republics Moscow considers irrevoca-bly in its sphere of influence, Russia has been remarkably consistent in respecting the rights of putatively recognised governments and upholding the principles of non-interference. In addition to the cases cited above, it has backed Asian states' efforts to check the United Kingdom's attempts at the Security Council to hold the government of Myanmar accountable for the brutal treatment of the Rohingya minority. Closer to home, it has continued to press for the closure of the international Office of the High Representative (OHR) in Bosnia and Herzegovina because it considers the OHR a channel for unwarranted interference in Bosnia's domestic affairs. China substantially shares Russia's approach. The root motivation behind it is a desire to preclude foreign involvement in their own domestic poli-tics. Neither has any interest in the advance of liberal democracy or cares a whit about vote-rigging, the suppression of protests, or the takeover of independent institutions such as legislatures, courts or the media. They uphold the unqualified primacy of a government over its population.

This marks a direct challenge to the world view of Western states. They generally favour and practise the promotion of democracy and human rights (including freedom of expression and association), fair elections, the rotation of power, the rule of law, civil-society activism and government transparency, and believe in independent institutions and the separation of powers. While they are not altogether consistent in calling out violators or in the level of effort they apply to redress their transgressions, these states are willing to consider punitive multilateral action against them. Although Donald Trump's election and tenure as US president has cast doubt on the West's status as a cohesive, values-promoting group, he has been as firm as any of his recent predecessors in promoting democracy in Venezuela – most likely because it would topple a hardline socialist government.

NATO's bombing of Yugoslavia in 1999 over its treatment of Kosovo was instrumental in confirming to Russia the importance of returning to a traditional approach to international relations. NATO's action came at the end of a decade when Western states had used their international primacy to promote concepts of humanitarian intervention that rested on the notion that the rights of a people could trump those of their government in some circumstances. NATO's threat and then use of force to drive Yugoslav forces out of Kosovo paved the way for the further partition of Yugoslavia and crippled president Slobodan Milosevic, who was ousted a year later and soon thereafter imprisoned.

A few years later, the US and several of its allies went even further, circumventing the Security Council to invade Iraq and topple Saddam Hussein. For Russia, this tore the very fabric of the system of international security. Moreover, beyond the concerns about Iraq's weapons of mass destruction, Russia discerned a clear US intention to change Iraq's regime and install a more pliant one. In 2010, France, the UK and the US toppled the Libyan leader, Muammar Gadhafi, by military force. A charitable interpretation of the Western powers' action would be that they applied an expansive definition of the remit provided under Security Council Resolution 1973 that sought to protect the civilian population of Benghazi. Russia's conviction is that those powers played Moscow by putting forward a resolution that was circumscribed by its terms to gain the acquiescence of Russia and China – both uncharacteristically abstained – all the while harbouring the intention to exceed those terms and oust Gadhafi.

By the time the Security Council was addressing Syria's civil war, Russia would no longer risk handing Western states a legal pretext for threatening intervention against a sovereign state.

III

In March 2019, Russia's prime minister, the establishment liberal Dmitry Medvedev, denied that the US and Russia were engaged in a new cold war. Rather, he said, the world was witnessing a struggle between international law and lawfulness on one hand, and 'unlimited permissiveness' on the other. The US, according to Medvedev, seeks to upend governments that it does not like regardless of international law. The difference in approach between Russia and the West may not represent an ideological chasm of Cold War proportions, but it is nevertheless a significant battle of ideas with global implications, and not simply a clash of interests.

Moscow and Beijing believe that the West wants to change their political systems. They have decided to mount a proactive defence, by blocking the US and other states from promoting liberal democracy or individual human rights in states where the sitting government is opposed to such developments. The rationale is that it is better to fight that battle in forward outposts, like Syria, Venezuela, Sudan and Myanmar, than to wait until their own domestic arrangements are under direct political attack. To regard this merely as the preoccupation of a handful of governments may be too sanguine. The principle of non-interference has appeal for many governments across the left–right spectrum, ranging from Mexico under Andrés Manuel Lopez Obrador to Recep Tayyip Erdogan's Turkey, and arguably including Benjamin Netanyahu's Israel and Narendra Modi's India.

That Russia has sought not only to uphold the principle of non-interference, but to proselytise for it, is very clear. At the 136th Assembly of the Inter-Parliamentary Union, held in Dhaka in 2017, Russia submitted a draft resolution on 'The Role of Parliament in Respecting the Principle of Non-interference in the Internal Affairs of States'. The first point after the preamble reiterated 'the need to respect absolutely and adhere fully to the Purposes and Principles of the Charter of the United Nations and international law, and in particular to respect the sovereignty,

independence and territorial integrity of States, and non-intervention in
the internal affairs of States'; the text was adopted by consensus.[1] Moscow
claims that over 95% of parliaments represented at the meeting supported
the declaration.[2]

In March 2019, the Federation Council, the upper house of Russia's
federal parliament, passed a resolution that called on other legislatures
to condemn NATO's aggression against Yugoslavia in 1999 and its consequences. The resolution characterises NATO actions as blatant acts of
aggression against a sovereign state and a clear threat to international
peace and security that violated the UN Charter. Thereafter, some NATO
states undertook interventions in Iraq and Libya without Security Council
authorisation, and tried to do the same in Syria. Today, the resolution
says, Venezuela, Cuba and Nicaragua are facing threats of similar action.
The resolution also notes that the Western-led 2008 recognition of Kosovo,
which followed the 1999 bombing of Yugoslavia, created a dangerous
precedent and damaged the international security system.[3]

Western governments, of course, believe that liberal democracy, in
all its variants, is the best system of government so far devised. Some of
them perhaps still nurse the delusion that the end of the Cold War settled
the global argument over politico-economic systems in favour of capital-
ism and liberal democracy. Yet even though non-state actors have gained
prominence in the last 25 years, information technology and social media
have empowered individuals and groups, and norms of outside intervention have become more permissive, states are still the most important
actors in the international system, which continues to favour them. Many
states suffer from instability, and the governments that rule them fear
losing power and appreciate Putin's call for the world to renew its commitment to the principle of non-intervention.

In turn, Russia's president can empathise with many of those leaders in
a way that those of Western democracies cannot. He has experienced first-
hand the turbulence that accompanies revolutionary political change. The
state he served as an intelligence officer disintegrated. Russia in the 1990s
suffered from lawlessness, separatism, de-industrialisation and humiliation. With the fortuitous assistance of recovering oil output and rocketing

oil prices, Putin wilfully re-imposed state power in Russia. Along the way he crushed opponents, weaponised the legal system and institutionalised corruption. Putin was also subjected to abundant Western sermonising about democratic freedoms and human rights. None of it persuaded him that free elections, the rotation of power, and independent courts and government institutions were the best way forward. He knows that if he is not in power, he could well be in jail or worse, as Gadhafi's fate demonstrates. At bottom, Putin advocates non-interference as a matter of his own regime security and self-protection. Yet in so doing he is pushing international relations in a direction inimical to Western interests. And he has, among the ranks of UN members, a large and potentially receptive audience.

Notes

1   'The Role of Parliament in Respecting the Principle of Non-intervention in the Internal Affairs of States', resolution adopted by consensus, 136th Inter-Parliamentary Union Assembly, 5 April 2017, http://archive.ipu.org/conf-e/136/item4.pdf.

2   See Committee on International Affairs of the State Duma, 'The Russian Resolution on Non-Interference in the Affairs of Other Countries Was Adopted by the Assembly of the IPU', 15 April 2017, http://interkomitet.com/international-parliamentary-organizations/inter-parliamentary-union/the-russian-resolution-on-non-interference-in-the-affairs-of-other-countries-was-adopted-by-the-assembly-of-the-ipu/.

3   The council did exempt Afghanistan from the list of condemned Western interventions because it was undertaken on the basis of a UN Security Council resolution – and presumably because it served Russian security interests.

Correction

Article title: Defence and Japan's Constitutional Debate

Author: Choong, W.

Journal: Survival

Citation details: Volume 57, Number 2, April–May 2015, pages 173–192.

DOI: https://doi.org/10.1080/00396338.2015.1026100

p. 179

The final sentences in the second paragraph have been amended to read:

In 1992, lawmakers passed the International Peacekeeping Cooperation Law (or PKO Law), overriding a resolution passed by the House of Councillors in 1954 that prohibited the foreign dispatch of the JSDF.[34] The PKO Law permitted such deployments, albeit under highly restrictive conditions – for example, peacekeepers could not be armed or sent into an area with ongoing hostilities. Nonetheless, the law marked the first revision of the policy on overseas deployment in nearly 40 years.

Note 34 was added, with subsequent endnotes renumbered:

[34] Akiho Shibata, 'Japanese Peacekeeping Legislation and Recent Developments in U.N. Operations', *Yale Journal of International Law*, vol. 19, no. 2, 1994, p. 312, https://digitalcommons.law.yale.edu/cgi/viewcontent.cgi?referer=https://www.google.com.sg/&httpsredir=1&article=1648&context=yjil.

p. 180

The second paragraph has been amended to read:

A few years later, when the 9/11 terrorist attacks on the United States led to the outbreak of war in Afghanistan in 2001, Japanese officials were eager to redeem themselves following the embarrassment of the 1991 Gulf

War. In November 2001, Japanese naval vessels carrying 700 sailors were deployed to supply American and British forces operating in Afghanistan. It was the first foreign dispatch of Japanese forces to an active conflict zone since the formation of the JSDF in 1954.[37] As Richard Samuels put it, collective self-defence at that point became a new 'fact on the ground'.[38] In 2004, by which time war had spread to Iraq, Japanese forces were deployed to a 'non-combat' zone in Samawah to provide medical support, restoration and reconstruction as part of the 'coalition of the willing' organised by the US. This deployment of 600 Japan Ground Self-Defense Forces troops was the first time Japanese forces were committed outside of a UN peacekeeping framework. While critics argued that the deployment violated Article 9, the Japanese government argued that it was legitimised by various UN resolutions.[39] In 2005, Japan sent 950 troops to Indonesia's Aceh coast on a humanitarian mission to aid victims of the 2004 tsunami. The operation was Japan's largest since the Second World War. The dispatch demonstrated the receptiveness of the region to the presence of Japanese peacekeepers.[40] For example, Jusuf Wanandi, a respected Indonesian scholar, said that he had no problems with the deployment so long as Japan did not go nuclear or trigger a news arms race.[41]

Note 37 was added, with subsequent endnotes renumbered:

[37] Bhubhindar Singh, *Japan's Security Identity: From Peace-State to an International State* (Abingdon: Routledge, 2017), p. 123.